THE
ARTS
IN MONTANA

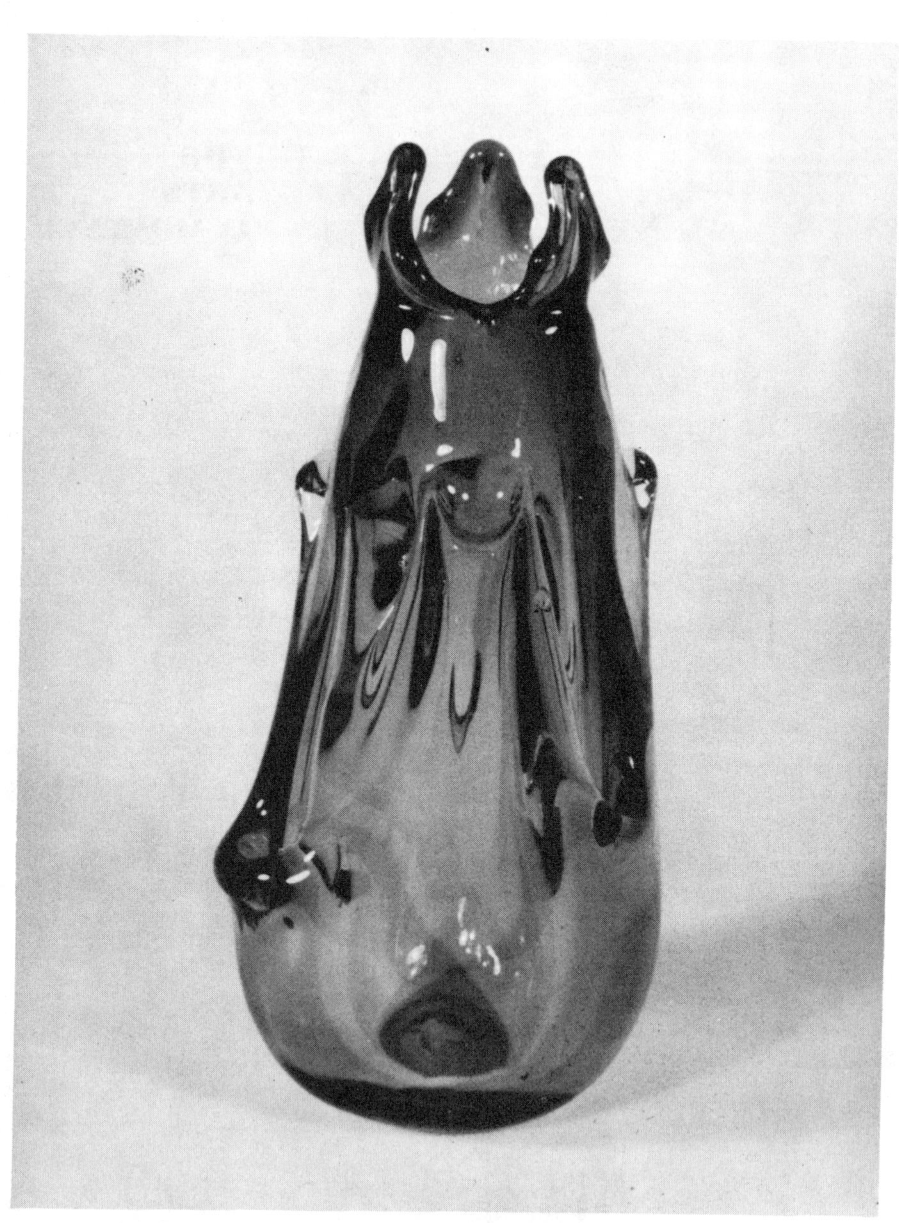

Glass, Dave Cornell

THE ARTS IN MONTANA

Collected and Edited by H. G. Merriam

. . . to preserve the heritage of the state as found in its history and folklore, to stimulate creative work in the several arts and to make these cultural resources available for the benefit and enjoyment of the people of Montana.

From the preamble of the constitution of the Montana Institute of the Arts.

MOUNTAIN PRESS PUBLISHING COMPANY
Missoula, Montana

Acknowledgements

Grateful acknowledgement for financial aid which has made publication of this book possible is offered to: The Ila B. Dousman Trust, Leif Erickson, Trustee, and these members of The Montana Institute of the Arts: Robert A. Athern, Dr. and Mrs. Ray Bjork, L.O. Brockmann, Merrill Burlingame, Harriette Cushman, Lawrence H. Gill, James M. Haughey, Archie Joscelyn, Fred Mass, Mr. and Mrs. H.G. Merriam, Frances Senska. LaDonna Fehlberg aided in the selection of illustrations.

Library of Congress Cataloging in Publication Data
Main entry under title:

The Arts in Montana.

Material originally published in the magazine
Montana Arts.
1. Arts — Montana — Essays, lectures, stories, poems, illustrations
I. Merriam, Harold Guy, 1883-   II. Montana arts.
NX510.M9A77   700'.8   76-58521
ISBN 0-87842-068-1

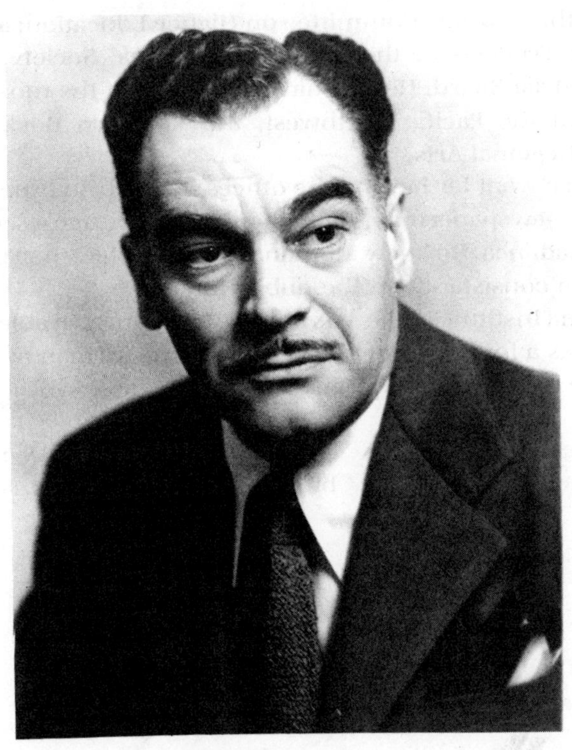

Dedicated to the Memory
of Joseph Kinsey Howard,
1906-1951

For many years Joe Howard was the voice of Montana to the rest of the country. His book, *Montana: High, Wide and Handsome*, won national praise as an outstandingly able economic and cultural study. In *Montana Margins, A, State Anthology*, he pieced together the colorful saga of the state as told in journals and letters of its pioneers, the novels, poems and stories of its more recent writers. Only a few weeks before his death he completed the manuscript of the heroic tale of Louis Riel and the Northwest Rebellion. His numerous magazine articles and stories proved the range and depth of his interests and his versatility as a writer.

Joe was a rare combination of scholar and man of action, an idealist whose feet were planted realistically on the good earth of Montana. He was the key figure in the Montana Study and its director for a time;

chairman of the Citizens' Committee on Higher Education; a member of the Board of Trustees of the Montana Historical Society, and of the Society's Editorial Board. He was director of one of the most promising movements in the Pacific Northwest, the Northern Rocky Mountain Roundup of Regional Arts.

His influence went far beyond the offices he held. An experienced and incorruptible newspaperman, he had an alert reporter's sense of news behind the headlines. He knew Montana politics as few men did and used his knowledge consistently in the public interest.

The Montana Institute of the Arts owes him an unrepayable debt for his contribution as a founding member, first state chairman of the writers' group and an advisor in every phase of its activities.

Extracted from In Memoriam,
by Paul A. Grieder, Bozeman, 1951

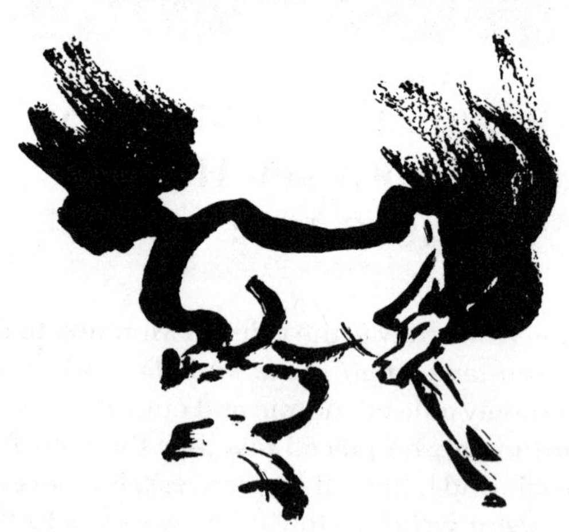

Gilberta Manker

Prefatory Note

A member of The Montana Institute of the Arts wearing a pendant made by a Montana artist was asked by a dealer in jewelry in St. Louis if it came from South America. "''No,'' she responded, ''it was made by a Montana craftsman.'' The dealer was surprised, saying that he had never thought of Montana as having artists. That idea about Montana may be fairly general in the country as a whole. However, artists and craftsmen have been living and working in Montana since it became a state in 1889. In art circles, and perhaps more generally, three Montana artists are widely known: the painters Charles M. Russell and Edgar S. Paxson and the writer Frank B. Linderman; but they are only three of several who deserve recognition.

The Montana Institute of the Arts was founded in 1948 and from that date has issued a magazine, now entitled *Montana Arts,* rich in materials about art in its various fields, about artists and with portraits of them and illustrations of their work. The materials in this book have been selected from the more than 100 issues of that magazine published between 1948 and 1975.

Final decisions about selection of materials have been the editor's, although twenty MIA members were asked for recommendations and responded with valuable advice. Limited space in the book made for exclusion of many writings which the editor would have liked to include.

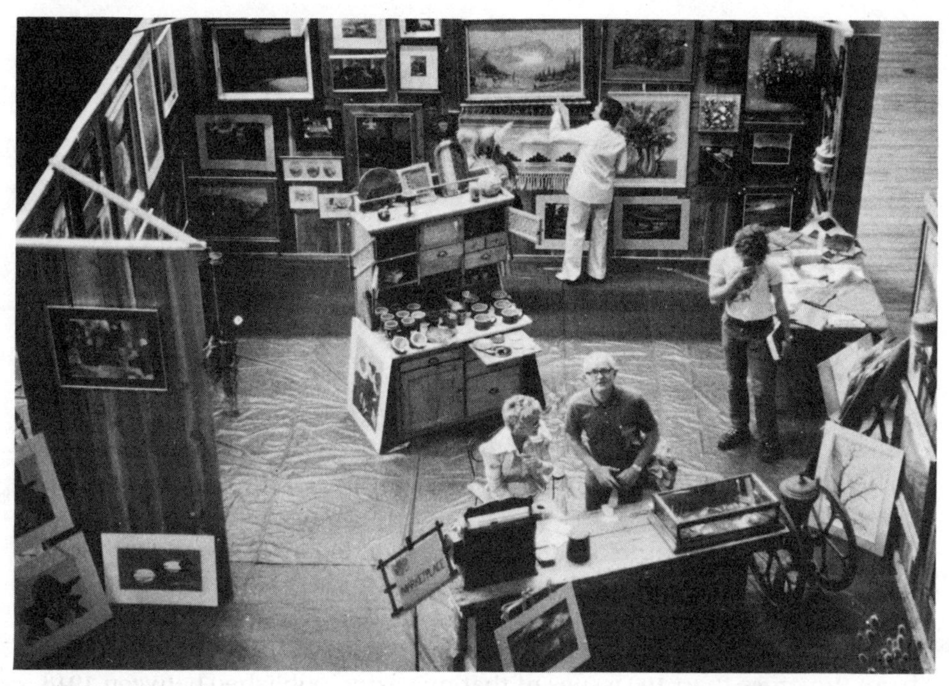

The Market Place, E.H. and Virginia Loeffler, Billings Festival, 1975

Challenge

Human life at best is ephemeral, a sometime thing. Man is small change and soon spent, and from the time when he reaches the age of reason every man realizes this, consciously or subconsciously. This realization powers one of the great drives of human existence, the abysmal urge to try to perpetuate something of himself...this basic human drive, this urge to create...is often subordinated and stifled by lack of opportunity. We, the members of the Montana Institute of the Arts, then, must aim our efforts and our programs at providing outlets for this basic creative spirit.

It would be smug and ridiculous to assume that from our efforts will come any great and world-striking results. Few of our writers will ever find a place in the world's libraries, few of our painters will receive recognition by famous museums; but we can give to many people the chance to round out their lives to a greater fullness by providing them with the opportunity to create something themselves, perhaps unique, perhaps beautiful, but in any case, no matter how crude or amateurish the product, something that is their very own, with the resultant satisfying uplift to soul and ego. Life is a compromise and if we in MIA can approach or even make a start toward any of our high objectives, we will have done something in which we can feel satisfaction.

Adapted from "The Essence of MIA"
by Robert McCaig, Great Falls, 1953

vii

MIA Was Formed

Adults see and hear with eyes and ears that have been conditioned by years of conventional living. Young people look on life with fresh eyes and hear it with fresh ears — the younger the fresher. Youth longs to express in some creative way much more than ordinary living has called out from them. That is why they are likely to be romantic and idealistic. Older people also yearn to express themselves but usually in terms of their experience in life. That is why they tend to be realistic. Young and old possess an urge, in varying degrees, toward expression. In the young it lies on the surface; in the older person it is deeply latent. However large or small that urge may be, it pushes them to find a voice for that something within them. The embodiment of that urge — in a writing, a painting, a sculpture, pottery, a song, a weaving, a research — brings relief, fosters pride, invigorates the ego.

MIA was formed to offer opportunities propitious to exercise of the creative faculties and to rouse to life latent urges in its members. It was also founded to look outward on the culture of Montana and take its place among the influences making for its health and vitality

H. G. Merriam, Missoula, 1958

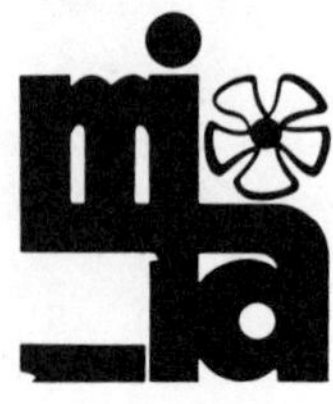

Introduction

Museums and art groups have been forming during the last few years in several sections of the state of Montana. The Montana Institute of the Arts is one of the oldest of these groups, perhaps *the* oldest, having been founded in Helena in the spring of 1948. This book, *The Arts in Montana,* composed of materials from the more than 100 issues of its magazine, shows what one group has been thinking and writing about art and who a few of the Montana artists are. A sketch of the activities of MIA indicates what has been and is being done by one group to enrich culture in Montana.

The purposes of the Montana Institute of the Arts are stated in the Preamble to its Constitution, namely, "to preserve the heritage of the state as found in its history and folklore, to stimulate creative work in the several arts, and to make these cultural resources available for the benefit and enjoyment of the people of Montana."

The activities furthering these purposes are eight in number: an annual Festival, a Little Traveling Festival, Traveling Slide Collection, Branches, a Magazine, a Marketplace, a Permanent Collection, and Publications.

At the annual Festival (the twenty-eighth one was held June, 1976 in Helena) art objects are exhibited, workshops are conducted, speakers, often from outside of the state, discuss art and MIA members in the several fields of art mingle friendlily. The exhibit is open to the public. From the exhibit a few paintings, ceramic and sculptural products and pieces of weaving and other arts are selected to travel throughout a year to twenty or more communities in Montana. In addition, a Slide Collection of art objects travels to high schools in the state that ask for it.

YMAS (Young Montanans Art Show) has held exhibits of art objects by artists of fourteen to eighteen years of age. In 1975 it was merged with MAI (Montana Art Interscholastic), which holds an exhibit in the spring of each year. *Montana Arts* devotes the larger part of one issue annually to young artists of Montana and their verbal and visual talents. The Permanent Collection has been growing since 1956 through the donation of paintings and other art objects by members of MIA. At the annual Festival a Marketplace is conducted which on the average totals sales of more than $1,000.

Montana Arts, the MIA magazine, is now in its twenty-ninth year. In its early years it served principally as a sort of "house organ," but since 1966 its editor has wished the magazine to be of interest and value to members through art discussions and many illustrations. The business of the MIA and the MIA Foundation is covered along with information about the Montana Arts Council. With the formation of the Montana Arts Council MIA has received grants from it for stabilization of art programs and for the expansion from a quarterly publication to the issuing of four to six numbers annually. SHARE (Service, Handling, Arts, Resources, Exchange) is sponsored jointly with the Montana Arts Council. It is a service initialed to provide aid to communities wishing to bring in artists and exhibits to enrich the cultural facets of their life. It helps locate resources, people and exhibits and aids in financing the travel and expenses, for instance, of putting on a workshop.

In order to serve statewide MIA has twenty-three Branches in twenty-three Montana communities. Each Branch may conduct general meetings, operate whatever groups its members desire to participate in: painting, photography, history and so on; set up exhibits; and use its imagination and energy in whatever artistic ways it wishes.

MIA has published, besides its magazine, six sixteen-page pamphlets of poems written by members, one fifty-page booklet, one paperbound collection entitled *Seedlings,* and one clothbound book of poems entitled *Seed in the Soil.*

These activities, it is believed, have been and are enriching the culture of Montana. Other art groups in the state likewise have enriched and are enriching that culture. This book bears a title which seems to represent generally art work in Montana and so it does, but it presents comments on art and artists and illustrations that are principally the work of members of MIA. The hope is held that sometime in the future, if art groups will get together, a larger and more inclusive magazine with more illustrations, some in color, which more widely represents more Montana artists and their contributions to Montana culture will be published. The *Arts in Montana* is a step in making known to Montanans and to Americans throughout the country Montana artists and their work.

MIA from its beginning in 1948 has harbored the hope that art groups in the state would come together in an organization that would be cooperative and would coordinate the activities of the many groups. MIA's first step toward such an end was the enlisting of affiliate members, but the project has not been followed up and developed. In such a cooperative movement exhibits instead of being shown in one community could be sent widely over the state, a larger and more representative annual festival could be held, the Little Traveling Festival, enlarged and circulated into still more communities, might be accompanied by an artist who would talk about art and explain its works, the aims of art and its importance to the state. The magazine could be twice as large with more illustrations, some of them in color. It could be a magazine to be proudly distributed over the United States. YMAS and MAI would reach more students and communities, and SHARE might become a large operation. MIA has also often discussed the operation of a traveling bus carrying art objects. These ideas are worth thought, and, perhaps, after much thought and planning, action.

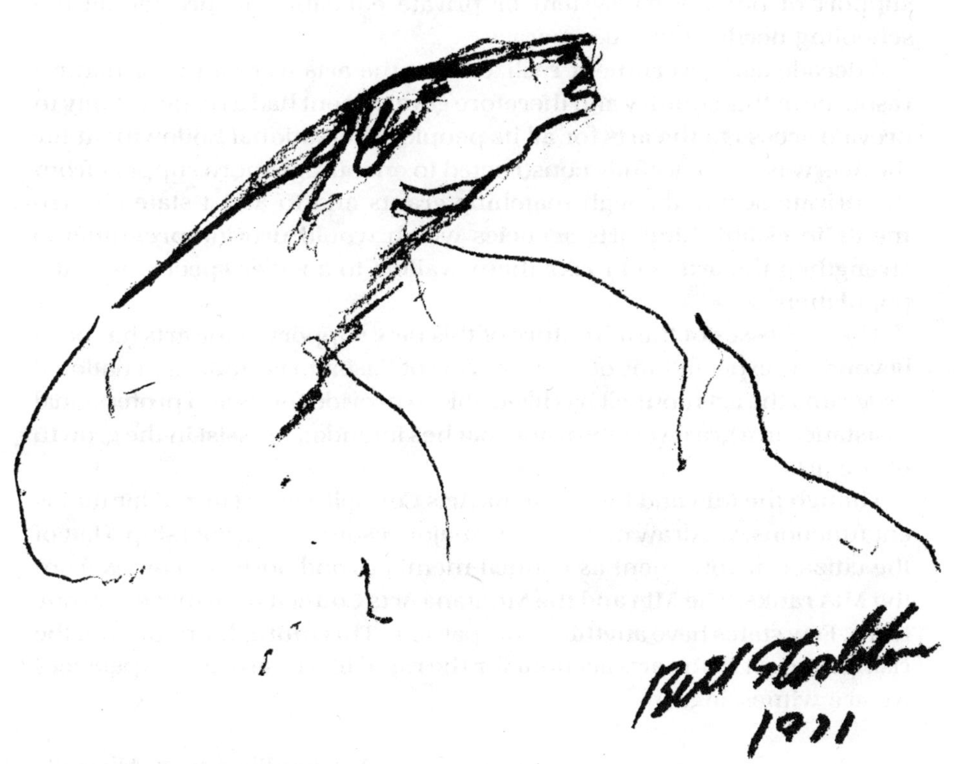

Montana Institute of the Arts
and Montana Arts Council

The goals of the Montana Institute of the Arts and the Montana Arts Council are similar. We share the belief that the arts are basic to human existence, are essential to a quality life and that Montanans have the right to be exposed to and involved with the arts in their many forms.

The MIA, as a broad-based, grass roots organization of many artists and friends of the arts, has through its membership and activities represented a major advocacy for the arts, and from its ranks has come a considerable amount of the private giving to the arts in Montana. However, for the arts to play their proper role in every American's life through private support alone would be comparable to asking writers and patrons to be the sole support of our library system or private education to provide all the schooling needs of our democracy.

A decade ago government realized that the arts were a major natural resource of this country and therefore government had a responsibility to provide access to the arts for all its people. The National Endowment for the Arts was very carefully constructed to encourage more support from the private sector through matching grants and to assist state governments in establishing arts agencies which would provide programs to strengthen the arts and make them availble to a wider spectrum of the population.

The successes of the adventure of this new support to the arts has been beyond the expectations of all. In its role of liason to regional and national programs the arts council has been able to provide funds and professional assistance to a great variety of approaches intended to assist in the growth of the arts.

Though the MIA and the Montana Arts Council are organized for different functions, we draw on the same major resource — leadership. Half of the citizens involvement as council members and advisors comes from the MIA ranks. The MIA and the Montana Arts Council have made a strong team. Few states have anything comparable. This mutual support and the rising interest in the arts account for the rapid increase of arts expeiences we are witnessing.

Maxine Blackmer, Missoula

Contents

Dedication   iii
Prefatory Note   v
Challenge   vii
Introduction   ix

Section I — The Arts
Paris, the End of an Era, Bill Stockton   2
The Arts in Living, Alfred W. Humphreys   9
Art is a Human Need, Robert T. Taylor   10
Mass and Elite Art, Robert T. Taylor   12
Art and Feeling Free, Robert A. Athearn   17
On Being an Artist, H.G. Merriam   18
The Years and the Wind and the Rain, Dorothy M. Johnson   21
The Fundamental Concept of Design, Earnest E. Bruffey   23
Art and the Coincidences of Life, Branson G. Stevenson   25
Gallery Talk, Albert Christ-Janer   30
That Wonderful World of Color, Isabelle Johnson   36
The Outer and the Inner Eye, Helen McAuslin   40
Music and Cultural Value, Robert A. Athearn   42
The Fascination of Weaving, Thomas Jermin   45
Art from the Ground Up, Branson G. Stevenson   50
History is Nobody's Property, K. Ross Toole   53
Photography, an Art, Denes G. Istvanffy   55
The Surface Hasn't Been Scratched, Norman Fox   56
Rockhounding, Betty and Max Hughes   59
Living with Jewelry, LaDonna Fehlberg   61
Studio 10, Thelma Gift   62
Montana House, an Adventure in the Hand Arts, Antoinette Jungster   65
A Community Complex, Kay Widmer   67
The Archie Bray Foundation, Viola G. Lindley   68
MIA and Indians, H.G. Merriam   70

Section II — The Artists

Architect
AIA Fellow   75

Carvers
A Personal Glimpse of John Clark, Mabel Bjork   76
With Paint and Wood: the Swenneses, Dixie Peltier   78

Ceramists
Frances Senska, Verne Dusenberry   79
Branson G. Stevenson, Jim Logan   80
Peter H. Voulkos, Lela and Rudy Autio   82
Rudy and Lela Autio, Maxine Blackmer and Frances Senska   86, 87
The Loefflers, Virginia and E.H. Loeffler   87
Peter Meloy, Lela Autio   89

Historian
A Search for Scribner, Audra Browman   91

Musician
Eugene Andrie, Maribeth Sawyer   96

Painters
Artist of the Year: James E. Dew, Aden Arnold   98
James M. Haughey, Jeanne Rhodes   99
Isabelle Johnson, Terry Melton   100
Val Knight, Verna Mae Banta   101
Elizabeth Lochrie, Helen Clark   101
Fred Mass, Mary L. Anderson   102
James Masterson, Myrtle Mockel   104
J.K. Ralston — Artist of Western History, Nancy Olson   106
Cowboy Artist, "Moquea Stumick:" Irving Shope, Helen Clark   108
Jessie Wilber, Frances Senska   109

Photographer
Rudi Dietrich: A Close-up   110

Sculptors
Lyndon Pomeroy, A Profile, Isabelle Johnson   111
Robert Scriver: He Knows His Subject, Mary Scriver   113
Jack Weaver: The Sculptor as Workman, Robert T. Taylor   115

Weavers
Margaret Burlew, Ethel E. Nelson   118
Marion Brockmann   119
Hilda Cunningham, Margaret Berlien   120
The Maloneys, Weaving a Life Together, Ruth Beem   120

Writers
Will James, Isabelle Johnson   122
The Mankers, Harriette Cushman   124
Meet These Writers — Verna Mae Banta,
Alice Schumacher, Archie Joscelyn, Fay Kuhlman,
May Vontver: Mildred DeCosse   126

Section III — The Various Art Fields

Architecture
Partners in Design, Dorothy Larson   131
Carving
Wood Carving, Arthur L. Roe   132
Out of the Woods, Betty McDonald   135
Enameling
Copper Enameling Is Fun, Frances Senska   136
What Is Good Enameling?, Frances Senska   137
Ceramics
Mining Camp Glazing with Kay, Mary McCourt Anderson   140
Rudy Autio's Architectural Ceramics, Isabelle Johnson   142
Waxing Eloquent with Was Resist, Branson G. Stevenson   144
History
Meagher Councy Centennial Year, Theresa Buckingham   146
Steamboating to Fort Benton, 1868, J. Lee Sedgwick   147
Trouble with Town Names, Stanley Davison   150
The Writer's West, Stanley Davison   152
Music
Montana's Community Orchestras: A Survey, Robert T. Taylor   154
Bravo Montana, Patricia K. Simmons   155
Montana Composers of Music, Alfred K. Humphreys   157
Red Lodge Music Festival, Mary Hauf   158
Painting
About Painting, Robert K. DeWeese   159
The Observer and Modern Art, James E. Dew   160
Why Paint Abstract Pictures?, Helen McAuslin   164
For What Is the Amateur Painter Working?, Isabelle Johnson   170
Encaustic Painting, James E. Dew   173
Photography
Photography in the MIA, Rudi Dietrich   176
Weaving
Summer Greens, Hilda Cunningham   177
Designing on the Loom, Marion Brockmann   179
Little Lost Lace Loom, Clista P. Wuerthner   183

Writing
Whence Came These Lines?, Elnora Old Coyote   184
On Form and Diction in Poetry, Robert T. Taylor   185
A Word to the Wise Poet, Don Manker   188
A Word or Two for Poets, H.G. Merriam   189

Section IV — Poems, Article, Short Stories
Poems
by William W. Chance, Mary Brennan Clap, Jaculyn Corry,
Harriette Cushman, Ida Isabel Donohue, Frieda Fligelman,
Irene Gilskey, Philip Gray, Paul A. Grieder, Nancy M. Harvey
Jean Hough, Dorothy Johnson, Marty Kelly, Margaret Kraenzel,
Berdina Lane, William Luckenbach, Irene McPherson,
James Magorian, Don Manker, Kit Miller, Bessie K. Monroe,
Elnora Old Coyote, Lenore Olsen, Julie Reid, Jo Stepanoff,
Walter W. Stevens, Robert T. Taylor, Veris Wessel,
Milicent Ward Whitt   193-218
Article
What's There to Lose?, Alice Schumacher   218
Stories
In Beauty It Is Finished, Helen Clark   220
The Weight Lifter, Margaret Kraenzel   223

List of Illustrations   232

Appendix
About the Montana Institute of the Arts   233
Presidents of the Montana Institute of the Arts   234
Secretaries-Treasurers   235
Editors of the MIA Magazine   235
Fellows of MIA   236
Founding Members of MIA   236
Publications of MIA   238

Section I

THE ARTS

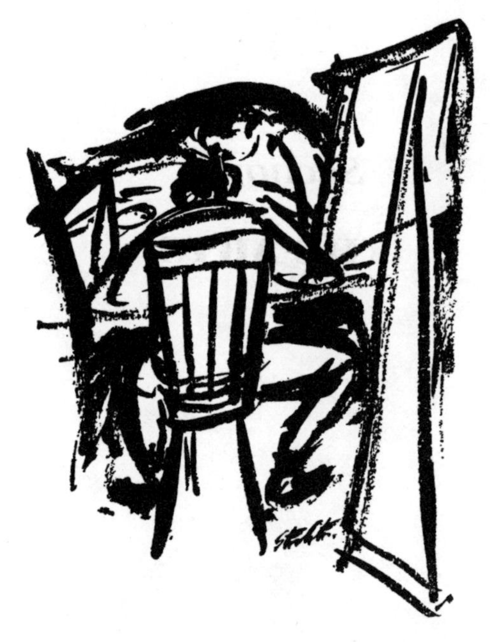

Sketch, Bill Stockton

Paris, 1948 — The End Of An Era

It was a forty-five minute subway trip from Villejuif, where I lived in the southern part of Paris, to the Ecole de la Grande Chaumiere, which was located two blocks from the Metro stop, Raspail, in the middle of the Left Bank. I made the trip five days a week. At first, it didn't matter at what time we got there — nine o'clock, eleven o'clock, one o'clock in the afternoon, or maybe not at all. Later on, the American Embassy decided the Americans on the G.I. Bill were "goofing off," and we were required to sign in. This was a great inconvenience, as most of the students now had to run across town, sign in, and then return to their little one-room apartments, where they could work without the distraction of several fellow students looking over their shoulders. Alas, the American educational system had come to Paris. It didn't matter now whether we learned, only that we attended. Really, this was as absurd as requiring a high school athlete to attend basketball practice. But how could the government know that an intellectual's only desire was the cultivation of his own mind, and that school hours meant nothing, and that he worked and read many, many hours after the school doors had closed. The French didn't like this new setup any more than we did. The French notion of a school was, "Well, it's here, take it or leave it."

I can still see in my mind's eye those old, worn, dirty stairs leading up to the three studios on the second floor of that old building. This was the Ecole de la Grande Chaumiere. Now, after all these years, I think I can remember the smell more than the image. It didn't smell exactly like Paris, yet in many ways it did. Do you know what Paris smells like? You have read descriptions of it, I suppose. Well, they're all right. Paris, the Paris away from the Champs Elysee and the Opera, the Paris of Frenchmen smells like violets, red wine, baked bread, Camembert, garlic and sidewalk latrines. But the Ecole de la Grande Chaumiere had an additional odor — it smelled of paint, poorly ventilated rooms and fifty or more perspiring aspiring artists.

They say the Directrice of the school was a Lesbian. She was married, and her husband, they said, ran a nightclub. Of course we never saw him. In the ten months I was there, I never saw her wear a dress. At that, she was a pretty good-looking girl in her late twenties. But she was rough and tough, and the common joke around school was, "Watch out for the Directrice, she forgot to shave this morning." Most of the time she minded her own business, which was chasing out little French kids who had sneaked into the studio to look at the models. She never ventured into the esthetic side of art; her only worry was to keep the Embassy off her neck.

The middle studio, directly at the head of the stairs, was given over to the Americans as a workroom. The other two studios had models posing for six hours a day, where one could paint and draw if he wished. There were no classes, only daily criticism (or critiques, as the American art teacher liked to call them) from several established artists. You could ignore them if you desired. You could also choose your instructor.

I still think of the hours I spent drawing arms, legs, necks, feet, torsos — endless arrays of them. This is how you learn to *see*. What is the magic of the human figure? What is that graceful rhythmic little thing? Even to this day, I have trouble fitting the stomach into the pelvic bone. This is how you learn why Michelangelo always bent the wrist; and Raphael, not knowing what else to do with it, bent it in the same way. So who is the artist? Picasso could draw them stiff as a board and still make them graceful.

It was some time during this winter of 1948-1949 that I finally came to realize what a drawing is. One learns somewhat accidentally at times, and this was due to Oscar. Oscar was a Norwegian from Minnesota. He lived in a tiny, attic room in an apartment building on Boulevard Saint Michel. The day I went over there, he was nursing a big boil on the end of his nose. In Paris you nurse a misfortune by forgetting about it and Oscar had almost forgotten his. He had been drinking hot rums most of the morning while he was working on a large painting. I mean it was large — it was nailed to the floor at the bottom and tied to a rafter at the top. Actually, it formed a convenient separation between his kitchen, which was a hot plate, and his bedroom, which was a cot. So we sat in the "bedroom" and looked and talked about the painting for a while. He asked me what I thought was wrong with it, and I told him that I thought his line was too fast — insensitive and uncomposed. He drew with a great facility, too easily. But it was at this moment that I realized what separated form from shape. "Of course, let Lautrec, Matisse or Picasso draw the simple shape of a rectangle and you have three separate forms. This one thing, their genius for creating line, edge and surface, is the charm of their style. No wonder all the second-rate artists in America were so occupied in imitating Braque. They couldn't draw! It was so much easier to imitate and arrange shape. And of course Braque was neat and decorative, and what more do you need to appeal to the feminine population?"

After this date I started to look at paintings with new eyes, and then the struggle began. I couldn't possibly imagine then that a few years later I would be sitting at the kitchen table in a cold, desolate shack in the middle of Montana making endless little variations on a line, and that I would

4

finally turn to the naive, sensitive drawing of my children for inspiration.

I had never seen any but a worm's-eye view of Paris. Even when I had been a soldier there during the war, I had always ridden the subways. It was Oscar who showed me the top of Paris by bus. He took me to those little out-of-the-way galleries where they still had unsold paintings by Modigliani. I remember one little gallery on the second floor of some building not far from Montparnasse where they had some drawings by Modigliani and Picasso, drawn undoubtedly at the peak of some party. I have often wondered why the snobs hadn't to date purchased these drawings and paintings. They were pretty good. Of course, that was only an artist's opinion, and they do have critics for such purposes.

Later that winter, Oscar did some very good lithography, I brought them all back to the States for a show that had been arranged for him in Minneapolis. I remember the customs official in New York had given me a bad time because I had made the mistake of saying they weren't mine, and he wanted to know how much the lithographs were worth. I told him they were worth nothing. After a bit of haggling, he let me pass, wondering, no doubt, whether I was smuggling in priceless art treasure. I could hear him comment: "Those damn artists." Well, that particular bureaucrat can sleep at night, for Oscar had the show and sold one lithograph. The show's arranger bought it.

I heard from Oscar again after my return to America; once, when he got married, when he sent us a "hand drawn" wedding card, very Rubenesque. (It had been a shot-gun wedding.) Again I heard from him several years later when he had a family and was working for the U.S. Government in North Africa. He no longer painted; and he, too, thought about it only once in a while.

Ben was a plump, little fellow from New Jersey. He read Chaucer and was quite an authority on English literature, especially old English literature. Ben had the type of memory that could recall almost every object in complete detail. It was a monthly occurence for him to get drunk. The American students who worked in the middle studio got so they looked forward to the parties he threw then. He always managed to pick up some girl in the street and he always "drug" her up to the studio. And now, the ball began. He would lead his reluctant find from one easel to the other. First, he would elaborately introduce his girl to each of us, and then in his most articulate, broken French he would explain the esthetic values of our individual paintings. This procedure would continue for almost an hour, or until Ben needed another drink. The next morning, no matter how early we would get to the studio, there would be Ben sitting in his isolated corner. His eyes would be swollen and bloodshot, and all day long he would draw with meticulous detail hundreds of Dali-like bulbous kidneys, swollen bladders and bloated stomachs. During this hangover period he would hardly say a word, and the strange part of it all was that he always followed the same pattern.

Despite all of Ben's peculiarities, I remember him most for his tomato soup. I had never asked him, but I think he was an orphan. The only correspondence he received from the States was a monthly food package from an aunt in Pennsylvania, and the package always contained a can of Campbell's tomato soup. Well, the day the package arrived I would buy a small bottle of wine and a loaf of bread. This was my donation to the meal. Once in a while, if we had enough money, we would buy a couple of what the French called "Biffteck de Cheval" (beefsteak from a horse) on the black market. Ben was the cook, and he always flavored the tomato soup with a clove of garlic. I guess that was why I always associate Ben with tomato soup. I always looked forward to these meals, for no matter how much of a Bohemian you might consider yourself, there was always a little nostalgia for America; and, after all, what can be more representative of America than a can of Campbell's tomato soup — sans garlic?

I wish I could say some flattering things about Ben's art. He had been a cartoonist for a small newspaper in America and when he wasn't drawing kidneys and bladders, or painting idyllic self-portraits, he would doodle out a string of cartoons. I think Ben was the average person's notion of an artist. If imitating shape can be called drawing, then Ben was an artist. Most people admire this little acrobatic ability that all artists have. It probably dates back to the sixteenth century when the artist was nothing more than the town photographer, and it has little to do with his ability to produce art.

I have wondered about Ben. Certainly, with his keen mind and his deep appreciation of good art, one could expect him to produce a more sensitive painting. Maybe he just recalled everything *too* vividly.

Most artists who can't paint well usually manage to do a good print. Oscar was this way; he did charming lithographs. I think this reverts back to their lack of appreciation of what is form. Any print medium will automatically create its own line, surface, and edge. This is because of the medium's limitation, whereas with painting or drawing, and where there is no limitation, the artist must produce these qualities.

There are many people and events I would like to write about if brevity weren't an issue. There was the little Armenian from California who always ordered raw hamburgers. He had spent the entire winter trying to imitate Modigliani. How often one sees this, an artist imitating the mature master without first being the immature, inexperienced student.

There was a big Irish kid from New York who also had been a cartoonist at some time in his career. He had been there longer than most of us and was more fortunate than we because he knew a girl with a father who owned a gallery a few doors from the school. So, for these reasons, he was the only American artist in Paris that winter who had a one-man show. The day his show opened he came bursting with the news that the American Ambassador had come to see his exhibit. We all went outside and, sure enough, there in front of the gallery was a big black car, and inside there was the Ambassaor performing his ambassadorial function, looking sideways at a wall of modern art. This was the Irish kid's big moment, and why spoil it by telling him that it didn't matter what the Ambassador thought of his work but that in the long run it would matter what *we* thought.

I had known Jim and his wife back in Minneapolis. Jim had wanted to be a writer and now here he was, the most non-objective painter in school. The Avant Garde movement had just taken hold, and several artists were experimenting with these new forms in the middle studio. I just sat and watched and listened to them speak of an artist called Jackson Pollock. I never dreamed that several years later I would look out my kitchen window on a bleak, winter landscape in Montana and there find inspiration for countless Avant Garde painting and that I would dedicate several years trying to give these new forms style, purpose and organization.

Several years later Jim was given a one-man show in New York, and the critics received it well. The following year he had another show and the critics panned it. He's back in Minneapolis now; and he, too, just thinks about it once in a while.

Orthon Friez, one of the original Fauves, was an instructor at the Ecole de la Grand Chaumiere. He died in the middle of the term. I remember him as an old man with very little left to say. He was well represented in the Musee d'Art Moderne with five or six paintings. Many of his earlier works were nice. In his later years he turned to painting pot boilers, and several of them hung in bars near the school. These pot boilers must have been painted with the American male tourist in mind, for most of them were sweet little paintings of nudes lying out in the forest. I never could figure out what those nudes were doing in the woods, because they really didn't look as if they were waiting for a boy friend.

Oscar and I went to see Bernard Buffet's first big show. The French had become desperate for a new school of painting, a new genius, and they had settled on Buffet. But what a poor substitute for those masters who had preceded him! Buffet was a good second-rate painter, nothing more. I was fortunate because I witnessed the passing of a great era. The year before, Picasso, in his last great burst of creative energy, had done his lithograph series, Rouault had just burned three hundred of his paintings and a few months later had published *Miserere Guerre.* Matisse was working on his chapel at Vence. These giants would never create again. In America in a short while, in the persons of Pollock and DeKoonig, there would be one last flourish added to the history of easel painting, then it would gradually evolve into the meaningless doodles of a pseudo-Bohemian cult called the Beatniks.

The average public has never fully understood the true Bohemian. The Bohemians whom Paris nourished for more than a century were intellectuals in search of knowledge. I don't believe that Paris will ever attract such people again. In fact, there will be no need, for in a few years the colleges and universities in America will have devised a system whereby they can crank out textbook geniuses on an assembly line basis.

In time to come, but probably not in my lifetime, a return to a more indigenous culture will occur and the artist will probably be a more integral part of his society. The artists of tomorrow will realize that Paris had taken easel painting to its ultimate apex, that Matisse in designing his chapel had pointed the way to go.

The easel painting has always offered the artist his greatest challenge — a medium without limitations, a medium that gave him his greatest individuality. Despite the admiration I have for the great paintings of history, I realize now that easel painting was the artist's greatest downfall. While, if he were lucky, it gave him a place among the middle class, it also offered the middle class the expensive, snobbish hobby of collecting. Neither of these conditions had anything to do with culture. In the future the artist will return to his natural role of craftsman and artisan; his role as the esthete will be minor. His talent and curiosity will be his education. He will become more and more involved in the art of architecture. He will realize that architecture, instead of being an engineering feat, can be a fine art. There will be a more understanding and natural development of the inherent, sensitive and artistic charcteristics of all people.

This is my wish. The artist with his restless, imaginative mind cannot stand still; he has only this one direction to go.

William M. Stockton, Grass Range, 1961

The Arts in Living

One of the most negative concepts influencing the future of all the arts is the all-too-common idea that mere spectatorship is an adequate expression of artistic interest. It has become the vogue in current society to let others paint our pictures, dance our dances, act our plays, sing and play our concerts, and write our poetry. The arts have been taken away from the lives of people and placed upon the concert stage, in the art gallery, in the theater, in the literature anthologies and in the ballet. Many of these art expressions are so far removed from actual everyday lives of people that they are often inexplicable and unsatisfying as art experiences for the ordinary man.

To be effective in any culture, the arts must be part of the lives of people. This fact is historically true, as any inquiry into anthropology will reveal. Primitive peoples *lived* the arts: they danced their happiness and sorrow; they sang and played on handmade instruments to express their joys and sadness; they painted and drew a beautiful and revealing record of their lives; they dramatized their myths and their ceremonies; they developed poetic forms of storytelling as a means of beautifying a common activity.

All art forms are symbolic in nature; they represent ideas and emotion which can be expressed in no other way. Mere words cannot reveal the emotional response aroused by the color and composition of a painting, the rhythmic beauty of the dance, the harmonic intricacies of the symphony, the subtle nuances of the poem. At least one quality is inherent in all art forms — the quality of beauty. It may not be an understandable kind of beauty, but it is there, and can be discovered only through an active kind of participation in the art itself.

Why did man in his early struggles for existence develop the arts as a part of his life? Perhaps it was because man has a basic need for beauty along with his other needs. Perhaps he *had* to bring some kind of beauty into his life in order to survive. Whatever the reason, man deliberately and voluntarily made the arts a part of his life, thereby bringing beauty into his existence.

We moderns may well take a hint from primitive peoples. Beauty should be a part of our everyday lives, not a spectator kind of beauty, but an active, participating kind of art activity. There is no substitute for participation in the arts, mere verbalization about an art form is irrelevant to art.

It is unfortunately possible that present-day man has been "civilized" away from participation in the arts, but, nevertheless, man must still have that need for beauty which brought about the arts, and it is certain that he could profit from beauty in his life today. Certainly, in the negativism of an atomic age, *any* way of putting beauty into the lives of men is appropriate. Participating in the arts is suggested, therefore, as one way of bringing beauty into current life.

Alfred W. Humphreys, Helena, 1956

Art is A Human Need

Recently I heard a tape recording of a speech by William Schumann, director of Lincoln Center for the Performing Arts. He pointed out that four or five percent of the population support the arts in America — music, theater, dance, painting, serious film. This figure shows, he remarked, the extent to which we have failed to make the arts important in American education and life. It has also been pointed out, although not by Mr. Schumann, that if more cultural opportunities are made available, the same group will take advantage of them, few new people will be attracted.

How serious is this failure?

There is a certain ambiguity in our American attitude toward the arts. On the one hand, we often pay lip service to the idea that they must be supported, even for this astonishingly small minority, because sophisticated industries will not come into a community without museums, live theater, and live musical groups. Many men and more wives will not live in cultural deserts, however glorious the scenery, however pure the air. At the same time, support of all kinds for our metropolitan symphony orchestras, to give one example, has failed to keep up with costs, and there are indications that a number may disappear in the coming decade. Some corporations contribute heavily to support the arts, but burning concern with American cultural life is not a universal attribute of the corporate mind. The Federal Government has put its toes into the water and has pulled them out again.* Military and other concerns use up the tax dollar. It is obvious that most politicians do not take the arts seriously.

Well, after all, how much outlay of public and private funds should be made for four or five percent of the population, about nine million people?

---

*Since then Congress has provided a fund for the encouragement of the arts.

10

There is one answer that would be difficult to sell. This is that human beings, all human beings, need the arts, and the arts deserve as much support as public health. An art center is just as important as a sewage plant. Is America wealthy enough to have both?

I believe that the need for the arts is built into the human nervous system. One way of describing the brain, even of the lowest animal, is a mechanism of selection and coordination. In a sense, the brain gives order and form to stimuli, order and form to responses. Like the fabled music of the spheres, our nervous system is making a kind of order or art from the raw materials perceived by our sense organs.

From the nervous system or even from brain to human mind is an unexpected jump, but it is reasonable to suppose that the conscious and unconscious minds long for order and form as well as give it to the world. The arts can be defined in part by their function of giving form and order to their data or materials.

The composer, for example, selects from all sound waves those of certain wave lengths, certain duration, certain quality, certain order. He selects rhythms which are found in nature. These he combines into meaningful structures having beginnings that excite curiosity, middles that develop and create suspense, and endings that satisfy — the trinity of the arts. The same may be said of all other artists, except that they choose from other data.

Every human being hungers for the order and harmonies of art. Religion also satisfies this hunger, in that it gives meaning to the individual life and meaning to history. The creation of the world is the great archetypal artistic act. On another level, TV westerns, pop and rock songs, popular fiction, hymns to beer and deodorants supply structure and harmony on a superficial and sometimes mean scale. Baseball is the ballet of athletics.

Every human being longs for form as an antidote to the formlessness of sense data and of individual experience in a complex and sometimes inhuman society. The arts and religion provide the most meaningful contacts with form — not TV westerns but great fiction, drama, and myth; not songs about soap but songs about love, God, truth, and experience; not foldouts but great paintings. The human being cries out for bread and is handed a plastic sandwich.

It is because men need the arts as creators or "consumers," not because the arts have some secondary effect on the economic growth of the community, that we should do what we can to encourage the availability of the arts in our communities. There is a whole unexplored frontier in public education and the training of teachers.

If fifty percent of the population were interested in the arts rather than five percent, William Schumann said, we would have opera in the small towns of America, art centers in the hamlets. We would have fifty percent of the population more fully alive, instead of four or five percent.

Robert T. Taylor, Butte, 1969

Mass Art and Elite Art

I. LEVELS OF ART

Throughout much of the history of the Western world, one or two arts have existed — folk art and elite art. In the last century and a half, a third kind of art has appeared — mass art.

Folk art is the art of the illiterate, the relatively uncivilized. While some have thought that it is the work of groups, what we know of creativity would seem to indicate that it was the work of gifted individuals, perhaps like the master poets of Wales, who perfomed as well as created their works.

Folk art, whatever the mechanics of its creation, offers more than entertainment to its audience, since it often embodies in it both the history and the ideals of a people. It is the source of epics. It may also be of religious significance.

At the same time, whenever the conditions of life have allowed an elite class to arise, there has been an elite art. Most of the art we know from the past is elite art, for it is the art of the literate. What we know of folk art we know because it survived into an age of literacy and was of interest to literate men. Usually folk art and elite art have existed side by side. The court minstrel would chant songs of chivalry to the lord and his retainers while the country singer would entertain the peasant with tales of Robin Hood.

However, with the gradual civilizing of the Western world, particularly with the transition to industrial and at least partially democratic societies, folk art almost ceased to exist. Where folk art survived, as in the hill country of the American South, it survived in isolated pockets and was, practically speaking, frozen and not actively creative.

Mass art, which was born with the industrial revolution, according to most accounts, apparently took the place of folk art for those of limited education and undeveloped taste. Mass art is art disseminated through mass media, that is, any media that reach huge numbers of people — magazines, popular books, television, radio, movies, newspapers. Its main purpose is to make money for its creators or sponsors or publishers or purveyors or all of them. Its secondary purpose is to entertain or, in some cases, to inform its audience. Although it may be the work of a single individual, as in the case of a book, it is often the work of groups, as a movie or television show, and the responsibility for it is scattered and diffused.

What we have called elite art (perhaps "minority art" would be a better term) is also in many cases disseminated through mass media, but to much smaller audiences. It is the work of individuals. Its aim is the communication of vision and, incidentally, the solution of artistic problems. It may be in the service of an idea — as a burning wish to reform a corrupt society, but it is not intended to make money for anyone or primarily to entertain, in the same sense that popular art is. It also, unlike the mass art of the Soviet Union, does not serve as a political instrument of government.

If we accept the definitions so far, we can see that elite art is closer to folk art than folk art is to the popular art which supposedly replaced it. Possibly this fact may explain why much past folk art of primitive peoples is acceptable to the usual audience of elite art. Both elite and folk art are the products of individuals; both are traditional; both are concerned with serious problems or irreverent laughter; neither exists primarily for commercial ends.

Since mass art must appeal to large numbers if it is to be profitable, it must be superficial and insipid. It cannot offend the prejudices of its mass audience or of any minority group in it. In the case of television, it cannot offend the prejudices or endanger the reputation of its sponsors. It cannot deal with great issues in a complex way, because the great issues are often disturbing rather than entertaining, and the mental, educational, and cultural limitations of part of a mass audience will cause them to turn the dial, or walk out of the theater,or throw away the book. Only villains can die. Sex is sometimes taboo (as in television) but meaningless violence never. Platitudes are a substitute for philosophy.

On the other hand, elite art exists because its creators have something compelling to say, and they must follow their own view of things so far as possible, no matter what prejudices and beliefs get trampled. Elite art is sometimes simple, but it is never superficial. It may on the contrary be ornate and complex, but its object is truth, never sale, never simple entertainment or watered down information. It is free, autonomous. It is *The Brothers Karamazov* compared to *Peyton Place*.

Edward Shils has suggested that perhaps a third level might be added to mass art and elite art — mediocre art. Mediocre art lies between true elite art — that which meets high standards of truth and beauty — and mass "brutal" art. It would include such diverse things as musical comedy and Sunday paintings of rural scenes. This level might be included for art which is primarily therapy or innocent self-expression as well as middle brow entertainment that do not reach large audiences but which also do not satisfy the tastes of the audience of elite art.

II. DEFENSES AND CRITICISM

From a certain point of view, criticism of mass art is inherent in its definition, as I have given it. Words like *superficial* and *insipid* are purposely words with strong connotations. Curiously enough, however, even its defenders often define mass art in about the same way, with the same negative and scarcely endearing qualities.

What then, one may ask, can they defend?

The most usual defenses are these: Well, what is wrong with entertainment? People get what they want. No minority has a right to thrust culture, however high, down the throats of the majority. This is a free country. There is still elite art for those who prefer it.

On a more sophisticated level, we have analyses of man and his societies. The greatest part of mankind, let us remember, has an I.Q. under 110, which everyone knows is only high average. The tastes of this majority, as well as its capacity for complexity and abstraction, have never been high. At any period of time, the limitations of mankind are a persistent fact. If at any period, the mass of men had had the buying power and if an entertainment industry had had the technological resources we have today, the situation in the arts would have been the same as it is today.

In other words, everyone admits that as mass art it is not much good, but on the other hand, it is nothing to be alarmed about. Elite art is still alive, and even mass media give it space; *Life* prints the old masters and the young ones as well as pictures of monkeys on bicycles.

Those who are not content to look on mass art complacently, viewing it as a tolerable phenomenon, if nothing very rewarding to men of good taste, are somewhat more alarmed. To them, mass art is a serious threat to elite art and to what we prize in civilization.

First, mass art tends to drive out elite art, partly because the devil has the money. The potentially great artist in the traditional sense is discouraged by the intense commercialism in the arts that makes it

14

virtually impossible for him to make a living. Elvis Presley for two songs recently made enough money to pay the average writer or teacher twenty years. Young American singers who have trained for years are often forced to live abroad, because there is no work for them in rich America although there is plenty for Fabian. The values of our society are plainly inverted, but the knowledge of this is not bread in the artist's mouth. The excellent but not popular book has increasingly fewer chances of being published — the cost in a competetive business world is too high. The artist of integrity has no opportunity anywhere to work as an artist rather than a craftsman in television, radio, or movies, unless he has the unique good fortune of an Ingmar Bergman. Good plays may go forever unplayed, because the cost of production on Broadway is too high, and where else, really, can you put on a play? So long as most of the money available for the arts goes to mass art, elite art is in danger.

Second, mass art tends to dull values for the audience of art, to substitute an inferior satisfaction for deeper experience. If we admit that experiences with great art are worthwhile, then we will be unhappy with anything less good. We can satisfy our appetite with sugar, but we must have protein to grow. Even if we assume that most men are clods by nature — a theory which some of us would not admit as fact — the sizable minority which could enjoy the innumerable pleasures of the arts are likely to grow up and old insensitive in many areas and content with drivel. Good potential is not a guarantee of performance, and the sight of scientists and specialists who are cultural barbarians is a saddening one. If most of a child's art experiences outside of school (where there is a little music, less painting and sculpture, and a modicum of first-rate literature) are with mass art, because that is all that is available in many areas of our land, then many women will not live as fully as they might if their potentialities for artistic experiences were realized. One of the ideals of democracy as we know it is a good life for every individual. Perhaps we should be somewhat concerned about a minimum cultural wage.

"Exaggeration!" the reader is likely to snort. After all *Life* does print pictures by Picasso in four colors along with pictures of Picasso's mistresses in one color, if the *Saturday Evening Post* does print Bertrand Russell along with soap operas, if T.V. does present *Jane Eyre,* however truncated and vulgarized, if advertisers do use the techniques of elite art to increase the sensibility of the masses, then elite art is not likely to be smothered or our children to grow up, as Ortega y Gasset said of Americans, a primitive people hiding behind the latest inventions. Yet such presentations of elite art are precisely what Dwight MacDonald in a provocative essay calls "homogenized culture." How can the unwary tell the value of elite art among the mass, if both are represented the same way? Is showing that Picasso is a sensual man (thus, as we would like to be) a key to experiencing his art? The voice of mass media is always shrill, and the values it finds in elite art are unlikely to be the right ones.

III. DECISIONS

All of this has significance in our lives, whether we are artists in any sense or simply the experiencers of art works. The artist in particular must choose, if he can, between God and Mammon. It may be that his talents fit him ideally for mass art, in which case he may count his money along with his blessings. There is nothing shameful in having an entertaining, popular mind.

Then, too, as history reminds us, few men in any age are great enough artists for their work to survive them. To forsake popular art is not necessarily to join the Olympians. One may be mediocre or Bohemian. To strive for greatness is always fraught with risk, in our time perhaps more than in any other.

If the artist can afford the luxury of his integrity, however, he must try to create out of his own vision, even if it is not a very clear one. His reward may be only his virtue and a sense of having done his best.

What we can hope for is not the death of mass art, which has a place apparently in our world, but rather some improvement in the state of affairs that tends to drive out elite art and deify mass art. Individuals can make themselves heard. Businessmen, we are told, are sensitive to criticism and praise. There is some hope that institutions may do more. Could not foundations pour less into group research and more into helping conscientious publishers meet the dictates of their conscience? Could not some of this money go into the arts, into repertory theater, more grants to artists of proven merit?

Would it be the red road to socialism if the government reworked the tax structure to favor the slow, cautious writer rather than the nimble hack? Might we think even of the possibility of government pensions for artists like those of many European countries, who count their artists as national resources? A great composer, a solid artist, and a writer of achievement are as worthy of protection as the Sequoia or Old Faithful. So long as the air theoretically belongs to the whole people, could we not ask for more FCC pressure to allow time on radio and television for programs that admittedly would not appeal to twenty million people but might appeal to one million? Many fear a Secretary of the Arts, but all government activity is not necessarily evil, except to anarchists.

16

Members of the MIA should be alert to the situation in the arts and alert to ways in which they may as individuals and as members of groups help to foster the arts in America. We should not denigrate mass arts or the popular artist, but we should be concerned that elite art has the opportunity to remain alive.

Robert T. Taylor, Butte, 1961

Art and Feeling Free

Art has always been, in its essence, on the side of human freedom, whatever attempts have been made to enlist it on the side of repressive *status quos*. An unfree art is, in the last analysis, a contradiction in terms, as perhaps one of these days the Soviet Union will find out. But it is this very freedom that has made many, from Plato on down, rather afraid of art. Our Puritan forebears were definitely up-tight about it. All authoritarian regimes fear it, often to the point of trying to take it over in order to control it, overtly as in the Soviet Union at the present time, or more covertly, more subtly, unfortunately, in much of the commercially-dominated culture of our own country where the take-over is often symbolized by the picture of the artist and his work on the cover of *Time* or by his exploitation by the television medium. We accept the artist's response, and therefore feel we don't have to do anything about it, thus defeating his essential purpose.

This fear of the arts is, as I say, essentially a fear of freedom — of that very freedom we all need so badly, the inner or spiritual dimension of freedom that many of us have to try to get from the psychiatrist, often without success, as well as the larger social freedom this implies and which is in turn implied by it. And there's a strong root-connection, therefore, though often rather deeply buried, between this fear and the fear of democracy that so marks our national life. (The more up-tight among us call it fear of Communism; but when the chips are down it usually turns out to be a fear of democracy itself). And this very fear itself needs the power of art to release us from it, strange as this may seem. By close familiarity with art, especially with the practice of it, and by becoming aware, as perhaps many of us are not, of its freeing influence on our own lives, we may come in turn to learn, convincingly, that freedom does not hurt us, that we need not fear it and that in the final analysis we need it at least as much as we need food and air and water and all the rest.

17

Thus even the humble molder of ceramic ashtrays is participating in some degree in the experience of freedom and is contributing to the inner and outer freedom we are all going to have to find, in far larger measure than we know it now, if we are to survive upon this earth. Anyone who thinks a nation's or a region's or an individual's art is merely the froth on the surface of life, a pleasant diversion from the daily grind, a harmless hobby that can safely and painlessly siphon off our tensions, is missing the real point. Art can and does do these things, of course, in its many protean forms. And those who fear art's freedom would hope that this is all it does. But any art that does these things also touches life much more deeply. It tells us, as individuals, what it means to feel free genuinely. Even as it expresses our tensions, it records a response to life in more or less significant form, articulating our response to the felt discrepancy between the real and the ideal that points to change, however infinitesimally, and therefore is incipiently revolutionary.

The cultural climate MIA helps greatly to maintain is the climate of freedom.

Robert Athearn, Middlebury, Vermont, 1971

On Being An Artist

In my day I have read thousands of student writings and a similar number of writings by adults, both prose and verse. Much of it has been uninteresting to me or anyone else simply because the writers had not thought when writing. All of them no doubt thought that they had thought. It was not that they could not think or would not but that the mother tongue and the mother wit had provided them with so much everyday material and expression that what they wrote rolled off the penpoint or the typewriter keys almost of itself.

Northrup Frye in his recent book, *The Educated Imagination,* expressed this idea: "We can't use our minds at full capacity unless we have some idea of how much of what we think we're thinking is really thought, and how much is just familiar words running along their own familiar tracks. Nearly everyone does enough talking, at least, to become fairly fluent in his own language, and at that point there's always danger of automatic fluency, turning on a tap and letting a lot of platitudinous bumble emerge." This faucet flow is what is used, unless we are deeply respectful of our minds, in a tea-time talk or in face-to-face dance-floor whispering or in a drawing-room conversation or, indeed, in any passing

18

conversation. Or we use it in faucet-filled letters, formal or informal. In social circles we call this "small talk" and the person who hasn't it is at a social disadvantage.

This fluency we acquire from social custom, from familiarity with objects around us, from repeated circumstances calling for repeated actions, from newspaper and light reading, possibly from all reading that is not concentrated in nature. In other words, simply existing supplies us with what has been dubbed "fatal fluency" — fatal to good talk and to good writing.

If we wish to be interesting, and who does not, we must examine our use of words and phrases and even whole sentences to discover whether they are those used by everybody else, used without thought, are merely cliches, are taken from someone else or from our reading and used thoughtlessly — from the top of the head. If in writing we use the language of everyday fluency our prose is flat and stale and our verse fails to appeal to any but automatic readers. So much for the writer's use of familiar words and phrases.

Another failing among these many writings I have read has lain in the writers having ceased to see really and to hear — except in familiar phrases and tones. This, like the preceding idea, applies to other artists than writers. When you paint, for instance, a landscape, you see familiar objects — a mountain, an old barn, a field of poppies. Very well, you *know* that poppies are yellow or golden, let us say, and so you paint them yellow or golden, but when you have finished the painting you have not painted the poppies you saw but the poppies your information about them told you they are. I once saw in an exhibition I was proctoring a painting which had in it a cow drinking at a stream; the cow was a greenish color. I sat down near the picture to hear the comments of observers. The drift? "A green cow? Absurd." But it wasn't absurd, for the light at the time of day depicted made the white cow green. You set out to throw the form of a pitcher on the wheel — What can you do to make it *your* pitcher and not any ceramist's pitcher? Your information about pitchers tells you the form a pitcher is: you make that form.

Not long ago I was reading Ernest Hemingway's account of his early days in Paris, *A Moveable Feast,* and came upon these sentences: "Since I had started to break down all my writings and *get rid of* facility and try to make instead of describe, writing had been wonderful. But it was very difficult." Hemingway broke down his facility by knowing closely what he wished to express and then questioning each word and phrase and sentence for its rightness in expressing just that. No curleycues, no fancy words, no trite phrases, no unnecessary words or phrases, no facile language, no faucet flow. By trying to "make instead of to describe" he meant a process like, for instance, a carpenter's when he makes something — he knows his materials and his tools and how to handle both, has in mind the image he intends to construct and proceeds to make the object.

Much writing has not sprung from *knowing* what was to be expressed. It made itself by use of familiar images or ideas and familiar words that ran "along their own familiar tracks." For almost every normal situation in life society has invented language, has made and set conversation, and we use just that unless acutely conscious of what we are writing or saying. The handling of tools, words and their relationships, is difficult. Because of society's ready-made ideas and ready-made language — whether in writing or painting or weaving or whatever — and because of the difficulty in handling the tools, in writing or any other art, we slip into familiar ideas and expression of them.

In writing, less experienced and less thoughtful writers rely largely upon adjectives and adverbs, the former changing the nouns to a more limited or a larger meaning and the latter changing the verbs similarly. Once in a class in writing A.B. Guthrie, Jr. read aloud a paragraph by John Burroughs which he admired; I asked him to count the number of adjectives and adverbs Burroughs had used; he examined the paragraph and, astounded, replied, "None."

Very simply illustrated, the difference between describing and making may be discovered in these two sentences: "The young man walked fast down the street," and "The youth strode down the street." Or again, the describer might write: "The round dying sun as it was setting turned the whole sky into a golden color"; the maker might write: "The setting sun poured gold over the sky." A much subtler distinction is seen in a sentence I ran across in John Mason Brown's *The World of Robert Sherwood;* he wrote, "When he walked down the street it became a boulevard." That is true making, not describing.

The describer tells the reader about something; the maker brings the scene alive by forcing the reader to use his imagination. What passed through your mind when you read Mr. Brown's sentence? A poorly written story gives you the materials for putting a story together, leaving it for the reader to do the making. The maker, the artist, puts life into the story so that you realize it. That is one reason why when you are reading a good story you don't hear a person speaking to you.

Similarly, the painter or any other artist unless he is thinking hard and is intent on creating is likely to follow what his information or his instruction tells him things are and thus becomes untrue to what he sees and hears (if he does really see and hear) and uncreative for the reader.

Being an artist — in words or paint or yarn or clay or tones — is difficult. It calls, too, for being one's self.

H. G. Merriam, Missoula, 1966

The Years and the Wind and the Rain

Almost every poet or fiction writer* has a helper to whom he can never give credit in public because of the name of the thing: genius. Sometimes he writes more profoundly than he really can, and he knows it. But he can't admit it. He can't give proper credit to his genius, because that would be boasting, which in our culture is not permitted. Therefore he must pretend that he did this fine thing all by himself — and that is not only boasting but a big lie besides.

The trouble is in the word "genius." We think of it as "extraordinary power of invention, native intellectual power of an exalted type." We equate genius with a high IQ.

One of the most obnoxious people I ever met managed to mention about once a week that she had an IQ of 147 and that 140 was supposed to be genius level. Of diamonds it has been said, "Them as has 'em wears 'em," but nobody ever gave leave to owners of high IQ's to flash their glitter on our eyes.

Fortunately for my peace of mind, I went through school before psychologists and schoolteachers worried about IQ tests. So there are no records anywhere to prove (a) that I'm not very bright, or (b) that, being especially gifted, I ought to accomplish a lot more than I'm ever going to.

Centuries before I progressed through the public schools of Whitefish, Montana without benefit of mental testing, genius had another meaning. The religion of the ancient Romans held that every person had his own genius. It was an attendant guardian spirit allotted to him at birth to govern his fortunes and determine his character and finally to conduct him out of the world.

This makes sense. What everybody has nobody can boast about. To an ancient Roman, it was no more remarkable to possess a genius than it was to have ten toes. They were all part of the package. I suppose a successful man could assume that he had an especially good genius, and a failure could find comfort in the thought that he wasn't entirely to blame.

We have lost, except in dictionaries, this meaning of "genius." Maybe everybody doesn't have a tutelary spirit now. Maybe it's still here but

*Or artist of any kind, or creative scientist, I suppose.

21

dormant, silent and powerless because we don't know about it or believe in it.

A creative artist is likely to know he has a genius, although he may prefer to let the world think that he wrote his book or composed his music or painted his pictures all by himself. Of course, the genius isn't always on the job. Many a book is written entirely solo and it would be an insult to one's genius to give it a by-line.

Now that I've gone into the antique meaning of "genius," I can admit that I have one, in the sense that everybody is entitled to one, and mine is free to help me because I recognize its existence and am grateful to it. The old gods pine and starve and die when nobody believes in them anymore. Zeus and Odin and perfect swarms of other deities no longer exist, after staying fat for centuries on the faith that fed them. Satan probably isn't looking very well, either. At least most Protestants don't hear very much about him any more.

My genius is a flibbertigibbet, here today and gone tomorrow, or more likely here yesterday when I was too busy to listen and unaccountably missing today when I have a couple of free hours and a fresh ribbon in the typewriter.

On page 199 of a book called *Northwest Verse*, edited by H.G. Merriam and published in 1931, appears this poem, which was first published in *Frontier*, a literary magazine that he edited:

OLD MINE

> Once there were men here.
> The pebbled dirt roof of the cellar
> Juts out from under the hill.
> A pile of tin cans, so rusty
> As to be almost a part of the earth, by now,
> Lies at the foot of the hill.
> The house is gone, and the men —
> God only knows where they have left their picks.
> Here are only their leavings
> And a gash in the earth that is almost healed.
> And the years and the wind and the rain
> Heal everything.

That was written by an eighteen-year-old girl, a student at Montana State University, who was describing something she saw from a train window. Nobody ever said it was great poetry. But I insist no girl of eighteen could possibly be wise enough to write those last two lines. They did not come from experience, from inside; they came from an attendant genius, who was wiser than the girl who wrote them down. The girl was, in fact, doubtful about that statement. *Did* the years and the wind and the rain really heal everything, or was she just guessing? I remember the circumstances vividly because I was that doubtful girl.

I am a girl no longer, though often still doubtful. More than fifty years of living have proved to me that those lines were truly written. I wish I could have been sure long ago. Certain subsequent events would have been easier to endure if I had believed my attendant genius.

For a long time after seeing the old mine I had the idea that there was something especially inspirational about riding on a train and always took along a notebook. But the skittish spirit doesn't always take the same train I do. Once, however, she shared my seat on a plane eastbound from Billings, and we wrote an awfully good story as soon as we got to a typewriter.

Dorothy M. Johnson, Missoula, 1961

The Fundamental Concept of Design

When engaging in the creative process a person tends to choose certain arrangements, proportions and color combinations that are pleasing to himself and to at least some of those people who view his results. It might also be noted that as an individual gains more esthetic experience in making value judgments with respect to design there is greater awareness of and sensitivity for the finer nuances and the more complex combinations of form and color. Two facts are significant: certain choices are made more frequently than others; and as the designer gains experience he is better able to discriminate between choices. A design element might be chosen either because of some cultural determinant growing out of the individual's racial, national, regional, family, or personal background or because of an emotionally felt empathy to the element which could also be a personal thing or something more fundamentally characteristic of race.

If the question were asked, "What are some of the basic principles of design?" the restrictions placed on the extent of the question and on its answer could become very complex and lengthy. I would like to restrict the answer to a single fundamental based on the individual's need for stimulation and for rest on the visual-neural level.

23

There are certain designs in paintings, buildings, and other forms of visual arts which have been accepted as being esthetically good. The basic principle of design that can be noted in each is the variety in unity or the unity in variety, depending upon which characteristic is predominant. Individual value judgments might differ on the degree to which lyrical unity should rule over changing elements. There have been periods in human history when sameness, conformity, repetition and refinements were the rule, eliminating variety even in the thinking of the individual.

But the point is that the beauty of wheat fields or of trees on a mountain side comes from the unity of color and shape of the related elements — without variation of light and shadow or of tree shapes interest would be lacking. An interesting example of the controversy of sameness versus difference or of integration versus contrast is the one between the so-called ''organic'' architects and the ''international'' — the former group make much of the unity between the structure and its surroundings. They experience a real visual delight in the blending of a building with its surroundings in which the unity of texture, color, and shape of the building and its materials tie it to the land. The internationalists, originating largely from the thinking of the Bauhaus school of art and architecture in Germany after World War I, admire the clean, measured machined lines of materials produced by our modern technology. They take pleasure in the maximum contrasts — variety — a carefully machined metal window frame working against a rough-hewn stone which in turn contrasts with the natural rock of the site. Others of this group seem to have gone to the extreme of favoring only smooth non-contrasting glass and porcelain and steel surfaces. Actually, the ''organic'' and ''international'' positions are not so far apart — aside from certain political and social implications which are outside the scope of this discussion — it becomes simply a matter of the degree to which unity or the degree to which variety gains attention in a particular design, whether it be a house or a pot, is created with sensitivity and understanding.

As has been suggested, the use of contrast is an expression of variety; so is the concept of ''dominance.'' The church or castle in a typical European village is an example of such dominance; so is a power pole in the middle of the front lawn, but in one case there is equilibrium which controls the dominance and in the other only an uncontrolled, dominating element or elements as opposed to the lyrical or static.

To carry the argument further, a created, man-made object might be said to have either unity with or opposition to the human nervous system in terms of empathy. If there is too much variation from what the human mind expects or desires the reaction is an unpleasant one; if there is too

24

much unity the observer is bored. If a thing functions too well it is taken for granted; but it must meet certain needs for visual delight or some mundane requirements or no one would bother to keep it around.

The artist, writer, architect, craftsman, or musician finds his creative effort, then, that of controlling unity and variety in the use of his medium to produce a result that will give a sense of pleasant, relaxing continuity and delightful, stimulating surprise for the esthetic pleasure of himself and others.

Ernest Bruffey, Havre, 1956

Art and the Coincidences of Life

Many, many years ago, about 1916, when I was, I think, a sophomore in Balboa, Canal Zone High School, I had by then had more than a vague beginning of the feeling that I wanted to be an artist. I saw some art which I admired very much that whetted my ambition to be an artist. The artist was Sidney Delevante, who had a signature I thought clever and distinguished. I admired him so much that I tried to make my own signature clever along the line of his and for years I signed my John Henry similar to Delevante's lettering. Some time ago I saw in *Art News* magazine in our Public Library some mention of a one-man show of works of an artist named Delevante, and the article stated he was teaching in New York City, at Columbia University it turned out. I took typewriter in hand and wrote him a letter, nearly fifty years after I was inspired by his works, and shortly received a most friendly letter from him in reply.

Another Panamanian, Fernando, Alegre J., a great friend of mine from high school days, wrote a letter in Spanish for me about 1919 which helped lead to a job in Colombia, South America. I worked for the U.S. Consul there. Later he became an agent of South American Gulf Oil Co. Since this man, Issac A. Manning, was a painter of lovely landscapes, I got encouragement to keep on trying to learn something about art. I drew all the time I could find and still have many of the sketches I did in my days on the Spanish Main.

Recently I found a postcard I wrote my brother Lon at Helena, on April 12, 1919, reading:

> I have made my primary step in big business. Am well satisfied with the American Consulate and the Gulf Refining Co., where I am getting both Spanish and English commercial experience. I am making pretty

25

good money here and expect to be in good position to go to the States in about a year where I hope to attend the Academy of Fine Arts in Chicago.

That letter resulted in my coming to Helena, Montana, in 1920. In the fall of 1920 when I was living in Helena, the State Fair was held there. I found that it had an art department for competitive entries and decided to enter something. The catalog stated that entries were open to two classifications of artists, professional and amateur. The former was "one who had not done China painting." I figured I was an amateur. I entered something and got an award of some kind and was again encouraged to keep on keeping on.

Soon after moving to Great Falls in 1921 I naturally gravitated toward Charley Russell. I also met Joe DeYoung, Russell's only protege. Joe and I bummed around together and, of course, had a mutual interest in art. One day, perhaps in 1924, Joe suggested we try our hands at etching. I had never seen an etching, much less made one, and no one in Montana was practicing the art.

About that time commercial art work for the Swanzey Advertising Agency of Great Falls brought me in touch with Mike Becker, owner of the Great Falls Engraving Company. Mike Becker gave me scrap copper plates to mess around with. After getting what meagre information I could, which was practically nothing, I scratched a drypoint etching of my wife-to-be and also a couple of plates of scenes along the Missouri River. Another man whom I knew through my advertising art work was a printer named Con Rumpff, who owned the Montana Printing Company. Con was good enough to let me have a key to his print shop and go there evenings to use whatever they had to try to make proofs of my etchings. Night after night I would fill the bed of his geared proof press with type furniture to enable me to bring my plates up close to the top roller. To get pressure I used padding of newsprint paper and now and then blotters. I used the tacky printing inks such as Con had for his regular commercial printing jobs and found them difficult to handle on the plates. Later I studied Lumsden's *Art of Etching* and learned to make my own etching ink. I also made a press, which I still have and use. I proofed on some pieces of deckle-edged papers that Con let me have from samples sent him by paper companies. I finally got some handmade papers, like Umbria from Italy, Kalmar from Sweden, Rives from France, and Tovil from England, along with some marvelous Japanese handmades from the old Japan Paper Co. My enthusiasm knew no bounds! I am still a "buff" for handmade papers; my latest acquisition is some "amate papel," such as made by the ancient Mexican Indians in pre-Cortez days and still made by the Otomi Indians near Cuernavaca.

Several years before World War II, I was on the Great Northern Empire Builder en route to Kansas City to attend a meeting of Socony Vacuum Oil Company, by which company I was then employed as their Montana manager. I was sitting in the club car and beside me was a Japanese. As he was very friendly we got to talking. He noticed my Flying Red Horse-Socony lapel button and asked me, "Where did you get that?" I replied that I worked for that company and he said, "So do I." He was an industrial engineer of the Yokohama Branch and was on his way to New York to a meeting. We corresponded over the years and each Christmas, except during the war years, I received from him beautiful Japanese prints, Christmas greetings. In 1962 Mrs. Stevenson and I went on a trip to Japan and the Orient, and on a stay-over in Yokohama-Tokyo we were invited to visit the Tonomuras, my friend and his family. Miss Iris Tonomura, who studied art in San Francisco, asked me if I'd be interested in handmade papers. She took me to a place where I got some, including the famous Torinoko, which paper I had studied about but never had hoped to possess. Since our return these friends have sent me a large box full of beautiful handmade paper, very suitable for proofing prints.

One day before I met Tonomura, a friend, Orlo Misfeldt, said to me, "If you ever get to Missoula be sure to look up Robert MacNab, manager of the Florence Hotel, as he has some rare fine prints of etchings and such." Not long afterwards I was in Missoula and asked at the hotel to see Mr. MacNab. The man at the desk was MacNab himself. He took me to a room off the mezzanine floor and showed me the finest collection of etchings I had ever seen — Callots, Rembrandts, Whistlers, Samuel Palmers, Frank Bensons and many other great names of art. I was simply amazed. When I got ready to leave a day or two later MacNab said, "Be sure to look me up when you are over here again, as I will have something else to show you."

A couple of months later I was there again, and the minute he saw me MacNab took me to the basement of the Florence, where, in a large well-lighted room, was an etching press, one imported from England, stacks of handmade papers from many countries, diamond-point etching needles, stacks of English hand-hammered, beautifully cut and beveled polished copper and aluminum plates, Kimber inks and burnt linseed oils, tarlatan wiping rags — everything needed by an etcher. I asked, "How come you have all this?" and he replied, "It's for you!" I said, "Come, let's back up, what do you mean for me? I only met you a couple of months ago." He said, in effect, "I knew you would come along, so here's the stuff you are to work with, now settle down this trip and start using it, and come back often." When I left he loaded me down with polished plates, handmade papers and a fine book on the printing of engravings and etchings.

One of the plates he gave me was aluminum. I put an acid-resistant ground on it that MacNab had from Kimbers in England, and when I returned through Helena I went up Last Chance Gulch toward the Spring Hill Mine and sat down and drew directly on the plate a drawing looking from there towards Helena. When I got home I tried to etch it in the usual acid I had learned to use with copper plates, but the acid seemed to have no effect on the aluminum.

I was about to throw the plate aside when my wife said, "Why don't you try to etch it with lye?" I asked why she thought that would work and she told me she once got some kitchen lye on an aluminum dishpan and it ate holes in it. I etched that plate in lye and it, with another etching, "Night Around the Roundhouse," a color aquatint, made the grade in the International Printmakers show at the Los Angeles Museum.

One day I was returning from Kansas City via Burlington route into Billings. In the club car a lady and I got talking. She turned out to be Ruth Starr Rose, a lithographer of the American Artists Group, New York. She was on her way to a dude ranch vacation. As we were talking about art I dropped the word that I did some etching, but had always wondered if I could do lithograph. Ruth Starr Rose said that as she had always wanted to do etchings, if I would write her instructions she would write some for me on making a lithograph. My letter to her on etchings brought one from her telling all about making a lithograph. She also sent me a grained zinc lithograph plate on which to make my first one.

I was so full of enthusiasm and curiosity and ignorance, that I proceeded at once to make a lithograph of a drawing I had made several years before of a Crow Indian watering his horse at the Little Big Horn River, when Jo DeYoung and I attended the 50th anniversary of Custer's Last Stand in 1925. It dawned on me that I didn't have a lithograph press to pull a proof of the lithograph I'd drawn. Enter the late Ed Oxy. At that time the *Tribune* of Great Falls had in their employ a lithographer of the old school, in Germany, who proofed and transferred the old lithograph stone designs they had of labels, letterheads, and such, to flexible modern zinc lithograph plates that are printed at high speed by offset rotary presses. I took my plate to Oxy, and timidly asked him if he could proof it for me. He kidded me, saying he'd never seen a drawing done right on the grained plates. I apologized for bothering him, but he insisted I stick around while he tried to get something out of it. He put it on the proof press bed and sponged it over with what I found out later was an etch of gum arabic and nitric acid. When that was swished over the plate he took a handful of rags and rubbed it dry as he twirled a fan on a stick with the other hand. After that was dry and he had lighted a cigarette, he took a rag saturated, I found out later, in turpentine and rubbed over it, dissolving out the crayon drawing. Lithograph grease crayon is soluble in turpentine but the undrawn sections covered with the insoluble-in-turpentine gum arabic are protected. Then he fanned that dry and doused the plate with a sponge full of water that dissolved the gum and washed the already dissolved crayon off the plate with the gum. As my drawing had apparently disappeared, I was ready to give up, but he told me to keep my shirt on and stick around. Then he leisurely rolled up his horsehide roller with oily lithographic ink and applied a film of water over the plate with a sponge. The water wet the undrawn portions but refused to adhere to the oil crayon-drawn parts. Then he rolled his inking roller across the water-damped plate; the ink adhered to the oily crayon-drawn portions but refused to ink the water-wet areas. Up jumped the devil — my drawing — in black ink just as I had made it! It was unbelievable to me, who had never before witnessed the process. Oxy then proceeded to lay some good damped paper on the inked plate, put a metal tympan over the paper, pulled the bed and press and plate edge up under the greased scraper bar, pulled the pressure lever down and ran it through by cranking the press. The proof was perfect! I finally found a second-hand lithograph proofing press for sale in Denver, and one place or another got some lithograph stones. So several coincidences finally made it possible for me to make lithographs.

The Montana Institute of the Arts was founded in 1948, and it was my good fortune to attend the founding meeting in the Placer Hotel Ratskeller. That was truly a milestone in Montana's art world. Do not let anyone ever make you think that Montana "is a cultural vacuum," as I have often heard. I believe that in proportion to our population we have more art interest in and creation of art works worthwhile in nature in Montana than any other place I have been in my checkered career.

I could go on telling of other personal coincidences of art. I could tell you about meeting a truly great art teacher, Sister Mary Trinitas of the College of Great Falls, who got me into clay working and pottery, and how that led coincidentally to the foundation of the great Archie Bray Foundation at Helena. I could tell of my great ceramic engineer pen-pal and friend, Dr. Paul E. Cox of Baton Rouge, or about discovery of interesting minerals of Montana such as Volcanillon, Volcanoula, and the making of "Bransonite" Montana turquoise from one of them. I could tell of interesting dreams that led to certain inventions such as clay-in-clay inlay, application of clay figures a la Wedgewood.

One Saturday a man who used to be associated with me brought his two sons for a visit to my basement workshop. I showed them how pots are thrown and I pulled an etching, explaining other art processes I work with. The following Monday in the office the father said to me that on Saturday evening at supper his youngest son asked, "Dad, is Mr. Stevenson a millionaire?" The father said he answered, "Why no, son, what makes you think he is?" The son rejoined, "Well, how could anyone have all that good stuff to play around with in his basement if he's not a millionaire?"

I'll sign off with this thought.

Branson Stevenson, Great Falls, 1964

Gallery Talk

At Pratt Institute we certainly don't refer to "minor arts" when we talk about industrial design or ceramics, and we don't talk about crafts either. I noticed that phrase used this morning. Let's put it this way: the whole idea of "fine arts" was a misnomer born of a misconception in the nineteenth century of what art really is. Arts made by people express the character of a people. A good pot, a fine piece of ceramic, classical in form, lovely in texture and color, altogether perfect technically, is a work of art. A bad painting laboriously imitative of nature, neglectful of the concepts and principles of art, is not art. A good piece of weaving, a fine piece of tapestry can be a work of art. As I often tell my students at Pratt, "If you will go to the Metropolitan Museum, enter the front door, turn sharply to the left and walk into the nearest gallery, you will walk into the 'pots and pans' sections of the Greeks." And that Museum, as you know, prides itself on handling only the finest of the fine arts. So, I would urge this group, as you develop, that you cease labeling certain sections of your presentation as craft or minor arts, and combine the excellent under the title of art.

Craft is that part of an art which is its technical content. We must know the craft of our art, but let's not, then, designate a whole medium such as ceramics a craft, with the implication that it is limited as a craft. Ceramics ascends to art when you see a piece like this, even though it is a utilitarian piece. This is a lamp base, and you can imagine how tasteful this lamp would be with the proper shade, and how practical — children couldn't push it over. It is beautiful in texture. It has subtle coloration which makes it stand out as a work of quality and not only as a craft.

30

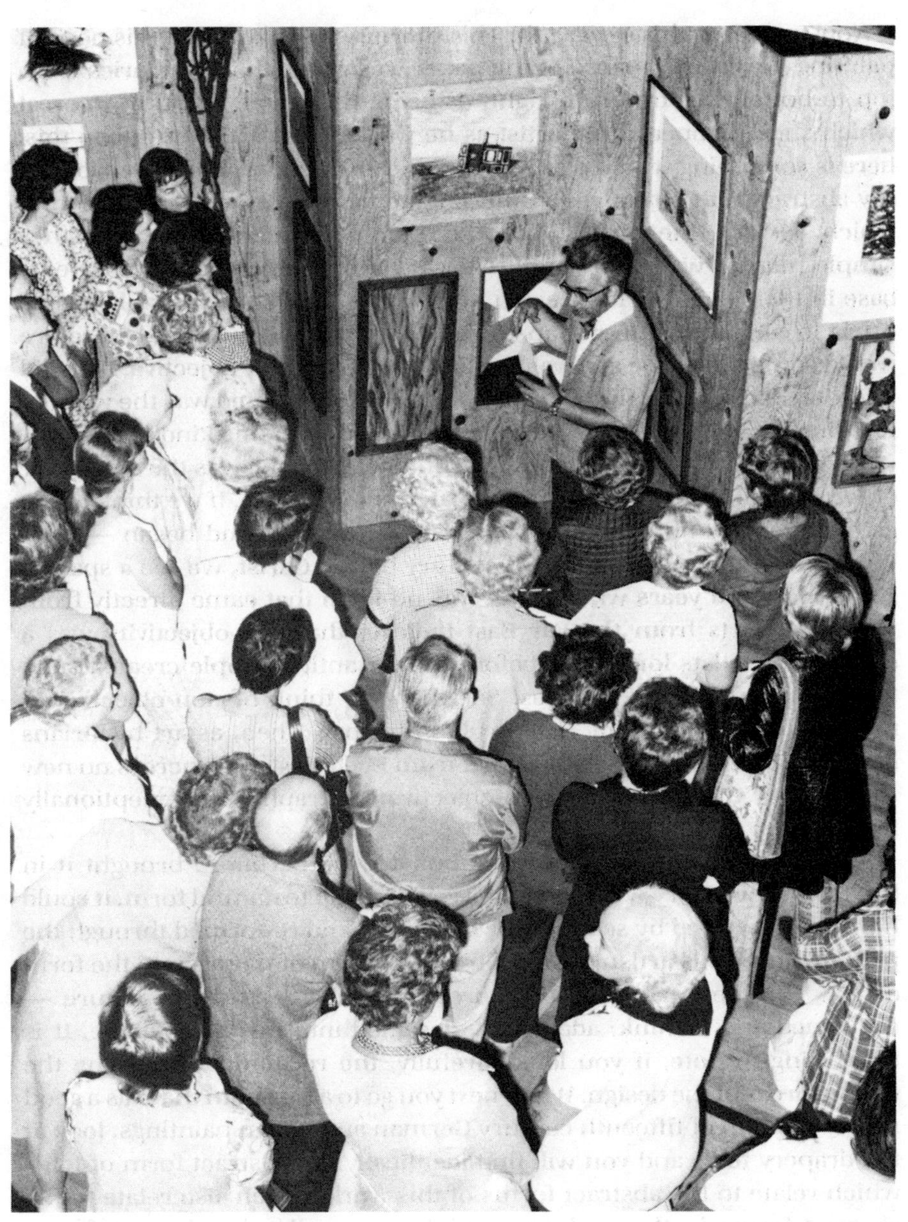

Gallery Talk, Festival, 1972

Now to turn to this serigraph. This morning I spoke about this need of painting the entire surface of the paper, regarding the boundaries from top to bottom, from left to right, as being the whole world of interest which should concern the artist as he works. This artist has done this; here is something which comes from the abstract non-objective world. I say abstract non-objective to differentiate from abstract. Non-objective, which is not the same thing as non-objectionable, is a rather simple-minded way, I guess, of referring to that which does not have its base in the object world — earth, tree, etc. — and so it probably has its origin in geometry. These shapes do not come from nature, and therefore would come under the general heading of abstract non-objective. Who did this kind of designing first? In our century the first noted was the work of Kandinsky, who as early as 1910 devoted himself to this kind of work...

...But we certainly cannot claim for Kandinsky that he was the originator of forms which do not come immediately from nature. If we think of the great Byzantine civilization which lasted until 1453 and began — who knows — in the second or third century before Christ, we see a span of some thousand years when there was no form that came directly from nature. Objects from the Far East indicate that non-objectivity was a concern of artists long, long before the Byzantine people created such forms in temples and palaces. So when we think of non-objective as modern we have to think back truly in history. Then, as art historians know, we can do nothing but repeat from Ecclesiastes, ''There is no new thing under the sun.'' This non-objective serigraph is an exceptionally fine piece.

This next work is non-objective, but it is borderline. I brought it in because it could very well have some relationship to natural form. It could have been inspired by seascape or landscape and re-formed through the personality of this artist, changed from the form of nature into the form of art. This next painting, of course, is nature — man in nature — re-formed and, I think, adequately designed into the given shape. It is interesting to note, if you look carefully, the relationships among the various areas of the design. When next you go to a museum that has a good representation of fifteenth century German and Italian paintings, look at the drapery folds and you will find identically the abstract form of folds which relate to the abstract forms of this work, which also relate to the abstract forms in the sculptures of the Acropolis, the abstract forms decorating Greek vases, the abstract forms of the Mesopotamian civilization, the abstract forms of Chinese painting. Study the magnificence of all those art forms. All these civilizations come to mind as we look at this little section of this painting.

There is a lovely cat here, which struck my eye this morning; it seems to be a watercolor drawing, a wash-drawing. The concept is quite original, subjective, personal. It reminds me of some of the pure drawings Matisse has done, and it shows what can be achieved monochromatically. Next is a black-and-white drawing with a relief in one color and how effective the result. I tried to select in each one of the pictures an illustration of what I stressed this morning: the main business is to cover the total shape. In no work before us is there neglect of the total shape.

Down below here is a painterly work. Plastically it has some of the charm that is lacking in the picture on the extreme right. But this artist has been strictly concerned with the plastic quality of the work and has altogether neglected drawing, in the obvious sense. He has apparently been concerned with two things: one, the patterning of the area, which has a very subtle interrelationing of structure; secondly, he has been concerned with paint. It may be somewhat influenced by abstract impressionism, though it is much tighter than many of those peoples' works who are pioneers in that field.

This is a little watercolor which I selected before I realized it to be the work of my sister, who began work — it is interesting how evolution takes place in an artist — as a water colorist largely influenced by Adolph Dehn. This artist has evolved through her own maturing, into designing of this original type. I have now seen four of these and I know there is a strong personal and permeating style, which comes from Marylon. May I pause a moment to speak about style? Style is that quintessence of character which comes from you. You cannot reach out for style; it must come from inside out.

Here is an interesting picture from two viewpoints. One, it has such a delicate design. I think it is beautifully balanced between the bold and the very delicate textures, the very small areas. I think it's a fine design. If you look carefully at it later, you will see that it has the visible evidence of that plastic quality which a good oil painting must have. A teacher cannot teach it. It's just something that comes out of the brush and suddenly it is there — something that is like natural perfect flavor in food.

Later on you might wish to see those beautiful pieces of weaving up there. I cannot lay claim to any professional knowledge of weaving. When my wife was weaving under Maryan Stringel I began to realize that color in weaving is achieved in a different way than color in painting is blended.

Here is a picture that interested me very much. It is not often that one finds a true primitive because we are so able to communicate now. It is almost impossible to be a primitive. The new magazines, say *Life,* for instance, presents a great museum of art in one year. So a sheepherder in the hills of Wyoming could actually learn much from reading about art. We are reminded by Malraux, who speaks of the "museum without walls": all the unlimited opportunity we have today to study the print, the reproduction of the picture. Nevertheless, in a general classification there is such a thing as a primitive and here is one. I think it is obvious to those of you who look at this artist's picture that he covers the given shape and is conscious of his obligations to work here just as he is conscious of his duty to work there. He is a designer. Like all primitives he works in a sharp and concentrated manner to express his design, withal there is a feeling of spirituality, which seems to be that quality of Henri Rousseau in the nineteenth century and which Kane, of Pittsburgh, showed during the end of the WPA days.

Above that picture is an encaustic. I took it over here for two reasons: first because it is an encaustic, a wax painting, which produces beautiful colors, and secondly because imitation of Rouault can only lead to disaster. Rouault is a man who does not allow any followers. Rouault, with his deep conviction, his life-long devotion, his self-criticism which caused him to burn 600 of his works, cannot be followed. So I would like to have here this one painting as a warning to all of us that the great cannot be followed, their trails are devious and they are high. No one should try to follow.

Here is another painting. May I comment on the very businesslike way in which he has handled the given shape. It is not to me a sensitive painting. The umbers and siennas, which are wonderful colors for mixing, are here used in a rather brutal way. The blues, which are of that same quality as Paynes' grey — again mixing colors — are rather harsh. But the design and the given shape are, as I say, a workmanlike job. Gouache lends itself beautifully to getting soft and beautiful colors. I should like to suggest that perhaps encaustic or gouache painting, as a little vacation affair, be practised. Then come back into oil, which might enrich the palette and offer a new vista of color to this artist, a very strong designer.

Our next study is a drawing in the classical tradition of drafting which architects employ. As a matter of fact, one can say that this really is a Renaissance type of drawing. I asked it to be shown because there are not many who concern themselves enough with this kind of drawing. At Pratt, the teachers in the final meetings of the college decided that next year would be drawing year. We're going to stop students in the hallways and say, "Reach for your sketchbook, pardner." There is too little drawing from students.

The next painting is a plastically interesting one. It looks to be a pretty good illustration. It shows how to look right in front of your nose and see a world there. There is no use running all over to find subject matter. The artist sees all before him and he draws it. . . You don't have to walk a mile to find the world you can paint.

The painting next to that one — the rather brown one — is interesting to me because of this: It reminds me of the number of times students have gotten into deep trouble with a palette which had everything from vermillion to black messed all over it. When that desperate stage comes, when you have drowned yourself in the rich possibility of color, you might limit yourself to yellow ochre, burnt sienna, black and white. Yellow ochre and black will give you a green; burnt sienna and white will give you a red, black and white will give you a blue; and then, if you're real good, at the end of the day, just for the hell of it, grant yourself one additional color. Such a limited palette gives you control again.

The next is a little watercolor which shows skill, both the charm and the possibility of skill, and also its limitation. It is an ordinary design, but technically it is handled with professional competence. It is again a limited palette, very satisfying, I'm sure, to the artist who did it. It lacks that particular quality which comes from a deep inner searching which makes Rouault a true master. This is not Rouault, but it is good clean craftsmanship. It is competent and deserves praise for that quality.

The last picture, the portrait of a man, is one of the best works in the show. It has all the quality that one likes to see in a good painting. It is well placed. It is designed. Its drawing is good, unfaltered. Its color is inventive. It's the kind of invention that a Courbet was concerned with. I hope this person goes on to investigate portraiture.

The weaving back there is a delight to the eye. If you go there, you will find that texture that is soft and altogether beautiful....I'm sorry I can't talk technically about weaving. My wife could. I'm sure that you have here your weaving chairman who is quite capable of telling. Please see her.

This pastel work, this collage, is the only example that I saw of a kind of art which began with Schwitters, a German artist of the early twentieth century. It is an attempt to overcome some of the surface limitations of painting. In many ways it has affected the artist who works in pure oil. Albert Mallory, one of the leading exponents of a new plastic form, showed with seventeen Americans at the Museum of Modern Art the possibility of joining some of the qualities of what you might call relief sculpture with that of painting.

I would like to close with one word, now, about subjectivism. I am working in the heart of "subjective land," which is New York. We have in New York City today the very center of painting in the whole world. New

York City, since about 1945 to 1950, has become to the painting world what Paris was to the painting world in 1910, when Kandinsky and Mondrian and Picasso and Matisse and Braque and Bonnard gathered there. The New York artists are leaders who are affecting whole civilizations.

Now I'll close by saying that I apologize to everyone whose work is not here in front of us. I couldn't get it all over here.

Adapted from a gallery talk by
Albert Christ-Janer of Pratt Institute
at the thirteenth MIA Festival, 1954

That Wonderful World of Color

How do you mix the color of skin? This is the beginning painter's first question in an instructed group or in conversation. The answer becomes the latch which opens or closes the door to that beginner as an artist. Too often the inquirer is given an answer which reads like this: A gob of white, a trace of yellow ochre, and just a wee bit of cadmium red. Such direction can only lead to the painting of the face of a bisque doll! And such direction destroys the excitement that comes with the discovery that each individual has his own coloring, and that coloring changes with sunglow, wind burn, illness or excitement. One finds the same changes in nature; the changes in green of a tree between sunrise and sunset, the tonal changes between the light yellow greens of April and the deep umber greens before the frosts of autumn, the change in blue water with each floating cloud, ripple or reflection. Yet in our misconception of painting we ask, "How does one paint water?"

Don Pater, Billings neon-sign designer, gives a "chalk talk" with paints. His equipment consists of an enormous canvas and house brushes with long handles. His palette has one-pound coffee cans containing red, yellow, blue, green, white and purple paints. His design is predrawn. He starts by telling his audience which area is sky, which is lake, hill, meadow, or cow. As he approaches each part of his painting he announces that "water is blue," dips his brush into the blue-filled can and covers the entire area. "Cows are red" and the red area is covered. "Meadows are green" and so on until no part of the canvas is unpainted. He then announces that breakers, clouds and cows' heads are white, and proceeds with his light areas. His remarks and quips while working make his act hilarious and delightful. He never fails to gain complete response and is much in demand by service groups, art groups and others. I doubt that he realizes how completely ironic is his take-off on the self-styled dilettante, the unserious amateur, the hobby painter or any other whose mistaken objective in painting is to "have a picture I can hang on my wall," to exhibit at the local fair, or to show to friends for prestige's sake.

These statements may sound unfair. They are tragic, really, in that the person who spends his time thus misses the excitement and joy he is seeking and his mind becomes more tightly closed to the doors opened by painting.

Among the joys he misses is an acquaintance with the wonderful world of color. Colors we have had with us always. What color is we have known a little more than a century. The discoveries that light is the source of color and that pigment consists of imprisoned rays of light led to the discovery of coal tar dyes. Synthetic pigments were soon invented to replace the old paints of ground earths or stones, used before 1840. Paints became more varied and less expensive.

While the scientist explored light, the artist explored color. His first result, the impressionistic paintings of such men as Monet, Degas, Renoir. Color soon came to be used as the means of intimate expression. Herein lies the first lesson of courage for the amateur. Study Van Gogh, that unhappy man who used unhappy colors to express himself, or, rather, who used colors in unhappy relationships to attain his effect. Turn to the work of the only happy period of his life. At Arles, in Southern France, life was for him filled with sunshine. To augment the yellow he punctuated with light blues. He wanted no harsh tones or contrasts to mar the reflection of his happiness.

Contemporary with Van Gogh, Gauguin used violent, deeply saturated yellow-reds and deep purples in large boldly patterned areas. Gauguin felt emotionally so strongly that he could express his feelings only in this way. His paintings are so intense that one Gauguin is magnificent, a room filled with Gauguin's works can make you ill.

While Gauguin and Van Gogh were developing the uses of color in one direction, Cezanne started in another. Discarding from his palette all pigment except the primaries, red, yellow and blue, he spent his many painting years in the vale of Aix-en-Provence studying trees, grass, sky, earth, trying to discover the realities of nature. He transposed as one does words in a sentence. He abstracted as one does in mathematics, and he discovered many things.

One of his discoveries was that earth in sunlight does not remain the brown of ancient or medieval painting but becomes a rosy ochre, a color which after his use of it became known as Cezanne pink. While this may seem an insignificant discovery, it illustrates what one means by the individual who wants rules to go by or who wants his work to look like "a picture." It seems unbelievable that for 1500 years earth's color had been accepted as brown. Actually, no one had observed the color of earth in relation to the colors of grasses, trees, shadows or sky. It becomes understandable when one realizes that most pigments were the ground earth of Umbria, Siena, and other areas where painting developed.

This one fact of earth sometimes being pink had far-reaching results. Picasso, as one example, painted whole landscapes in Cezanne pinks. This he did at the time psychologists were exploring color. To him pink was a happy color and for three years he painted everything in shades of pink. In the next year he became disillusioned and confused over poverty and injustice in cities. He went from the "pink period" directly into a "blue period," which was a direct contrast. During his "pink period" he painted scenes of family life or happy subjects. When the "blue period" started he chose beggars, outcasts and the oppressed as subjects.

Since that time in the early nineteen hundreds color has been developed in many directions. Often artists have gone in tangents, thinking in terms of color to the exclusion of all else, even forgetting subject matter, which is something a painting must have. The wildest orgies, however, have taught something about what can or cannot be done with color uses.

Seventy-four-year-old Marc Chagall is considered one of the world's great artists of today. Of his use of color Jean Laymaire writes in describing Chagall's Jerusalem Windows:

> The essence of the Jerusalem Windows lies in color, in Chagall's magical ability to animate material and transform it into light. Words do not have the power to describe Chagall's color, its spirituality, its singing quality, its dazzling luminosity, its ever more subtle flow, and its sensitivity to the inflections of the soul and the transports of the imagination. It is simultaneously jewel-hard and foamy, reverberating and penetrating, radiating light from an unknown interior. Chagall's palette is inexhaustable, quick in sharp or subtle contrasts and, as in the latest paintings, it can enliven with infinite nuances a vast expanse dominated by a single color. So many things he does with color. And there are many more things to do if one has the courage to learn.

Immediately, the reader queries, "So much for Chagall. How can I learn?" The answer is not too difficult. Think for a moment about that picture you want to paint. Are you certain you don't have someone else's picture in your mind? If you have, try to eliminate all preconceived ideas of how a painting should look. With your canvas before you determine your subject. Forget some of the drawing this time. Mark your areas out simply and be ready with the palette. Looking at your subject select the area of color you would like to try first. Look consciously from your subject to your palette. Confer with yourself. Select that paint which is most nearly like what you think your subject color is. With your palette knife put a very small quantity of that paint in the mixing area of your palette. What color can you now mix with that color to get the value and shade of that area? Should it be a bit lighter? Darker? A little more yellow? Red? Mixing the colors on the palette, hold a knife-full against your subject. Getting near to the color? Try again, and again. If you work on this one color during the entire period allotted for your painting, you will have gone far in cultivating your consciousness of color. Once you find one color the next is easy until you begin to see not only colors but their effects, one on the other. In your color mixing be provident. Use almost minute quantities of paint. Once you find the color you can remember how you arrived at it and mix the quantity you may need.

You may want to express yourself intimately — your thought and feelings, as did Van Gogh, Matisse and many others. (Matisse always expressed himself happily as Van Gogh did unhappily.) Forget how other people use color and use the colors you feel in your mind's eye and your imagination. This canvas you are doing, not for husband, wife, or neighbor, but for yourself, so have courage to fail if necessary. After all, you did not express all of your body rhythms successfully the first time that you danced.

Another interesting experiment is to paint an area somewhere on your canvas in a shape that you like with the color you choose for today. Complete filling the canvas with colors and shapes that you feel go well with the first shape. When you have filled the surface you will have many shapes in various colors. Work on these, adjusting here, changing color there, varying the textures and so on until the canvas pleases you. This will be a design rather than a painting. Better a good design than a bad painting. And it is good exercise in developing sensitivity to color. You may even want to put this design on your wall until you will have learned how to do that painting.

There is danger in discussing the uses of color as a subject alone unless we remember that color is only one facet of painting or of art. Color in today's world has become a challenge. It is much misunderstood, especially when it comes to painting the human figure. To the amateur who asked, "How do you mix the color of skin?" I should like to quote the pronouncement of Gustave Moreau, one of the greatest modern teachers, regarding the work of one of his students:

You have the tonal aspects but nothing of its depth, its intimacy . . . you have caught nothing of the grain of that skin, greenish in certain passages, then red, blue and that lovely gray, which are all contained there and give the whole so intense a poetry and make that flesh so truly exciting. No, there is no profundity in your tone, . . . you must think color imaginatively. You must copy nature imaginatively, that is what makes the artist. Color should be considered, pondered, reflective, inventive. You paint flesh that throbs, you must paint a head that thinks . . . . Believe me, the only painting that will endure is that which has been dreamed about, thought about, reflected on, created in the mind and not simply with manual facility.

The student or beginning painter who strives alone should remember that stress on the simple mechanical craft of painting with formula or rule means a low aesthetic and intellectual level of instruction or study. If he will adopt the spirit of the words of Moreau he will soon be entranced by that wonderful world of color which he will have entered.

Isabelle Johnson, Absarokee, 1963

The Outer and the Inner Eye

The modern artist lives in a world vastly different from the world in which great art of the past was produced. To understand what a modern artist is trying to communicate, we must understand the nature of the society in which he is working.

The artist of past times lived in a stable world, with accepted standards of social and religious beliefs, with a fixed code of good and bad, beautiful and ugly, with a scientific view of the world as a closed, static universe. Under these conditions the great art of Giotto, Rembrandt, El Greco, the great art of the Renaissance and up to Cezanne was produced.

It is never easy to analyze the causes of a profound change in ways of thinking, but there is no doubt that a new and quite distinct type of art arose in the five years preceding the First World War. There was a desire on the part of many artists to reject the copying of nature and to establsh an "art of pure form." Some explanations for this are the development of the camera, particularly color photography, which made the hand copying of a landscape in oil rather obsolete; new scientific discoveries of nature and phenomena, which altered concepts of space and time and their interaction; the mechanization of civilization, so that machine-imagery filled everyone's mind; and lastly a spiritual and intellectual insecurity and a breakdown of established standards. While the individual

40

artist may not have been aware of the effect on him of these changes, they influenced his unconscious processes.

At the end of a long line of realistic painters, Cezanne forged a new trail. He is universally regarded as being the chief source of modern art, and his understanding of the basic qualities of the Old Masters, and his use of color in design paved the way for the Cubists and later painters. Cezanne did not copy nature primarily, but painted his objects in space with emphasis on geometrical shapes, and painted the same object as seen from different viewpoints at the same time.

The Cubists — Picasso, Braque, Gris, many others — continued in Cezanne's footsteps but "distorted" the object even more. They showed superimposed views of an object, and the picture was no longer recognizable as a copy of nature.

Now, in a continuing development, artists like Mondrian, Gabo, Arp, Pollack, DeKooning and many others give up entirely the representation of nature, and hold these views, well expressed by the following statement of Gabo and Pevsner: "To communicate the reality of life, art should be based on the two fundamental elements, space and time. Kinetic and dynamic elements must be used to express the real nature of time. (The dance and music are examples of this). We deny volume as an expression of space. What is space if not impenetrable space? We announce that the elements of art have their basis in a dynamic rhythm."

Furthermore, new materials and new tools are used by many contemporary artists. They may use hand-shaped thermoplastics, cellophane, wood, wire, glass, resin and cement paints; among sculptors the old method of carving, chipping, or moulding clays, stone and wood may not always satisfy and they try new materials, such as plexiglas, steel, iron, aluminum, wire, plate glass. The old concept was of a piece of sculpture on a base, immovable, heavy; now, in an attempt to indicate motion in space, the sculpture may move, be a mobile, which indicates volume relationships and interpenetrations.

Speaking for myself, painting is an attempt to create forms and colors on the canvas with a life and relationship of their own, without reference to the material world; to divest the picture of anecdote or illustration to the point where the emotions of the spectator will be wholly aesthetic, as when listening to music. Since I have lived in Montana I have an enriched awareness of space and time — caused by the mountains, the space, the great distances around us. This quality I attempt to indicate in my paintings and sculpture.

The work of Arp shows the entire absence of any derivation from nature. He is quoted as saying, "Art is a fruit growing out of man. While the fruit of the plant never strives to resemble a balloon or a president in a cutaway, the artistic fruit of man shows for the most part a ridiculous ambition to imitate the appearance of other things. I like nature but not its substitutes. Illusionistic art is a substitute for nature."

Naum Gabo, in one of his recent works, expresses his artistic vision: "The reason I make constructions in transparent materials (though I do not limit myself to such materials) is because transparent materials give me the chance to dematerialize as much as possible my idea for the content of my work of art. By de-materialization I mean to make it as near as possible to a spiritual object — that is to say, an object more appealing to our minds and our feelings than to our crude physical senses."

The formal integrity in his art is the timeless quality in art, and makes him part of the tradition of great art in the past, but his use of contemporary materials to solve contemporary spiritual problems makes him a product of our time. Quoting Herbert Read, "Much of modern art is in the nature of a protest; it is a negative reaction to the decadence of our civilization. But the art of Gabo is positive and prophetic, and looks beyond the convulsions of our epoch to time when a new culture based on an affirmative vision of life will call into being an art commensurate with its grandeur."

To understand the work of Gabo and any other vital contemporary artist, we must look with the inner, not the outer eye. With this vision we may then see that the present day artist is searching for an order and faith in life, and perhaps expresses as an individual that for which the collective human mind is also searching.

Adapted from an article by
Helen McCauslan, McLeod, 1955

Music and Cultural Value

One of the prices we pay for being so all-fired civilized is a certain loss of perspective, or at least a tendency toward such a loss. Take music, for example. We are learning more about this fascinating art every day. Musicologists seem to be flourishing, and most of what they're doing is good. We can never know too much about such things. But it so often seems to me that in the search for "facts about" we lose sight of the essential nature of music.

Along with all the arts, music suffers from the fact that we devote much more time to its dissection, analysis, and understanding than we do to using it as a source of valuable experience. For music exists primarily to give the listener rewarding experience, just as the novel, the drama, the poem, the painting do. Yet so many people are kept from the fullest enjoyment of music by the ridiculous notion that music is something that has to be understood in some largely cerebral fashion, or it's something designed to create quasi-visual pictures of some kind in the mind's eye, or to convey certain ideas.

Those who are musically educated become adept at telling where the first theme of a given composition leaves off and the second theme begins. They can distinguish between a symphony and a sonata, tell us which came first, Bach or Buxtehude, and explain the differences between an acathistus and a zarzuela. But it is often open to question whether they are equally skilled at grasping the experiential import of the music and using it to make broader, deeper, and more human persons of themselves. We need to remember that, as Friedrich Hebbel put it, one doesn't approach the piano in order to use it for the demonstration of mathematical truths. It is foolish to try to say in tonal language what can be much more clearly stated in discursive form, just as it is stupid to try to do with a brush and oils what a camera can do much better.

It isn't enough to know what a certain shape in an abstract painting means; the essential thing is to grasp the feeling it exists to convey. How often in the art gallery, and in like manner in the concert hall, do we find people, especially those knowing people who should be setting examples of the proper approach to a painting, overly concerned with cognitive meaning, on how the artist achieved his effects, rather than on those effects themselves. This is almost as great an obstacle to the spread of real value in works of art as is that form of "cultural" snobbery which assumes that art and culture in general are the special concern of the "upper classes," a buttress for social prestige, and the reward of wealth. These two things, with all their protean ramifications, are the greatest obstacles to culture there are. To say that one must know a certain amount or that one must possess certain extraneous social graces in order to partake of the vital springs of the human spirit is to set up a sort of Hindu heirarchy that relegates the ordinary human being to the class of the culturally untouchable.

Works of art, the highest and purest manifestations and products of human culture, exist primarily to preserve and make available valuable experiences. Music does so through patterned tonal symbols — tones in patterned relations as to pitch, rhythm, intensity, timbre and perhaps a few more qualities which, because of such patterning and because of past human musical experience, come to acquire evocative significance to those capable of grasping their import. These tonal patterns "symbolize" or call forth certain attitude-patterns and their attendant feelings in the hearer. And any given work of musical, as of other, art is justified and valuable only insofar as the experience it calls forth is a valuable one.

Works of art are the peaks that rise up from the plain of human culture, the concentrated essences of human experience. Culture makes it possible for what is valuable in the human past to continue operative and effective in the human present. It is the avenue through which the beneficent human spirit speaks to the individual and through which the individual may himself speak.

Culture holds the human community together just as the cells of the body are held together to form and maintain a living organism. The great works of art are generalization of and abstraction from general human experience, an ingathering of diverse elements fused and made relevant in the white heat of the creative individual personality, an intensification and focusing of experiential essence, an integrated pattern of significant human feeling. To recognize art's value, it is necessary that we approach it with the proper perspective — as an expression of the human spirit to be experienced as such, something we should permit ourselves to be affected by, to the depths of our being. To merely understand is not enough. The study of music, just as the normal approach to it, must always be in perspective, with full recognition of its basic expressive function.

Another obstacle to the full enjoyment of music is the misconception of its proper function. It assumes that one's response to a work of art must be in terms of "like" and "dislike," that the artist's principal concern is to please someone or other. In the first place, this condemns one to the limitations of one's present taste, of a piece with that sort of asinine (I use the word advisedly) narrow-mindedness typified by the person who, having once been deeply moved by a rendition of Sullivan's "The Lost Chord" on a mighty organ, proceeds to judge all his subsequent musical experience on those terms and dares any and all composers and performers to meet that impossible standard. If one's taste in art remains the same for more than a few months, one should take appropriate measures to ascertain whether one is or is not alive. In the second place, the assumption that the artist is concerned with catering to a limited taste, with pleasing every listener or viewer, is ridiculous on the face of it. Many of life's most valuable experiences are not pleasant in the undergoing of them, and their value doesn't seem to have a great deal to do with whether they are pleasant or not.

The only really fruitful question to ask of any work of art is not "What does it mean?", in the cognitive sense, "How is it done?", or "Do I like it?", but rather "What experience does it give me?", "What effect does it have on me?", "What does it do to me?" If it does nothing for any given individual, it is not thereby condemned. That individual should ask himself the further question, "Do I know how to grasp the experiential essence of this work?" It isn't enough to be exposed to all the great and noble expressions of the human spirit in the course of our factually-oriented education, if we are not also given the ability, and the incentive, to grasp and make use of these expressions. I look forward to the day when an integral part of the upbringing of every individual will be training in how to make real and vital contact with the evocatively significant human cultural expressions, showing him how they relate to his own life as a human being and a member of the human community and to his own emotional needs and interests.

Robert Athearn, Butte, 1952

The Fascination of Weaving

We are living in a time of magic created by modern industry. Never before have so many beautiful fabrics been manufactured in such quantities. Chemistry has provided an amazing array of new materials from which to make cloth and hundreds of new colors for dye. Artists and designers work steadily contriving countless combinations of weaves and prints ranging from conservative and restrained to exciting and flamboyant. And yet, in this mass of commercial output an exquisite piece of handwoven material stands out like a gem.

High regard for hand work is not a rebellion against the machine. Rather, in spite of all the benefits and abundance of beauty produced by our mighty industrial system, it emphasizes the fact that man is still our focal point of interest. Herein lies the basic fascination of hand weaving.

Oddly enough, it was neither a commercial weaver nor a manufacturer who invented the power loom, but an English clergyman. In the 18th century, the Reverend Edmund Cartwright, desiring to spare weavers of his days the many hours of drudgery, conceived the necessary mechanical arrangement to make the loom automatic and capable of being driven by power. In 1814, Francis Cabot Lowell, an American traveler in England, brought back the idea of power weaving to our country. Thus a new industry was developed which nearly eradicated the art of hand weaving. Without mass production of goods in mills, however, hand weaving might never have been appreciated as an art.

45

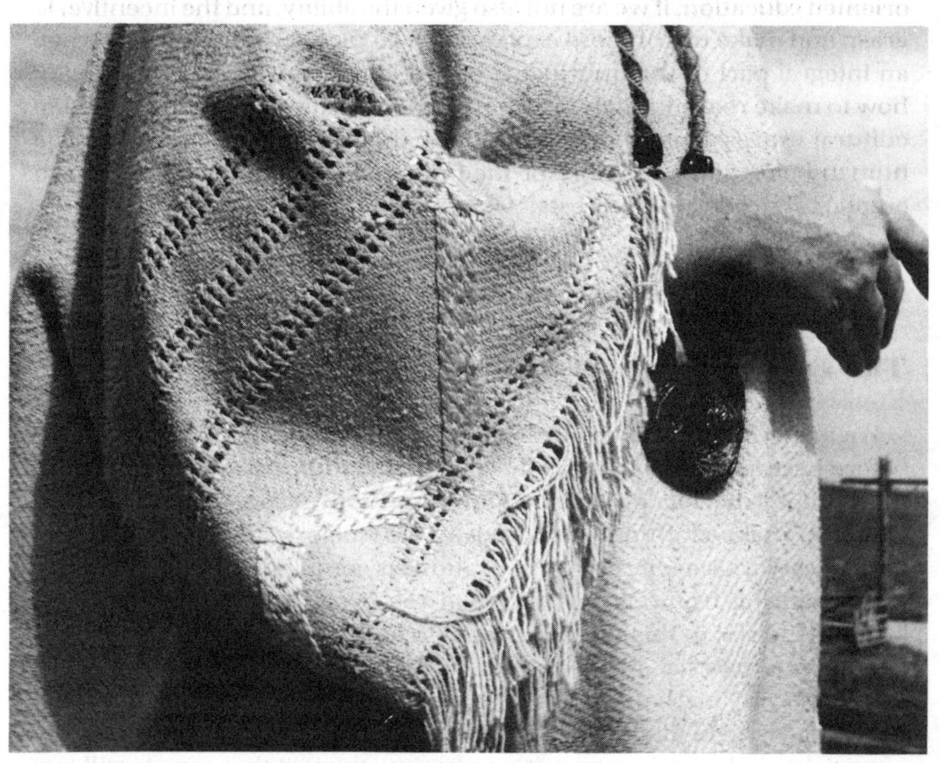

Caftan woven by Sue Geering

Fortunately, a few hand weavers persisted in remote areas of our country and, to a greater extent, in the Scandinavian countries. Hand weaving also continued in other parts of the world untouched by the progress of the machine age. Early in the 20th century a new interest in hand weaving developed. This rediscovery of the art instituted one of its fascinating sidelights, that of being a detective. Here was a delight akin to antique hunting. Museums were visited, dusty trunks in attics were searched, and auctions regularly attended to find samples of early American hand weaving. And when old treasure was discovered, it had to be analyzed and a draft of the pattern drawn so that present-day weavers could again weave the traditional colonial patterns.

Mary Meigs Atwater of our own State of Montana was foremost in the nation to revitalize the craft. She was like an art connoisseur with the distinctive ability of not only making the beauty of hand weaving known to the public, but discovering how to weave precious fabrics and passing on this knowledge to all interested. She was an accomplished weaver and visited many parts of our land and several foreign countries in search for weaving patterns and methods. Most of her notes are available in published form.

Weaving has a certain captivating quality. Like pottery making or silversmithing, the end product is usually something useful; yet in the creation of this product, the artisan makes full use of his skills, his sensitivity to color and design, and above all, his imagination. This fascination appeals to many and their admiration for weavers grows as they see more and more products of the loom.

But how does one change from an admirer to a weaver? Usually it is through the good fortune of being able to watch a weaver at work; to see how rapidly threads become cloth; to see the pattern appear as the warp is changed for each new shot of weft; to hear the rhythmic beat of the comb as each thread of weft is brought snugly into place. The whole operation seems so simple, the effect so intriguing that the observer is soon imbued with the desire to become a weaver.

The initiate naturally would want to weave a little on his own. Happy day for him if the work being done by the weaver would permit it. To hold a shuttle for the first time is something of a thrill. Here is a little instrument carefully carved from wood, smoothed and varnished so that its lovely grain is revealed. It is graceful and functionally streamlined. Loaded with colored yarn, it slips through the shed of the opened warp with such ease as to delight the eye. A pull on the beater and the weft is in place. A shifting of the warp and a return shot of the shuttle. Back and forth fifteen or twenty times with changing treadling, and a delightful sensation becomes most satisfying in the realization that here is a means, a medium of expression which will give vent to many heretofore repressed creative desires. Fascinating? Definitely!

Before the novice can weave those dreamed-of stoles, coverlets, towels and suiting, he must master a lot of rudiments of weaving. The mechanics of the loom, his tool of trade, is most important. There is nothing difficult about learning to operate a loom, but just the loom itself fascinates many people. At this point a few become sidetracked in one of the ramifications of weaving and find that the construction of looms becomes their prime objective. Indeed, many homemade looms deserve admiration, like pieces of beautiful furniture.

There are literally thousands of interesting patterns and variations which may be woven on a four-harness loom. Many weavers find complete satisfaction in duplicating colonial coverlets, tablecloths, aprons, and numerous other articles. Technical perfection is their fascinating goal. They are like some photographers whose only ambition is technically perfect prints. But this type of weaver and photographer is a boon to both crafts in the maintenance of high standards.

Weavers are no different from other artists in seeking new forms of expression and reflecting the times in which they live. Hence we have contemporary weaving. New homes demand draperies, curtains and screens which can be woven only by hand. The materials used, such as doweling, split bamboo, and even glass rods, defy fabrication by a machine process. The result is a distinctive, a custom built job for a particular use. Color, texture, and above all, purpose, must be considered by the weaver. Truly, such an order is a most fascinating challenge.

Scarcely another art form has such a variety of texture. Cloth varies from heavy to light, from solid to lace. It is within the weaver's power to choose the texture he desires, even combining two, three, or four of the extremes in any degree. Using the same weft as warp, texture may be obtained by the pattern of the weave. Twill, tabby or plain weave, herringbone, damask and satin are all different textures obtained by pattern. Texture may be obtained by the use of warp and weft of different sizes. Simple use of alternate large and small threads in the weft or warp will produce an interesting texture. Regular or irregular spacing of the warp or weft will give an altogether different effect. The combination of different kinds of material such as linen with cotton, silk with wool, cotton with ramie, and a host of other materials affords combinations which are limitless. The facination of texture in weaving is that it is not only a delight to the eye, but to the sense of touch.

Weaving becomes truly exciting when color is added to the myriad of

48

patterns and textures. It is like changing from charcoal drawing to oils or watercolor. Skeins of colored yarn are like tubes of paint. One may choose a low key pallet of subdued colors, or the bright and gay hues. But colors in cloth do not mix like paints. The weaver must approach the problem as did the impressionistic painters. Each little nub of colored thread retains its own color, but in relation to adjacent colors it appears to change. Here is the opportunity to create vibrant materials or the softest of color combinations.

With all these possibilities of pattern, texture, and color, hand weaving appeals to the artist for its limitless possibilities for development. It provides so much latitude, so much potential for creation of original fabrics. Whenever a special cloth is needed he has all these resources at his disposal to create the desired material.

A good piece of weaving is not accidental. Once the final product has been envisaged, there are many questions to be decided. What materials should be used for the warp and weft? What colors will make the desired effect? Should the goods be heavy or light? How many threads to the inch? Should the warp be spaced or solid? All these things and many more must be decided before the warp is even put on the loom.

Many creative weavers use color crayons or pastel chalk during this planning stage to assist them in design and color balance. Once the color selection and design have been crystalized, the weaver next works out the weaving pattern best suited, usually plotting it on graph paper unless he makes use of one of the well-known weaves. Occasionally a little experimentation is done on the loom before the weaver is satisfied that he has just what he had planned.

There is no law which states that a thread of weft must go the full width of the material. It may end at any point and its place be taken by another thread of a different color. With this technique tapestry weaving can be done on a loom. Thus, another fascinating field of weaving appears. The weaver is not limited to the patterns of the treadles or harnesses, but is free to weave into the fabric whatever design he desires.

Tapestry weaving is not new. Tapestry has been found in old Egyptian tombs. The weaves of Navajo Indians and Mexicans are tapestries. The "Golden Age" of tapestry weaving was from the mid-fifteenth century to the mid-sixteenth century when artists wove pictures into cloth. While the Renaissance is sometimes thought of as the rebirth of art, it sounded the death knell for tapestry weaving. The influence of Raphael relegated weavers to the inferior position of copying paintings slavishly; even the ornate frames of oil paintings of that period were woven into the borders. Whenever originality and creation stop in art, that field of art ends. By the late eighteenth century, tapestry weaving had diminished in size and production.

Newsweek magazine of March 30, 1959, contained a most heartening account of how tapestry weaving has revived in France during the past two decades. Picasso designed tapestries. The late Fernand Leger turned out a dozen bold designs which were on display in Paris. This spring the work of twenty-one designers was displayed at New York's Museum of Contemporary Crafts. This show included three forceful abstractions of Mathieu Mareugot. The attraction to tapestry weaving by artists might be explained by Leger, who felt it gave warmth to his work which had coldness on canvas.

A few Montana weavers appear to have sensed the possibilities of tapestry weaving. It is hoped that they will pursue this form of art, and will attract other artists to this medium.

And there you have it, the fascination of weaving, the creation and weaving of a dream.

Thomas E. Jermin, Great Falls, 1959

Art From the Ground Up

The Great Falls *Tribune* that autumn morning said Ludwig's alfalfa haystack burned down during the night, twenty-five tons of it, fire of unknown origin . . .Hadn't I just been reading in the bible of the potters, Leach's *A Potter's Book,* about use of wood and vegetable ashes in glazes? What're we waiting for? I phoned my ceramics mentor, Sister Mary Trinitas, head of the Art Department at the College of Great Falls, and that afternoon found two good Catholic Sisters of Charity and me, a Mason and a sinner, albeit a potter, filling cans and boxes with Ludwig's alfalfa ash. And what a nice, cool-hued, sugary textured glaze we made after washing the stuff and sieving through a 100-mesh screen! No, I did not set that stack on fire!

I'll never forget the look of consternation Mrs. Stevenson gave me when she looked out of the kitchen window and saw me toting some pails of wheat husk ashes into our basement. But that's another story. Them there wheat ashes made some mighty nice effects in glaze developments. These ashes, brought into my furnace room contrary to the normal direction of ash hauling, were from the General Mills plant at Great Falls, so now I can eat my Wheaties from a bowl made of Ryan clay dug near here, glazed with wheat ashes from the makers of that breakfast food.

50

Perhaps ours is the craziest household but we did make two gallons of good maple syrup that spring, the first time it had been done here. In getting acquainted with my maple trees I corresponded with some Vermont experts and they had me make them some jugs. I developed a liquid-tight closure with ceramic screw thread and wedge lugs. They sent me about fifty pounds of chunk-stove-burnt hard maple forest green high-fire glaze; used without any metal oxide colorant this maple ash produced a mottled pinkish and smoky effect in a stoneware glaze.

While we're hauling ashes I might as well mention a good glaze I got by using a year or so accumulation of cigarette ashes in our home. Have to use it sparingly — there wasn't much of it after washing thoroughly and sieving.

I have made some unusually satisfying stoneware glazes from minerals obtained in the Wolf Creek Canyon and the Canyon of the Missouri River between Helena and Great Falls. Red stone from the sheer walls of Wolf Creek Canyon produced a greenish tinged glaze and the green stone from the same place made a bright orange high-fire glaze.

Some Georgia potters near my father's farm in the Blue Ridge mountain area of north highlands of that state told me how to do local salt glazing (one pot of salt glazed without affecting other portions): "Just like bread dough." A combination I developed with a Missouri canyon mineral containing chlorite over an engobe of Armington A.C.M. Company fireclay mix gave me a reticulating glaze similar to salt glaze; with full control of application and color on any part of the pot giving added beauty

Waste products and valuable metal oxides, made at plants in Montana refining ores, provide, in pure as well as in impure form, many interesting glaze materials, such as manganese dioxide impure, all of which give quality color effects in glazes when fluxed with varieties of feldspar such as that from the Lewis and Clark caverns of Montana. An unusual waste iron precipitate from Anaconda gave rich reds when fired high, oxidation, and gave celadons when reduced. The Lewis and Clark mineral, by itself, is a good golden yellow at cone 8 to 9, and its mutation goes into a turquoise beauty when modified with small percentages of copper oxide and cobalt.

And speaking of cobalt — shades of Ming and Sung — the asbolites of Old China streams have a worthy successor in the blues, light and dark, already achieved (and more to come) from another material derived from Montana's smelting industry; it has a name like "alphacobalti-naphthalinabeta," something or other like my name spelled backwards, Nosnarb Nosnevets, which I use when potting in Yugoslavia! It produced blues of depth and character and helped make near jet black when combined with some muscovite, garnet, feldspar conglomerate from the

Missouri River canyon, called "Best Availability Canyon" because it was the easiest to climb up to get in the high canyon walls.

Some other glazes are made of a mineral from that canyon called "Canyon 45 Mile" because that's how far it is from Great Falls. I mustn't fail to mention that a good yellow comes from our vanadium pentoxide, a name that seems to give Mrs. Thelma Chase, Montana potter, pentup delight whenever I mention it. Thelma has made some wonderful lovely glaze effects using high grade copper ores and galena finely divided and applied by blowing, or other ways, into still wet glaze surfaces before firing.

There are the Kalispell, Whitefish, Lewistown slip glazes and the colored clay bodies covered with transparent glazes. One Sunday Pete Meloy, potter of Helena, took his nice family for a drive out toward the Missouri River in Helena Valley and stopped to gather some loam from a field beside the road. This made one of the most beautiful basic loam glazes I've ever seen, maturing at a high fire. Pete says there's acres of the stuff. These natural materials, available freely to the observing potter, give varied results when prepared and applied by grinding, sieving, ballmilling, underglazing, overglazing, pouring, dipping, brushing and spraying. I have also devised a method of making pastel type glaze crayons out of any glaze formula, and of course crayon drawing technique of application will produce different effects from the same naturalistic designs which may be drawn in these crayons with granulation according to texture of biscuited clay bodies — and blending, hatching can be carried out according to the artist's intent.

We get the subtle beauty of translucence in our true hard porcelain made from the country's purest kaolin in the South Moccasin Mountains, and our own "petuntze," plasticized by a secret process using an ingredient that completely burns out in the fire and is self-reducing.

Of great significance in decorative processes of glazing is the amazing wax resist by many individual methods of manipulation using the water soluble wax, Ceremul A, first used and developed for this purpose about five years ago in Montana. This emusion wax has obvious advantages over the old cumbersome and awkward use of melting paraffin wax, with its difficulty of application to the cold pot.

I have used some unusual materials such as seed sapphires and rubies from the world famous Montana Yogo mines, also radioactive carnotite mined near Boulder and Basin, Montana, which produces yellow to iridescent color effects that click, even on a Geiger counter.

We started this out like a stack on fire, but we're about burnt out now. It is my hope that sincere creative potters will grasp these objectives and ways of working and experimenting and feel some of our enthusiasm for this down-to-earth-art-craft, making use of the seemingly inexhaustible minerals of Montana's field and roadside. All you need to follow this "art from the ground up" is enthusiastic alertness to possibilities lurking along the countryside, in highway cuts, mountain streams, mines, industrial plants and maybe a burning haystack or two!

In this way I believe anyone, anywhere, can get happy results — your *own* glazes, neither obtainable commercially nor likely to be stereotyped or duplicated, even under similar procedures. Wouldn't that be deeply satisfying personally?

Added variety from the same materials comes also from different kinds of firing, oxidation, reduction, open fire or saggered.

This could go on and on, so let's get out and start diggin' some dirt.

Branson Stevenson, Great Falls, 1953

History is Nobody's Property

It was, reputedly, Henry Ford who said, "History is bunk." Some unidentified wag is said to have remarked, "The only thing that history teaches is that history teaches nothing." A great many professional historians seem to feel that history has legitimacy only when considered in the lens of their own meticulous camera and, all the while, the average person is pretty much bored by the whole business.

Maybe it all depends on the definition of history, but the fact is that almost everybody is interested in history if the definition doesn't arbitrarily and sometimes arrogantly exclude them. In the first place, history is not a five-credit course in a not-too-hot schoolroom from the mouth of a pedant. Neither is it a family tree nor an exclusive club. It doesn't belong to historical societies and needn't, perforce, smell of dust. It can't be frozen in museum cases and nobody has as yet confined it simply to old timers. Anyone who was ever born became an old timer if he was given time. History doesn't start at St. Louis and move up the Great Muddy to Fort Benton and then stop. Nor did it stop on May 1, 1867, here or any other place.

History partakes of geography, anthropology, economics, geopolitics, theology, physics and cybernetics, but it is none of these things and all of them. It is any aspect of the passage of man through life from the beginning to the end, from the seed to the dust. Nobody owns it. Everybody lives it, some incalculably small part of it at least.

It is human, intensely and passionately so. That's why it is a pity to define it narrowly, claim it as property and argue about who owns it, who can practise it and who is excluded from it.

Take your own town. You say you have no interest in history. Your town is four dimensional. It has an existence in time, in place and in change. You cannot be interested *only* in its present because its present is past the moment you conceive of it. You cannot be interested *only* in its future because there really isn't any such thing independent of the present and the present is immediately part of the past. This is no syllogistic trick. It is simple truth. Both you and your town are caught up in continuity. Trapped, if you will, together. So with you and your river valley, you and your state, and you and your nation, the world and the human race.

We think of ourselves sometimes as having free will. The question may be debatable theologically but it isn't historically. We act and are in context. We are the product of our history and we can function only on that basis. It is not merely a matter of genes, ids, egos and minds. It is a matter of history. So it is with your town which is where it is and what it is because it grew that way historically. It is really a little foolish to say that you have no interest in history unless you are quite sure you have no interest in yourself. That is like saying you have no interest in a partner who accompanies you through a dark and fearsome journey.

The next time you walk to the postoffice consider the sidewalk and the thousands of feet like yours that have trod there. Consider the hopes, the fears, the years, the loves and hates that have made your town what it is and you what you are. Look at the buildings, consider the dates on the corner stones and consider that you walk in the midst of ghosts so close they are nearly visible and whisper so near to your ear they are nearly audible. And remember that whatever mark you make in your own quick passage through time and place others were here before you, feeling as you feel, that only the present matters and only the future is interesting. Yet all that is now in the past.

We should not think of history as anyone's property, anyone's prerogative. It is the stuff all of us are made of and it is as interesting as life itself, because that's what it really is.

K. Ross Toole, Helena, 1955

54

Photography an Art

Many times when people are viewing my photographs they will ask, "Just how did you *see* this picture?" It is the human eye which recognizes a pleasing composition and carries the result to the brain. Through that as yet unexplainable human computer the final result emerges. The maker calls it, hopefully, a work of art. Well, who is to say whether or not it is?

Whether of not photography is an art has been a matter of argument ever since photographic images appeared on the scene. I am a firm believer that it is an art, that any rendering of an impression, whether it is by paint and brush, clay, welding torch or a camera lens should be considered art provided that the results are pleasing to someone. To recognize it as such we may have to put it in the dimensions of time. The primitive Plains Indian drew figures and symbols on rock surfaces, perhaps to commemorate some event; yet today it is treasured as Rock Art. Copies of them decorate many homes.

Photographers have a handicap not confronted by other artists: they have a subject and have to make the best of it. If there is a TV antenna on that picturesque log cabin the film will record it. A painter may simply leave it off. If an expression on a face does not fit the desired mood, an artist's knife can change it in the clay. We photographers are stuck. We have to work harder to make that ugly telephone pole part of the composition.

Philippe Halsman, one of the greatest living photographers, says in one of his books that there are those who take a photograph and those who make one. The taker photographs a scene of a situation developing before him. In order to have any artistic value the photograph must contain the best compositional elements, lighting, angles and perspective available. Even if he used every component in the most advantageous manner he may only have taken the photograph.

Many times a photographer creates an image in his mind. Sometimes an idea comes as a flash. Again, it might be the result of an agonizing search for the right solution over a period of time. But when the photographer conceives an artistic picture and successfully makes it he has created a photograph.

In my estimation each form of photographic expression serves its purpose, and I am certain that they overlap in the work of an individual photographer. For instance, an amateur who snaps the Yellowstone Falls has taken a picture. When he arranges his kids at the picnic table to form a group he has conceived an idea in his mind, he is making a photograph. But who would say that a harbor scene at sunset with a seagull in the foreground could not be considered an artistic expression? But on the other hand, when a photographer goes out with a piece of branch, sticks it in the snow, photographs it in a strong cross light which makes the snowflakes sparkle it is the realization of a preconceived idea. Of course, it is also art.

When the urge to create something overcomes one and the results are satisfying the feeling of accomplishment is undoubtedly greater than recording a pretty sunset. It seems it is largely a question of what an individual is striving for or what his mood may be at a given moment.

Photography offers many ways to create the unusual even from an ordinary subject. At the time of picture taking one can utilize various light effects, use various focal lengths of lenses, different angles of view, filters, each of which emphasizes certain elements of the picture — blur figures to give motion or throw the background out of focus to help concentrate attention on the figure in the composition.

After the picture is made there are many techniques available to be used in the darkroom before the final form takes shape. Use of different grades and surfaces of paper, cropping in unusual ways, differing chemical processes and texture screens are but a few tools to make an ordinary picture an outstanding photograph.

The finest camera may be the weakest link. The art in an artistic photograph originates in the mind of the artist operating the camera.

Adapted from an article by
Denes G. Istvanffy, Billings, 1967

The Surface Hasn't Been Scratched

He was a bright young man of Manhattan, lately graduated to fiction editor of a slick magazine for men, and we had sold him a yarn dealing with Fort Benton and the last steamboat to leave before the ice closed the Missouri for the season. A man named "X" had stalked through our story. Any Montanan would have recognized our character as the forthright and formidable X. Biedler, but the bright young man knew Montana mostly as a place of legendary gunsmoke and gallop, of cowboy and sheriff and rustler. And so he plied us with questions as we sat in his office high above the roar of traffic.

We talked of Lewis and Clark that day, and of the fur trading era and John Colter and all the wild rivers that had known the canoe and the bateau and the mackinaw and the keelboat, and we got to the first discovery of gold. He had thought the only Virginia City of fame was in Nevada. Henry Plummer walked with us a way, and Granville Stuart, and soon all the pageantry of the open range was paraded. Yes, our man had seen Russell's painting, "Last of the Five Thousand," but he hadn't known about the tragedy of the hard winter of '86 and '87. He'd heard of Custer, but the fighting skill of that red strategist, Chief Joseph, was new to him.

We got to the war of the copper kings, and to another war, when Montana's men had swarmed to Butte to form a roughriding cavalry to free the Cuban from Spain. The homesteader influx intrigued him, and the county splitting and Jim Hill's dream of empire. What about Shelby? Hadn't there been a world's heavyweight championship fight staged there? But he hadn't known about wheatland baseball, when big league players had been imported in the 1920s by such towns as Scobey and Plentywood. Nor had he heard of another sport, the deadly game played three-cornerwise by Federal men and rumrunners and hijackers on the Bootlegger Trail down from Canada.

We talked of the wars with Germany, the first and the second, and of how air bases and military installations had sprouted in our prairies. We remembered troop trains rolling under a darkling sky, and the mournful hoot of locomotives echoing from the buttes, and were reminded of the long struggle that had attended the spanning of Montana by a transcontinental railroad. Later a certain Kid Curry had held up a train on another railroad at Wagner. And so our talk shuttled back and forth across all the time and space that is Montana.

At last the bright young man leaned back in his chair. "It seems to me," he said, "that you fiction writers haven't even scratched the surface of the material you've got in Montana."

He wanted to know about the people and the industry. He could use fiction and so could several other markets that had its basis in the workings of an industry. We talked then of sheep ranching and mining and smelting and lumbering. We talked of mighty Fort Peck dam and the forestry of oil derricks in the Shelby-Kevin-Cut Bank area and of how a couple of boys with a vision had started a ski run at Whitefish and another had launched a newspaper at the boom town of Hungry Horse. Hutterites in Montana? What were they? And did we actually mine sapphires out there? And that irrigation business and rural electrification? Weren't there stories in them? Ah, yes, and a hundred more we hadn't time to touch upon.

The clock had ticked to the hour of parting and we shook the hand of the young man; and the wonder in us — knowing the many Montana writers and their contributions — was why so much we had said had been new to the young man who dealt in fiction. Then we realized how our own closeness to Montana had blinded us to the sparsity of our writing population, great though it is in ratio to our over-all population.

Thus we went away with the knowledge that a treasure trove of material was indeed ours; but no one from a state that deals with raw materials so largely could escape the fact that the raw materials were one thing and the processing quite another. And so we saw our work cut out for us.

Where, then, could we do our digging? The gold lies in our history books and the files of newspapers and the stories of old-timers. We thought of Merrill Burlingame's *Montana Frontier* and were happy that it is to be found in so many libraries, for the chronological table at the back of that estimable book is itself a springboard into a thousand fiction stories. Or read the roster of names in the index — Benetsee and Bozeman and DeSmet and Dimsdale and the myriad others. These were people, but they were also stories begging to be told. And what of the nameless ones, the sheepherder toiling at his stone monument, the circuit-riding parson gladdened at eventide by a ranch light showing on the horizon?

Yes, we knew where to look for color, but our work would have to mean more than sluicing out the bare facts of history or enterprise or character, for many of the facts might have belonged to any region or to any people, and our real wealth lay in what was indigenous to us, the individual feel of Montana, the treatment on paper of an event or a person so that the finished manuscript would hold the breath of Montana. We thought of the pay dirt heaped upon the shelves of the Historical Society Library at Helena. And we thought, too, of what was ours through MIA — the meeting and the mingling and the sharing with others of attitudes and perceptions.

We foresaw the danger, though, for we remembered that the bright young man of Manhattan had been conditioned by a flood of fiction across the years that had led him to believe that only the cowboy, the sheriff and the rustler had existed in Montana. We had been given the chance to show him the many faces of our land, and the many people, but he was only one editor. Others with whom we had no personal contact had presumed that some of our fictional pictures of Montana must be fantasy, for they didn't fit with the time-honored tradition of gunsmoke and gallop.

We knew then that we were faced with a challenge that called for a special skill, for we must please the editor by giving him the product dear to his public, yet into this product we would weave with integrity the Montana we knew.

We would study his magazine, we promised ourselves, and see where his vulnerability lay. And we would remember, too, that the past is often a remote and forgotten land until it is linked with the present. Bridge-builders we must be. We thought then of the Cree Indians who fled into Montana to seek sanctuary after the Riel Rebellion in Canada, and we remembered the term "misplaced persons" that is new only as nomenclature. One bridge is built!

But mostly we thought of what the young man had said about the surface not being scratched, and we itched to get at the hundred places where we might do our digging. Surely the pickaxe is not a strange tool to the hands of a Montanan. Surely we would all mine this wealth and process it and bring it to market. And so great is the scope of possibilities in our native heritage and history that we need not journey far to begin our digging. Indeed, no farther than our own backyards.

Norman Fox, Great Falls, 1952

Rockhounding

First of all let us say that we are amateurs; we don't claim to be experts. Our rock hunting fever started a few years back in Helena. Betty, while attending a women's club convention, panned gold at the concession stand (they guarantee color) and she got her first taste and thrill of seeing gold appear at the bottom of the pan after much slushing and swishing. Well, that was it. No rest now but we must go out into the hills and look for gold. From the attic came gold pans used by relatives in earlier days. We spent many, many pleasant days looking and washing our hands in mountain streams. But no gold.

We, however, so much enjoyed being out in the fresh air and sunshine that we decided to look for more rewarding rock hunting and turned to river agate. In boats, by foot and swimming we spent sunswept days on the river, examining the shores and islands. We found big rocks, little rocks, crooked rocks and very few river agates. But what fun! Max polished some of the smaller rocks in a tumbler and Betty now wears a set in melted silver as a necklace. People upon hearing of our rock hunting began to tell us of places to go and soon all of our weekends were filled with rock hunting trips.

One of our favorite trips is to the sapphire mines near Philipsburg. The sapphire diggings are some 23 miles west of that town on the West Fork of Rock Creek or 38 miles from Hamilton over the Skalkaho road, a beautiful drive. Our first trip was in 1958. George Carter, who was in charge of the mines then, took us up Malay Gulch. The topsoil had been removed over a

59

wide area. Neither of us had ever seen a sapphire in the raw. George helped us look and provided screens and taught us how to use them. Betty's mother, who sat on the bank watching us, suddenly asked, "Is this what you are looking for?" and held up one of the nicest and largest sapphires we have ever found. Like gold, sapphires are where you find them.

To dig sapphires you need at least two screens; some people use three. The present owners of the mine, Bill and Sally Eaton, have screens for rent. If you care to make and take your own the following meshes are most commonly used: a ½ inch screen to remove larger gravel is held over a ⅛ inch screen which retains the small gravel and the sapphires. The third screen, if used, is a ¼ inch for in-between gravel. As the screening is usually done wet there are water pools at the diggings. The screen is shaken back and forth and rotated much as a gold pan is. After the final shaking the screen is held to the light at a slight angle to drain off the water. The sapphires are then visible and what a thrill it is to see them pop into view! We have hit good pay dirt and found as high as fifty sapphires in one screening, but this is exceptional. Ten to twenty gems are the average to a screen if you count small ones. We were told by the Eatons that several 15- and 16-carat sapphires have been found this year.

Another rockhounding trip we found enjoyable was to Fernwood, Idaho, looking for Idaho garnets. Some of the garnets star and are very lovely tumbled. They may also be faceted. We spent several days and dug all the garnets we cared to have. Garnet digging, like most rock hounding, is hard but rewarding work. We left our car and hiked up the creek bank about a mile. On the way we watched the water and found some nice garnets lying in the creek bed where they were easily visible. Diggers were at every level and likely-looking spots on the way. Finally, we found a clear space and started to dig. Using the screen method again we washed, shook and rattled the screen and like the sapphires the garnets appeared in the bottom.

We have spent many sundrenched hours on the banks of Hauser Lake east of Helena on what is known as El Dorado Bar. We went there originally to hunt sapphires but ended picking up hematite. Sapphires and rubies are both found there. After a good rain you can pick them up on top of the ground, but the largest and best are found by — you guessed it — hard work. You dig, shovel, dry screen and then carry your gravel to the lake edge to wash and, we hope, to find sapphires. We found the hematite more rewarding for us. It may be picked up off the ground almost any place on the shore, especially where people have dumped their screens in search of sapphires. It is sometimes very shiny and almost completely polished by nature. We tumble ours to get the shine. Hematite is iron and the majority of the pieces are very dull and very odd in shape. When polished it is called "black diamond."

We believe that for a local trip our most enjoyable times have been spent up Lolo Creek hunting for quartz crystals. We have walked most of the logging roads as well as the main highway looking for them. You may spend an entire day or only a few short hours in this manner and the only skills required are sharp eyes and strong walking muscles. Our daughter Ann found a pocket of smoky quartz in a cut of the road. We have found clear quartz and every size and color degree of smoky quartz. Each crystal is an amazing work of Mother Nature.

Max and Betty Hughes, Lolo, 1963

Living With Jewelry

I am convinced if I had lived in the era of the caveman I would have been one of the first to have a bone hand-shaped into a ring for my nose.

We have been living with paintings, pots and sculpture by Montanans. Quite automatically and gradually I have been acquiring jewelry hand-crafted by our Montana silversmiths. While the paintings, pots and sculpture remain at home the jewelry works of art cling to me wherever I go.

In some cultures (Indian, African) jewelry was a handy way of showing off wealth by hanging "money" around one's neck, from wrists and ears. In ours it satisfies the esthetic side of oneself.

It is startling to realize the many forms jewelry can take for both men and women. Besides earrings, pendants, cuff links and tie tacs I have some handcrafted buttons, all by Margaret McFarland Ames of Billings. She created our *new* wedding rings. She explains her jewelry as functional sculpture, a three dimensional work designed for the purpose of being worn, to enhance rather than decorate the owner.

My first handcrafted jewelry was a pair of silver with African coral earrings by Frances Senska of Bozeman. When I wore a pounded brass pendant by Bill Sage to the St. Louis Museum of Art some years ago the shopkeeper asked if it had been made by someone in South America. I boasted it was made by a Montana artist and she commented that she never thought of Montana as having any artists. She soon found out differently.

Maxine Blackmer, Missoula, has told me it sometimes took a month or more to visualize the design statement she wishes to make with a particu-

61

lar stone or material. In commissioned work she insists the piece suits the individual's personality and requirements. She feels that a beautifully designed piece in precious materials is cold and impersonal unless worn and enjoyed.

The craftsmen I have mentioned all are exceptional artists in other media, which enriches and gives a depth to their work in jewelry. A commission usually is based on a certain gem or object that offers a challenge to their creativity. I respect their work as being of heirloom quality, but they also have the responsibility of designing and creating jewelry that will survive and become the artifacts of our times.

When I was in Seattle in October for the architects' conference I shopped in the Northwest Craft Center and Gallery several times. In conversation with the shopkeeper Ruth Nomura I found that the work of Montana craftsmen is in great demand; she urged me to encourage them to send more of their work — a far cry from the St. Louis incident.

I must admit that our house has some jewelry too. A small box has a bronze knob by Bill Sage and our punch bowl ladle has a cast silver "bauble" to enhance the handle by Margaret Ames.

There are several other silversmiths in our state also creating jewelry that is not only a joy for an individual but enters the exhibition realm. I will endeavor to become better acquainted with them and acquire some of their work. I'm anxious to see what a contemporary craftsman can do with my two pre-Columbian clay beads.

LaDonna Fehlberg, Billings, 1967

Studio 10

Tuesday evening around eight o'clock the sounds of footsteps are heard ascending the stairway to the second floor of the DeMolay Memorial Building to the studio. Some of the footsteps are light and quick as those artists hurry up the staircase in anticipation of the evening before them. Other footsteps heard are burdened and labored as the artists puff up the stairs carrying canvas, paint cases, and what have you. However, each has a sparkle in the eyes as they eagerly enter the studio door. Perhaps they are thinking that tonight they will get that one likeness or painting they have been dreaming of. Regardless of how they arrive young and old alike are there to create in their own way using favorite media to make their impressions of the subject of the evening. Their main aim is to find a way to express their art with brush, palette, knife, pencil, chalk or charcoal. Quite often a "pinkie" is used. In losing themselves in their work the silence of creation is often a studied quietness.

Perhaps their models that evening are the category of the ones they have had before. Children and teenagers have been favorites, possibly because of their freshness. These have been of many nationalities. Of course, they have been the character type models, such as the aged mother in her rocker reading her Bible, the itinerant white-bearded old man who wandered into the cafe on the first floor of the building, the hippy with his beads and uke, a rancher, an Assinniboine Indian in full dress. For action studies we have had a boxer, dancers, youth in sport activities. Each member is responsible for getting a model or setting up still life.

Often we have a "Do It Yourself Night." We then have fifteen or twenty items placed on a platform table, items such as fresh and dried flowers, glassware, bottles, driftwood, antiques, pottery, rope, and cloth draped in various textures. The artist is on his own; he composes his own study, paying close attention to highlights and shadow, form and color. It is quite interesting to see the results. Masterpieces are seldom born here but creative ideas abound and the embryo of an idea is stored in a mental sketchbook.

Some members are dyed-in-the-wool traditionalists and others lean toward the modern and the abstract. This is well and good, both stimulating and progressive. Once the eye of a traditionalist painter twinkled as he watched an abstract take form. He began dabbing with an experimenting brush striving to make something abstract. He tried, but he went back to his first love — that was what he enjoyed. Well, he tried, didn't he? The modernist experiment with tradition? Sure, why not?

As they did the same study each artist found that techniques differed, each person and individual and no one forced to change his technique.

This paragraph from the constitution shows what Studio 10 is and what members do:

> It shall be the object of Studio 10 to further art in the individual and the community by maintaining a studio where members can work at all times; providing a place to show their finished work to the public; by presenting art shows, workshops, field trips, and any other stimulating instructive or constructive activities that are possible and practical.

This statement grew when a group of 10 artists met in May, 1957: Marilyn Christ-Janer, Connie Servoss, Lois Hawks, Lela Tonkin, Mildred Bowen,

Morrie Weissman, Ned Lambertson, Branson Stevenson, Bill Deno, and Al Gordon. These artists decided that they needed a place where they could meet, paint, and not be interrupted by the jangle of the telephone. Today the membership, though limited, is about twenty-two. The constitution states that anyone shall be eligible to become a member of Studio 10 who is a working artist in any media or field of art, who is seriously interested in the purposes of the Studio, and who can show a number of his works to the organization.

Recently it was voted to add a second group to Studio 10, the Tuesday Afternoon Group, TAG. They have outdoor sketching quite often, as well as group painting in various media, as the evening group does.

Studio 10 is a learning, working, creative group. The principal aim is to further art in Great Falls, in Montana, and within themselves in their growth as artists.

Since 1958 the Studio has offered to the public one or two workshops a year, one of the original desires of the ten founders. The first workshop was held on May 14-18, 1958, by Leo Beaulourier. It was followed by two others in the spring of 1962 and one in watercolor in October, 1963. In October, 1958, Jim Logan held one on "Light and Color," followed by one in 1960, and in 1967 one on "Acrylics." John Segesman held a workshop on "Composition," in 1959 and another on "Color and Composition" in 1964. Dr. Jordan from Choteau in 1962 held a workshop featuring "Oil Painting," and Rosemary Morris demonstrated and held a workshop in 1964. Charles Mulvey of Long Beach, Washington, gave a very successful watercolor workshop.

In 1961 Studio 10 reached another goal set up by the original 10: a gallery became a reality. Though the exhibitor is not charged a small fee is asked to help pay for insurance on the art works exhibited. Guest artists are chosen by a committee, which tries to fill the calendar for a year in advance. The public is admitted free of charge to view the art work at any time when the Memorial Building is open.

Studio 10 conducts a few other activities. In 1968 the Lions District Convention needed decoration for their festivities. They asked the Studio to paint a mural 35 by 13 feet for a background of the stage at th Rainbow Hotel. Four members buckled down and did the painting. Since September, 1969, members have had exhibits each month on KFBB-TV and different artists have held demonstrations each month.

Adapted from an article by
Thelma Gift, Great Falls, 1969

Montana House: An Adventure in the Hand Arts

A beautiful new building is going up this fall in Glacier National Park, the future headquarters of Montana House, a retail shop which specializes in authentic arts and crafts. Behind the project are two people: Hans Jungster, a graduate forester who never expected to be doing this at all, and his wife, who is telling this story. The summer of 1960 will be the fifth year for Montana House, which had its start elsewhere in the wholesale and manufacturing business.

The basic plan for Montana House has been substantially unchanged from the beginning. It will remain a regional craft shop emphasizing in particular the work of Montanans, an outlet for the artist who makes a few exceptional pieces, and for the producing craftsman who turns out more volume designed with a general market in mind.

Will people actually buy locally produced crafts? The answer is, Yes if they are genuinely useful, of good design, and of good quality in materials and workmanship, and fairly priced for what they are. The great problem is the source of supply. By word of mouth, by advertising, by traveling to shows, by purest accident, we find out who makes what. That is only the beginning; can he make more of it, can he do it efficiently, can he get more material, can the design be modified to make it more useful, and, futhermore, does he want to bother at all? Usually negotiations break down — he "hasn't time." Few and far between are those delightful persons who come in with a good craft item that is fully developed for marketing and available for marketing.

Another side of the supply problem is getting good design from people who have a craft skill but lack creative ability; they wait to be told what to make. We listen carefully to customer suggestions, study the gift trade, rack our brains and plan an item, but it's another thing to get it produced. The established artists, equipped with well formed work habits and amply supplied with ideas, cannot be counted on either. He may be absorbed in a variety of professional activities, usually does not depend on his creative output for a living, produces a relatively small number of highly creative pieces which find their own market. Other facets of the supply problem include getting variety in style, design and materials; having an adequate size and color range, in the case of clothing; having a good range of prices.

The second great problem of this specialized type of retailing is the exceedingly complex one of pricing. When a handmade article stands in a store with a price tag on it, what is behind that tag? Assuming that it came directly from the maker without benefit of agent, there are two sets of expenses involved, the craftsman's and the retailer's. The craftsman sets his own price; he counts the cost of materials and equipment, figures his wage and profit which he thinks he has earned. The retailer adds up bills for heat, light, maintenance, office supplies, advertising, display time and materials, rent, fixtures, wages, wrapping supplies, freight, telephone, transportation, and figures the per cent of profit that will keep him going. To come out ahead he usually must have a minimum mark-up of forty percent. Just one thing, though, finally determines that retail price of a craft article and that is the attitude of the potential purchaser. If it *seems* right to him, if it is close to the value he himself places on the article, he will buy it; when all the costs involved add up to more than *seems* right he leaves it alone.

The attitude of the person who comes walking into the craft shop is extremely important to both the craftsman and the owner of the shop. The attitude which he, or most likely she, brings with her as she looks about has been formed by a variety of factors. The first of these is other craft shops. Well-known craft items, similar wherever they are made, have to be about the same price, a prime example being the handwoven wool border skirt of two lengths of fabric. The purchaser is also conditioned by commercial merchandise. If he cannot see that something is handmade, if it actually resembles a factory product, the customer will not pay for the hand work involved.

If a substantial amount of quality hand craft is sold at cost within an area, certain things happen. The people who buy it unconsciously begin to value it at cost price; since no value has been put on the craftsman's skill and originality they don't value those either; the cost price begins to seem like the right price. The producing craftsman, who is the work-horse of the craft movement, may want to make similar things but he finds that he cannot compete; the price has been set for him; he must accept a below minimum wage, lower his quality, or turn to something different.

The interrelated complexities and subtleties of pricing hand work have a threefold effect on what can be offered in such a shop: 1) things that duplicate so-called "fancy work" are eliminated, though if better and more original, they may succeed; 2) work must be top quality in design and workmanship to justify the price; 3) work that competes directly with commercial goods and imported crafts will lose out. The craftsman does best when he follows his own inclination, developing and perfecting his own ideas and technique. The people who browse through craft shops are looking for just that, and chances are good that they will recognize it when they see it.

Our plan for the future is to continue what we are now doing, hoping to do it better as time goes on. We are truly grateful to the people who have made their work available, some since our very beginning. We are also making plans to sponsor the best work of Montanans in the arts. The final hope is that in the not too distant future we will be able to provide facilities where artists may come and work, instruct, and demonstrate. By providing a dependable outlet for the craftsman's products, by making Montana House a well-planned, well-managed show window placed before thousands of people, we hope to provide a year-after-year oportunity for craftsmen and artists.

Adapted from an article by
Antoinette Jungster, Apgar, 1960

A Community Complex

The lady came into the Country Bookshelf soon after the doors opened in the morning. "I've hired a baby-sitter for the day and I've brought my lunch. Would you mind if I just stayed here and browsed?" She had come to the perfect retreat from household routine. Marguerite Kirk and Vivian Canfield, owners of the Country Bookshelf and Paperback Barn, have created an atmosphere of hospitality and comfort in their establishment that tempts visitors into creative work or browsing. While their main business is selling books, they are also building a community complex where persons interested in various arts may gather to study and work.

The buildings of this center date back to the 1870s and were erected by Miss Kirk's grandfather, a Pennsylvanian who liked to spend summers in the Gallatin Valley. The ranch buildings, located on the outskirts of Bozeman, included the family home, a bunk house, a chicken house, and a big red barn. Then, in 1958, survey work for the new U.S. 191 began and it was learned that the highway would cut right through the chicken house. Because it was too good a building to tear down Miss Kirk had it moved closer to the house and remodeled it into the Country Bookshelf.

The attractive book shop boasts a fireplace and a floor of picture rock from Logan. It is furnished with antique furniture brought to Bozeman from New Jersey and Pennsylvania. Local art such as ceramics, silk screen printed articles, hand painted greeting cards, and jewelry is displayed and sold here, providing artists with an outlet for their work. Across the courtyard, which, in summer, is bright with flowers, is the bunk house. Its outside wall serves as a bookstall, and inside is an antique loom, which weavers may use at their convenience.

After the big barn was converted into the Paperback Barn, Miss Kirk worked with Joe Fitch, director of theater at Montana State University, to transform the hayloft into the Loft Theater, a summer playhouse which offers four plays a season, Tuesdays through Saturdays, from June into August. A lobby furnished with antiques and decorated with old theater posters, contributes to the Gay Nineties atmosphere though the plays range from the tragedies of Ibsen to the sophisticated humor of Thurber.

The latest addition to the cultural center is a small church which Miss Kirk rescued from the demolition squad. The first Catholic church in Bozeman, it was dedicated in 1885 and since then has been at various times, a Mormon church, a secondhand store, and paint shop. In the future it will be used for art exhibits, special musical concerts, and meetings of cultural groups.

Montana writers are featured in every department of the shop, from the children's reading room to the history shelves. Ask for a good book to read and the proprietors will say, "We have a new book by a Montana author."

Asked what project they are planning in the future, Miss Kirk said, "We are ready to leap in any direction so long as it is for the cultural improvement of the community." Then she mentioned a large autograph party she is planning for Montana authors.

Can you think of a better place to spend a day's vacation?

Kay Widmer, Bozeman, 1965

The Archie Bray Foundation

One man's dream has become a reality in the Archie Bray Foundation for Ceramics; which is to be dedicated October 13, 1951, in a shaded grove just three miles west of Helena.

At an original cost of more than $20,000 Archie G. Bray, one of founding fathers of MIA and one of the Capital City's most active music and drama sponsors, has established the best equipped and most unusual center of its kind in the Northwest. It is a center dedicated not only to the development and preservation of one of the world's most ancient and honored arts, but also it will provide headquarters for advanced study, testing of various materials, and exhibit of prime examples.

The doors of the low brick building are open to anyone. There are no restrictions, no entrance requirements, no set fees. Bray emphasizes that the foundation and its facilities are to be used by any person with an interest in ceramics — pottery, sculpture, porcelain. Charges will be based on materials used, and in some cases they will be forgotten.

The foundation is the answer to the lifelong dream of Bray, who as a boy tried to construct a potter's wheel — although he had never seen one — a dream that persisted even after he worked his way through Ohio State College to receive a degree as a graduate ceramist and after he had traveled in the Midwest and had seen the small man-made wheels driven by waterfalls.

Complete in every detail, the Foundation is located at the Western Clay Manufacturing Company, with which the Bray family has been associated since 1886. The brickyard was founded 20 years before the turn of the century and was managed by Bray's father, a Cornishman, who directed its first major steps.

Power for the company and for the foundation is provided by a 150-horsepower Corliss engine that at one time furnished power and lights for the city of Helena. More than 50 years ago it was located at the present site of the Great Northern Passenger station.

Of interest to both ceramic enthusiasts and the general public will be the Foundation museum, which has been established to display outstanding examples of ceramics work. Already it contains two of Bray's prize pieces, which are over 200 years old.

Bray plans annual, autumn and spring shows in the spacious room, attracting the work of nationally and internationally famous ceramists, as well as examples created by more novice Montana artists.

In 1952 Bray expects to bring to the Foundation Bernard Leach of England, the world's most noted ceramist. As a Foundation guest and instructor, Leach would spend two weeks in Helena.

Complete facilities for testing all types of clay have been installed at the one-story Foundation building, and any individual is invited to send samples for testing, free of charge.

The main building of the Bray Foundation, symmetric and artistic in design, covers more than 2,400 square feet. It contains a light and well-planned workroom, measuring 20 by 40 feet; a glaze room equipped with every type of glaze used by modern potters; a kiln room with four types of ovens, including a Harper and a Blobar, latest development in kilns with every imaginable type of control. Bray says it "will do everything but play records."

Students at the Foundation will have access to the famed Blossberg clay, which is reputed to be "finer than any synthetic compound." It contains the most valuable ceramics properties and is susceptible to any glaze.

With a ceramics graduate as a full-time instructor, the Foundation can accommodate classes of 12 persons at regular two-hour sessions. Conferences may be made at any time, day or evening, seven days a week.

First of the competent instructors at the center is Miss Lillian Boshcen, a native of North Carolina, who has received her Master's degree in ceramics and who has exhibited at some of the most outstanding invitational and national shows. She has studied at the California College of Arts and Crafts, Mills College, and San Francisco School of Fine Arts. By November 1, Miss Boshcen will open classes in every department and will instruct on the kickwheel, which she brought with her.

Working with Bray this summer in completing plans for the Foundation and in furthering their own creations were three of Montana's best known artists, Pete Voulkos, Rudy Autio, and Kelly Wong, all Montana State College graduates and frequent exhibitors at MIA festivals and other Treasure State shows. They have the distinction of being the first to use the Foundation facilities.

Voulkos expects to return to the Foundation after completing his work for his Master's degree in ceramics at the California College of Arts and Crafts. Voulkos concentrated on pottery this summer, while Autio developed his sculptural techniques.

At the invitational dedication dinner, October 13, the clay cornerstone will be laid. It will contain the brief history of the Foundation. It will establish a means of fulfillment for others who dream of a place to work.

And Bray, not yet content, is still looking to the future. He wants to be able soon to bring advanced students from Montana and neighboring states to the Foundation to complete work for their degrees. "As a final thesis I'd suggest they design, construct, fire and test an old-style beehive kiln," Bray says. "All the materials are here and there's lots of room."

Then looking across his property toward the hills, he adds, "Wouldn't it be something to put a stone bridge across the creek and build a little theater?"

Viola G. Lindley, Helena, 1951

A third article, by Jerry Metcalf, entitled "Today at the Bray," is in vol. 28, No. 2, Winter 1976. *Montana Arts.*

MIA and Indians

Verne Dusenberry, third president of MIA, an anthropologist primarily interested in the Indian and his culture, noted in the spring 1958 issue of the MIA magazine that Indians were members of MIA but that the Institute had given little attention to Indian culture — "Projected plans to recognize the Indian as part of the cultural heritage of the state have not materialized." He credited Mable Bjork for "championing the cause of John Clarke, the Indian sculptor"; establishment of the Joseph Kinsey Howard Memorial Funds, whose moneys "were to go to the worthy Indian young people who want to attend college and specialize in the arts"; Alfred Humphrey's movement "to secure representative recordings of primitive music from each of the [Montana] Indian tribes"; "minor recognition given Indians at the Festivals in Havre and in Kalispell"; and assistance given by the Missoula Branch in the preparation of an art exhibit held during the first annual Institute on Indian Affairs at the University of Montana. He hoped that "as an Institute we may become in the years ahead more interested in the Indian as an individual citizen of Montana and find ways and means of assisting him."

A number of articles concerning the Indian have appeared in the MIA magazine. The winter 1961 issue carried an article by Grace Threthewey on Indian paintings in the vicinity of Kalispell. At the 1961 Festival Joe Medicine Crow presented a history of the Crow Indians, which was reported by Gretchen Jellison in the summer issue. An illustrated account of the "Center for Indian Studies" at Rocky Mountain College appeared in the autumn 1967 issue with a map locating the Indian reservations in the states of Montana and Wyoming. Dr. Hap Gilliland of Billings, who noticed that the history book used at the Lame Deer School on the Cheyenne Reservation had "one-and-one-half pages devoted to the history of the Indians and Mountain Men," has developed an Indian Intelligence Quotient Test and has published books about Indians. Nancy Olson, in the 1971 spring issue wrote of an Indian Cultural Series of publications — "By June 1, 1971, there will be sixteen softback 32-page books off the press." Of these books John Woodenlegs of the Northern Cheyenne Tribe, said, "These books are stories about our way of life, our problems and our progress, our history and our hopes for the future. They should help all children to have a better understanding of Indian people."

In the same issue, October, 1967, Walter Woodcock, a worker in the Bureau of Indian Affairs in Billings, wrote "About Indians Today"-"Montana is the home of many tribes, the Salish and Kootenai on the Flathead Reservation, the Blackfeet on theirs, the Chippewa and Cree on the Rocky Boy Reservation, the Gros Ventre and Assinniboine of Fort Peck, and the Northern Cheyenne and Crow of their respective reservations. Of the 34,477 enrolled Indians in Montana about 20,000 live on or near reservations." The issue also carried a review of Peter Nabokov's book *Two Leggings: the Making of a Crow Warrior,* by Ann Whitmack, writing by Yellowtail Tioneeta and Elnora Wright on "A Lesson from the Wild Geese";

Mabel Bjork's account of John Clarke, the Indian carver at East Glacier; Georgia Carter wrote a note about Joe Medicine Crow, an anthropologist and Dale Burk about Gary Schildt, "Lone Bull of the Blackfeet," a painter — "I try," the artist said, "to bring about an emotional involvement between the viewer and the subject matter."

Elnora Wright in the March 1969 issue recounts the remarkable career of Dr. Barney Old Coyote, a Crow Indian, and in the next issue outlined the Indian part of the program of the 1969 Festival in Bozeman which had the theme, "Redskin Roots," and in the June 1960 issue wrote "Redskin Roots in Retrospect," together with the address at the Festival by Dr. Old Coyote, entitled, "The Indian Heritage." Dr. Old Coyote said, "He [the Indian] prays in the morning and at night so that physically, mentally, and spiritually he may be in rapport and harmony with all creation at any given time of the night or day . . . . As Indians we learned that we are but one big family and that we are all children of one Great Spirit which is in our souls and which can be understood and enriched to fit the times of our lives, today and forever." At the Festival young Indians of the Crow, Sioux, Arapahoe, Shoshone, Northern Cheyenne, Assinniboine and Chippewa tribes, members of the Indian Club at Montana State University, presented dances in authentic costumes and narratives on buffalo tanning, the war bonnet, and Indian legends — "from children to grandfathers the show went on through prayer, legend, song, and dance . . . . An enthralled audience," wrote Elnora Wright, "got a picture of the Indian in all his beauty, his culture, his fun, his prayer."

An account drawn from
many articles by H. G. Merriam

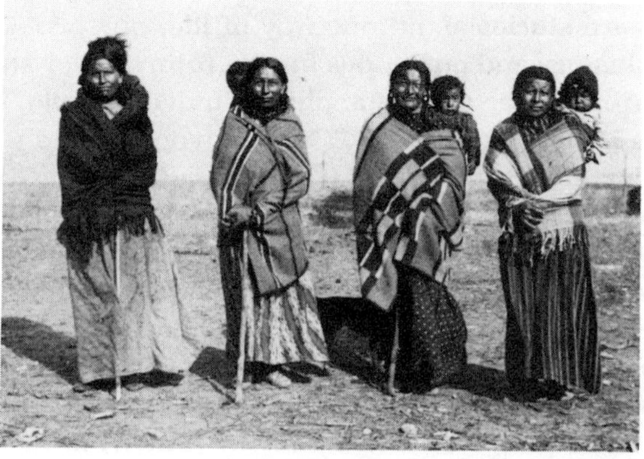

Indian photograph, circa 1899

Section II

THE ARTISTS

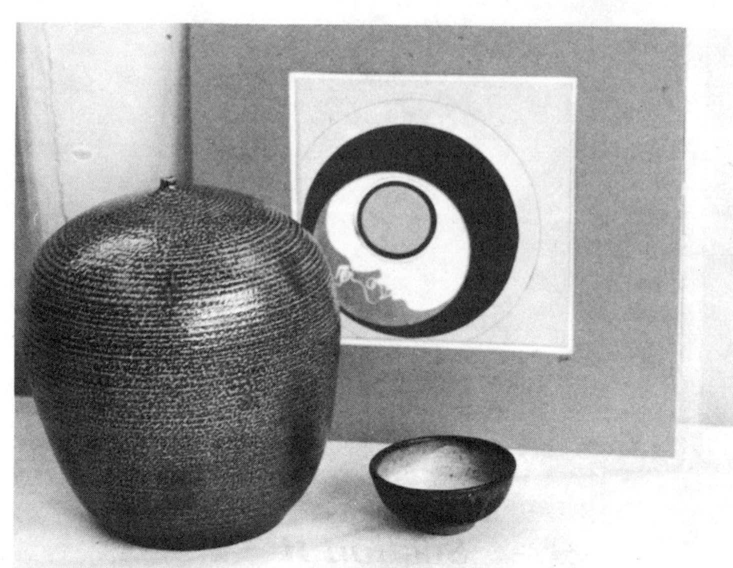

Stoneware bottle, Ken Edwards
Moon Struck, cut paper collage, Jim Jiede
Stoneware berry bowl, Mary Tavener
1971

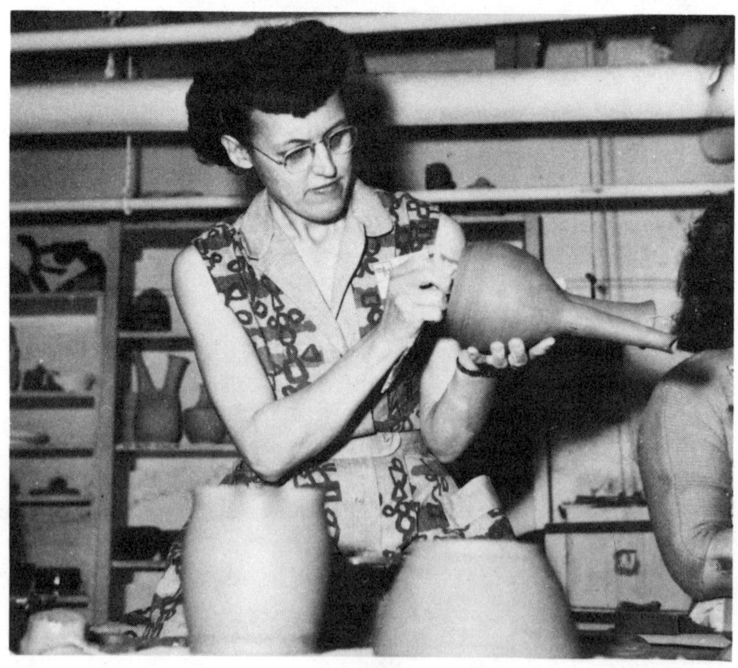

Frances Senska, 1957

ARCHITECT

AIA Fellow

Robert E. Fehlberg, partner in the firm of CTA Architects/Engineers/Planners, has been elected to the College of Fellows of the American Institute of Architects, an honor given to architects who have made notable contributions to the advancement of the architectural profession.

Nominated by his peers, Montana Chapter, AIA, in recognition of his contributions in the areas of public service, architectural practice, and service to the architectural profession, Mr. Fehlberg has engaged extensively in public activity.

At the local level he was largely responsible for bringing the Yellowstone Art Center into being. With his experience with this Center he served as consultant for the establishment of the Lewistown and Copper Village Art Centers. He has been consultant also on the development of the art center in Missoula. He has served as President of the Billings Art Association, the Montana Institute of the Arts, the Montana Institute of Arts Foundation, the Yellowstone Art Center Foundation, and the Yellowstone Art Center Commission. He has been a member of the Montana Arts Council and has chaired two committees for the Yellowstone Art Center. One of his photographs was selected for the Permanent Collection of the Montana Institute of the Arts.

Mr. Fehlberg's contribution to architectural practice is symbolized by design awards received by CTA for which he has had significant responsibility. A few of the projects meriting special recognition by the Montana Chapter of AIA are the Physical Education Building and the Liberal Arts Building of Eastern Montana College; the AOP Sorority House in Missoula, the Montana Corporation Office Building in Billings, and the Montana Crippled Children and Rehabilitation Center in Missoula.

Mr. Fehlberg's service to his profession is indicated by his positions of leadership. He has served as President and Vice President of the Montana Chapter of AIA. He has been president of the Billings Architectural Association. Mr. Fehlberg has been, since 1971, a Director of the American Institute of Architects for the Northwest region. This responsibility requires him to represent fifteen chapters in seven states.

Mr. Fehlberg was accepted formally into the College of Fellows in ceremonies in May, 1973, at the San Francisco Convention of AIA. His introduction states: "The work of Robert E. Fehlberg shows the outstanding contribution of an architect to his state and to the business and cultural life of his community, while maintaining an active and successful practice and unselfishly sharing his time and talents with fellow professionals.''

LaDonna Fehlberg, Billings, 1973

CARVERS

A Personal Glimpse of John L. Clarke

John Clarke is busy carving but takes time to roam about. He searches the high altitudes for weatherbeaten trunks and roots and the lakeshores for waterbeaten pieces, which he poetically calls drifty wood. He incorporates into his sculpture compositions burls and twisty pieces more than ever before.

He neither acts nor appears the part of one aged eighty-six. Besides a lean athletic body he has an investigating mind, fine sense of humor, and good eyesight. He seems to miss little in his constant search for the interesting and the beautiful. Undoubtedly the same qualities contribute towards his quiet evaluation of people.

John L. Clarke is Montana-born of Montana-born parents. He has had an art career for over sixty years. He can be considered an outstanding soloist when it is realized that he has reached his accomplishments without the ability to hear since age two, which also results in lack of speech. Although there are conflicting views as to how the deafness took place, the important item to keep in mind is that he built a good life in spite of the loss.

Assuredly it has required the best qualities from his three-fourths highclass Amerindian ancestry and the best qualities from his highclass Americaucasian ancestry plus a considerable environment to achieve the status he holds nationally and internationally as a wood sculptor.

Like most men, John Clarke profited by having a wife who not only enriched his daily life but believed in his skills and capabilities to the extent that she did something about it. She knew when and how to do some of the things he could or would not do. It was Mamie who got his work into large exhibitions in the largest cities, placing him under the test of vast audiences and hard-headed jurors. She visited by the hour with people from all over the world in the sales-shop part of their studio home. She wrote the letters and took care of the financial matters. She also had to be the reminder that orders for bears, goats, deer, and elk were unfilled when he went off on delightful tangents such as carving a baby skunk or fashioning a delicate dragonfly.

John and Mamie Clarke and their little blonde adopted girl became friends of my mother and myself when I maintained a studio next door to them, the summer of 1941. During these months I learned how well-known John Clarke is among European carvers. I recall especially a father and son team of Oberammergau wood carvers who remained in Glacier Park the whole summer specifically to observe Clarke and his techniques. I also saw Montana carvers come frequently for help and criticism.

I became fully aware that Europeans, New Yorkers, and west coasters know this man and his products better than most Montanans. It took purchases by noted men out-of-state to awaken interest within the state. Just a few years ago a Montana welfare worker was a guest in a Viennese home. She told me that one of the thrills of her entire journey was sighting a John Clarke carving in that home.

Today many fine pieces of Clarke's earlier work are to be found in dwellings of far-sighted Montanans. The Museum of the Plains Indian at Browning and the hospital at the same place have good examples of his skill. The Historical Museum owns a cottonwood panel about four by thirteen feet presently on loan to the University at Missoula. The Permanent Collection of the Montana Institute of the Arts, on display at the Historical Museum, includes an outstanding carving in cottonwood by Clarke. I saw several exceptional pieces purchased out-of-state before they left his shop. Many went into private collections of noted people. There are pieces also in eastern and western museums and at least one at the Chicago Art Institute.

In 1918 he was awarded a gold medal by the American Galleries of Philadelphia for the wood sculpture of a bear. He has participated in leading exhibitions, received many honors and been written up favorably in major newspapers of the country. There were exhibitions in New York, Philadelphia, Atlantic City, Boston, Milwaukee, Chicago and other cities.

I noted on a recent visit that John keeps his mail in a good-sized carton. When he wishes to refer to a letter he carefully lifts those on top so as not to disturb the chronology. In replacing the item he does so with the same precision. Undoubtedly he re-reads what he receives but from our experience of the past two years one should not expect a reply. A new freedom for any of us when we become over eighty-five should be freedom from answering most letters. With this in mind, there may be several MIA Montana Arts readers who would enjoy adding to the reading material in that carton without thought of return mail.

In the thirty-six years since I first met Mr. Clarke I certainly should have become a sign-talker. For the few times I would see him it never occurred to me to study toward greater enjoyment of future visits. This is how short-sighted one can be, consequently it is only with the laborious written word that we converse even today. His sign for those who talk too much was directed at his sister and myself as we visited on this recent trip at the home of Mr. and Mrs. L.W. Goss in Browning. The man naturally had a good laugh. His signs for tough steak or utter disgust or sadness are crystalized dramatics at their best.

His face becomes lighted with eagerness and pleasure as Ray and I appear at his door and is enough to cause us to wish we were going back next weekend. The best we can hope for is that he accepts our invitation to spend a fourth Christmas with us in Helena.

Adapted from an article by
Mable Bjork, Helena, 1967

With Paint and Wood: The Swenneses

Selecting a couple for our Libby Writer's group interview assignment was no problem. Buck (Donald) and Bernadine Swennes immediately came to mind. We are proud of their "dedicated to the arts" attitude.

Their art careers started in 1965 when Buck gave Bernadine paints for Christmas. Since they are people who do not believe in idle hands they put the paints to good use and what started out as an enjoyable hobby has now become an important part of their lives.

While Bernadine has continued to paint, Buck now specializes in wood carving. He works evenings in his basement workshop when he's on day shift at his planer-operator job at St. Regis Paper Company.

Bernadine has a small studio tucked away in the corner of an upstairs bedroom where she paints daytimes. She also works at an easel in the dining-room. A proud moment for the Swennes came when she sold her first painting. Her paintings have now been shown all over Montana and have found their way to other states as well. At present Bernadine's paintings are displayed in various buildings in Libby and the Magic Mushroom Gallery in Missoula.

Bernadine paints mostly in oils in a style all her own. Her portraits of Indians bring an immediate question, "Who is this?" Their facial expressions make you want to know their story now! One painting draws attention at every showing. It is of an Indian youth. Bernadine has used umber and crimson tones in her series of Indian paintings.

Buck began carving in 1967, having been inspired at an art show in Kalispell. Carving mostly in cottonwood bark, he also uses pine, juniper and other local woods. He uses cottonwood bark for Indian faces because it takes a good finish and detail is easier to carve. After one or two coats of varnish, the sculpture is covered with colored wax for a finish.

Buck carves animals and figures out of harder woods, pine and juniper. Juniper with its red tones and light streaks provides a beautiful natural finish. One of his carvings is a juniper frontiersman.

He carves pine when it is wet and green. Then he lets it dry slowly so that it won't check or crack. A large table-model grizzly bear was carved out of pine.

Buck states that "animals must be carved in exact detail to be very realistic." Study and practice enhance the skill required to bring out the life-like features and characteristics common to the different species. The coyote, grizzly bear and buffalo are his most frequent animal subjects.

Buck has also made Indian heads out of hydracal, a form of plaster of paris, only stronger. But he doesn't care for molds as well as he does for carving. With a half-dozen simple tools Buck makes animals and figures come alive. But he spends much research time beforehand among his stacks of reference books on animals and their natural surroundings.

Both Bernadine and Buck consider their creative fields limitless, with many possible and various goals in the future. The reason they are able to produce steadily in spite of everyday commitments is the mutual appreciation and respect each has for the other's work and the cooperation of their three children.

Dixie Peltier, Libby, 1973

CERAMISTS

Frances Senska

Although Frances Senska's major fields are pottery and design, she has also received national recognition in lithography. The Brooklyn Museum, the Library of Congress, and the Princeton Library, in addition to the Binet Gallery of New York, are among the purchasers of her lithographic prints.

Miss Senska received her training in lithography at the University of Iowa, where she took her B.A. and M.A. degrees. She has also studied pottery and design at the Institute of Design in Chicago, the Cranbrook Academy at Cranbrook, Michigan, and the Pond Farm at Gurneyville,

California, where she studied under the famous Marguerite Wildenhain.

To visit Miss Senska's home in Bozeman is to see the effects of a sensitive and trained artistic talent applied to practical living, for she has designed much of her own furniture, pottery, and silverware.

The broad interests reflected in Miss Senska's training and her artistic productions reflect an equally broad and varied background. Born in Africa, where her father was stationed as a medical missionary, she saw a good portion of the world, its peoples, and its art at an early age.

She is at present serving as assistant professor in the Montana State College Art Department.

Verne Dusenberry, Bozeman, 1952

Branson G. Stevenson: Artist in Many Fields

The name of Branson G. Stevenson must appear in large letters wherever the names of Montanans are listed who have worked long and hard for the advancement of the arts and artists in our state. Branson's name will also appear in the record of artists who have made unique contributions to the culture of our times by the amount and quality of their works. I have had the privilege of knowing and working with Mr. Stevenson for over twenty-five years.

Two qualities stand out in Branson Stevenson's artistic make-up in unique amounts. The first is his enthusiasm for almost all of the various media of art, together with the fact that he has developed much skill in the use of so many of them. The second outstanding quality is his keen curiosity and scientific investigation into each project that he undertakes, whether it be lithography, pottery, silkscreen printing or the physics of color in light and pigment. Both his enthusiasm for the virtues of a particular medium and the fruits of his research on technical frontiers are always graciously shared with fellow artists and interested laymen.

The traditional concept of an artist as a long-haired irresponsible escapist from the contemporary business world most certainly does not apply to Branson Stevenson, who holds the position of Montana manager of the Socony Mobile Oil Company (1959).

My first meeting with Branson came about when I stumbled onto an article about dynamic symmetry which Branson had written. His hospitality and encouragement when I as a high school student had mustered the courage to call on him and introduce myself has not diminished to this day. At that time Branson was perfecting his technique of printing etchings and I was privileged to use his tools and printing press. When he had secured the materials for lithography and had learned the process of printing lithographs, he urged me to use his stones. Really Branson's generosity is phenomenal.

Whenever a club or organization wanted to learn about some phase of art, Branson would take the time to present a talk. Each time an art group would form in Great Falls, Branson would put his shoulder to the wheel. At various times we have had an American Artists Professional League, an informal life drawing class, the Great Falls Art Center Association, the Russell Memorial Gallery Committee, and finally the Montana Institute of the Arts. Branson is a founding member of MIA and, since he took my wife and me to the Helena meeting in 1948, so are we. The Archie Bray Foundation at Helena has taken much of Branson's time and energy since its very beginning. Since shortly after the death of C.M. Russell, one of his innumerable friends, Branson was active in trying to establish a memorial to the cowboy artist, and now that the Trigg-Russell Memorial Gallery is a reality, he has the responsible and time-consuming job of chairman of the exhibitions committee. For many years he has been the Superintendent of the Fine Arts Department of the North Montana State Fair.

Despite Branson's almost unlimited expenditures of time and effort toward furthering the numerous projects and activities to promote the encouragement of creative expression and the showing of worthwhile art and craft exhibitions, he still finds time to create an imposing quantity of fine paintings, prints, and ceramic works. Among the various media in which he has worked with outstanding success are: life drawing, wood engraving, etching and dry point engraving, lithography, silk screen printing, oil painting, true fresco, water color painting, ceramic pottery and sculpture. In the field of water color painting Branson originated a technique of using an emulsion of wax mixed with the pigments to derive a new range of effects which are striking and expressive. In his ceramic works he has originated some novel methods for the application of decoration to pottery and has done extensive research and experimenting in the use of native clays and minerals. The thorough study which he has made of every medium in which he has worked is typical of his approach and concentration.

In 1945 Branson was commissioned to paint a fresco in a private home in Great Falls. True fresco painting, the method used by Michelangelo in his famous paintings in the Vatican, is an extremely permanent medium.

Because of the amount of preparation required before the actual painting begins, this method of painting is not often used in this high-speed age, and Mr. Stevenson had to do considerable research and hunting for the correct materials before the project got under way. He generously hired me to assist in the mural and it was only after we had finished the entire wall area in one continuous painting period of about eighteen hours that we realized why modern fresco painters cover about ten square feet a day. We had completed an area of over one hundred square feet, which I feel confident is a record of some sort.

Every artist is unique in at least his personal philosophy of art and the development of his own style. Branson has always been positive in defending the right of each artist to work out his own personal style. I feel that the approach which he feels is right for him is a rational one based on research into color harmony, the logical development of dynamic space relationship, the utilization of recognizable themes and the exploitation of the particular virtues and strengths of each medium in appropriate ways. Every work that I have ever seen by Branson has been a demonstration of complete control of the materials used.

Proof of the correctness of Mr. Stevenson's approach is seen in the number of places where he has had his work exhibited: in Washington, Oregon, California, and Colorado, as well as in New York and Washington, D.C. Some of his ceramic work has toured the world in an exhibition of American Artist-Craftsmen.

Jim Logan, Great Falls, 1959

Peter H. Voulkos, Potter

The young man who arrived at the entrance of the building which this fall housed Pomona's big *House Beautiful* show was probably ill at ease and too modest to mention his name when he told two policemen that he had forgotten his invitation. Like any gate-crasher he was reminded the show was only open to those with invitations and left to wander awkwardly about the foyer until a friend went through a back door to fetch the proper officials to identify him. His name is Peter Voulkos. His new position is head of the Ceramics Department of the Los Angeles County Art Institute. And his pottery was generously represented in Pomona's show.

At the age of thirty and with only six years of experience behind him, he has gained national recognition as one of America's most important ceramic artists. The American Craftsman's Educational Council has just presented in the American House Gallery of New York City, a one-man show of his work, of which it says, ". . . massive in concept, striking in design and decoration. Students and those who love fine pottery will find much in this exhibit for both study and pleasure." "Massive in concept" could be used to describe Pete's whole ceramic career. Examples of his work are in collections of fifteen different museums throughout the country (1954).

One of the best things that have happened to Pete during these six years of making pottery was having a good start with a good teacher, Frances Senska, pottery instructor at Montana State College. For, instead of complaining about the fact that he worked all night instead of during the day, used all the clay they could make and littered the floor with heaps of trimmings, she went on supplying him with plenty of material and some dry humor, realizing she had the insatiable student a teacher finds once in ten years.

From Bozeman he went to Oakland, where he took a Master of Fine Arts degree at the California College of Arts and Crafts, spending his time exclusively in the ceramics department. Amazingly enough, while seeking employment during the summer of 1951, he met Archie Bray, a brick-maker in Helena and a patron of the arts, who was building a pottery and looking for a good potter to take charge of it. That whole summer was spent at hard labor: handling bricks in the yard for eight hours, laying bricks until dark on the new pottery buildings, and throwing pots late at night while dead tired. The next spring after graduation, he returned as manager of the new pottery, which was named the Archie Bray Foundation. In the three years that Pete has lived and worked at the Foundation, his development has been spectacular. Students have come to study with him from all over the country and his pots have sold by the hundreds.

To watch Pete throw a large pot is a fascinating show that invariably draws all the visitors and half of the other potters working around him. The centering of fifty pounds of clay requires both skill and strength. Clay and water fly as it spins; Pete strains to push it into shape and after a few minutes begins to sweat from the effort. Soon the mass magically grows to 20, to 25 inches, is shaped, straightened out, and shaped again with the top of the whirling cylinder in his armpit. Up it goes to 30 inches, sometimes 35; the lip is shaped, cut and smoothed deftly, and the pot is thrown.

A day or two later, sitting in the midst of half-a-dozen of these giants, a pot of red iron, a pot of blue slip, a jar of liquid wax, and a few brushes, nails, and pear pitters, he begins to decorate. If he is making a line drawing he may brush in briefly large shapes with wax and scratch the design into the clay with a nail; then spinning the pot on the wheel and holding a brush dripping with red iron against it, he makes line, color, and pattern appear instantly and spectacularly in the areas not painted with wax.

Decorating with brushwork directly, he may use two or three colored slips or wax, relying merely on his superb dexterity with the Chinese brush to design the pot. His slip trailing is as decisive and sure as his line drawing, practiced so many times and done so quickly it seems effortless. Pressed down with the thumb, it sometimes becomes a thick flat line, sometimes a thin thread.

Some of Pete's ideas about pottery are of interest to all artists whether they are potters or not. Peter believes that the first requirement of a good pot is that it be a unified whole. No one part of the pot should exist as a separate attraction. Decoration, for example, should not be so intensely interesting in itself as to detract from the form but should enhance it; a painting on a pot is rarely as successful as a decorated pot. The same is true of necks, feet, glazes, and every other part; even the slightest nuances in form, color, decoration and glaze must belong to the total idea, a principle true in any work of art. For this reason, Pete has never made a fetish of glazing techniques. In fact, he does not do exhaustive glaze testing, relying instead on a half-dozen glazes, which he uses excellently. While he values a thorough knowledge of the technical end of pottery, the main objectives in his work are strictly esthetic, the making of a pot that will stand on its own merits as a thing of beauty. All of the separate aspects of pottery are subordinate to the single esthetic aim.

During a discussion about the teaching practices at a certain school he was told that the students there had compiled an unbelievably large number of glaze tests, totaling thousands. "Sounds good," he remarked, "but I wonder if they'll ever get around to make the pots to put them on."

Pete's resourcefulness is in everything evident in his workshop. All sorts of shortcuts are taken whenever practicable; sandpaper for smoothing, a stick with nails for scratching textures, throwing many pieces from a single lump of clay, electric wheels for large pots, mixing clay in half-ton batches, voluminous quantities of glaze, roto-tools, dentists's amalgams — any means to an end is all right if properly used. When trimming or turning the feet on some of his gigantic bottles (a seemingly impossible task to most potters), he uses a large sewer pipe as a turning chuck and sets his bottle in it for shaping. This results in a towering, turning structure at least four feet tall, which means that he has to stand on a stool to work on it.

There are few potters who have used native clays and earth glazes to the extent that Pete has used them. While still at Bozeman, he was fond of utilizing the red clay and "trail creek glaze" found near the town, and much of his earlier work is characterized by these materials. Pete now thinks that digging clay is nonsense if it is cheaper and more practical to buy it. The same is true of glazes. Earth or slip glazes are all right to use but their virtue is not in the fact that they are earth glazes. In contrast to Pete are the purists, who dig and refine their clay, fire with wood, insist on using the most primitive equipment and perhaps spend so much time "grubbing the earth" they have little to show for their effort. On the other hand, all of the niceties of ceramic equipment such as hi-fire reduction kilns and spray equipment do not furnish the easy means to fine pottery. A good potter can make good pottery under the most limited circumstances; some of Pete's finest work has been done using low-fire kilns and other meager equipment.

The sources of Pete's ideas are numerous. Pete believes that all artists, potters, sculptors, and painters should experiment constantly, investigating new techniques and adapting them if they are sound and useful. His ideas stem from both traditional and contemporary pottery, ranging from ancient Sung, American Indian, and Greek to contemporary Swedish and Japanese ceramics. No era has passed without value in it as inspiration for his work and no art, whether ironwork, basketry, weaving, painting, or sculpture is overlooked. At one time while visiting the livestock show in Great Falls, he was tremendously impressed by an enormous Black Angus bull in the pavilion; this impression may have coincided with a keen interest in the drawings of bulls by Picasso. Nevertheless, bulls have been appearing in his pots ever since. He has also used abstract flowers, leaf repeats, humorous faces atop horses and inside chickens, and a delicate reindeer in simple brushwork which has practically become a trade mark.

Pete disagrees with the interior decorators and other customers who have made lamp bases out of his rice bottles. It is singularly disturbing to him when others fail to see the simple, decorative purpose of his pottery. Since potters cannot compete with the large volume of technically flawless factory ware, they must concentrate on each piece as a work of art, perhaps even sacrificing its functional purpose for its decorative one. And although Pete makes many useful pieces (bowls, cups, teapots, urns, wine sets, compotes, coffee pots, salad sets, tureens, etc.), each piece is conceived as a new and different art object. If it is vase or bottle and prospective customers ask, "What shall I use it for", Pete usually says, "To look at."

Lela and Rudy Autio, Helena, 1954

85

Rudy and Lela Autio

Lela and Rudi Autio, both native Montanans, are the most widely known couple working in the arts in Montana. Rudy was born in Butte, Lela in Great Falls. They met and were married while they were both students at Montana State University in Bozeman. At graduation time, along with another art graduate, Peter Voulkos, they demonstrated in clay at the MIA Art Festival in Virginia City. Also at the Festival was Archie Bray, owner of the Western Clay Manufacturing Company in Helena and an art patron with a dream. From this meeting actually came the working beginning of what is now the internationally famous Archie Bray Foundation. Lela, Rudy and Pete worked in Helena that summer starting the construction of the pottery building; then, after two years of study at Washington State College Rudy received his MFA degree and he and Lela returned to the Foundation to stay for five years. Pete also returned after completing his MFA in Los Angeles. This period in their lives was one of hard work and meagre finances. At this time Lela worked mainly in enamels and Rudy in clay sculpture. They both taught classes and became acquainted with the "greats" in the pottery world. At the Foundation Rudy executed several ceramic mural commissions for public buildings around the state.

In 1957 Rudy, as assistant curator of the Montana Historical Society Museum in Helena, constructed the large Lewis and Clark diorama. About this time the University of Montana Art Department expanded to include ceramics in its curriculum and Rudy was hired to set up the ceramics studio. Rudy and Lela with their four children have lived in Missoula since this time. Their home and studio in the Rattlesnake area are well known to students, townspeople and visiting artists. Their casual, delightful hospitality is enjoyed by many.

Lela went back to college in Missoula and earned the master's degree with honors in painting. She has since pursued her own career, teaching at the high school level, night classes in ceramics at Seeley Lake and Sentinel High Schools, art education and crafts courses through the University of Montana Continuing Education program. Since 1968 she has been the art director of the University High School Art Camp. Under her guidance this program has been expanded. Lela has also instituted summer programs for junior high school students and pupils in grades four to six. She has a sincere interest and concern for young people and their involvement in art activities.

Maxine Blackmer, Missoula, 1970

Rudy Autio

A major piece of welded steel scupture by Rudy Autio has been installed at the country home of Miss Helen McAuslin at the mouth of the Leveridge Canyon south of Bozeman. Autio, who is well known throughout the country for his work in sculptural ceramics, has recently turned to work in welded steel and cast bronze . . . . His ceramic sculpture adorns many buildings in Montana: a library at Cut Bank, churches in Great Falls, Anaconda, Butte and Missoula, the Liberal Arts building on the campus of the University of Montana and the Library of the University in Bozeman, and a very long relief panel depicting the early days of Last Chance Gulch is back of the tellers' counter at the Gold Bank in Helena. This past year he has completed a welded steel sculpture for the Metals Bank in Butte as well as the piece for Miss McAuslin and a bronze grizzly for the University of Montana.

His work in pottery is in many public and private collections. He has won awards in shows in this country and his work has been sent to international shows by the State Department as representative of the best of contemporary American art. Besides his teaching he has been on juries of many regional and national shows — most recently the Ceramic National at the Everson Gallery in Syracuse, N.Y., the most prestigious show of ceramics in the states.

Frances Senska, Bozeman, 1970

The Loefflers

"An artist is not a special kind of man, but every man is a special kind of artist" said Eric Gill. None of us are alike in total, but rather we are all striving for some sort of self-expression in all of the things we do. We accept the responsibilities of our own personalities, with fear of the mistakes we might make, but being confident that what we do is our own expression. We are self-conscious of our own tastes, yet try to achieve a product that is both an expression of the inner self and a rewarding document of one's labor. And, so it is with us in our lives and our creative efforts together these past years.

Our moving to Montana provided us with the impetus we needed to make art expression into a very big part of our lives. MIA was the fuel that fed the spark of excitement in us to continue our creative growth and to reach levels we had not imagined possible before. The atmosphere of working with others in MIA in many areas is one of the most worthwhile experiences we will carry with us wherever we might be. The banding together of people in a group such as MIA is truly one of the finest movements of its kind for Montana people. Giving our time to MIA has been a truly satisfying endeavor and has repaid us many times over.

Our concept of living is being with people and surrounding ourselves with the many things we enjoy. Our eclectic home, our antiques, our art work and our traveling consume most of our available time. Anyone visiting us in our various homes in the past years might well attest to that. We've acquired antiques and art work from our travels through the British West Indies, Canada, Mexico, Guatemala and many areas of the United States. Most recently Montana has been a vital source for our collecting. We seek out the collectable items that interest us most and use them in and around our home and in our daily living. Traveling has become a way of life for both of us, traveling the Rocky Mountain region on business trips and pleasure trips to new and remembered places.

Our studio at home continues to grow with each passing year. Ginny's paintings, sculptings, and printing all vie for space with Bud's potters wheel, kilns, glazes and great number of tools. We continuously find new interests, as well as trying to remember and maintain old skills. An old printing press has been added to our studio this spring, with its associated type cases, tools and paper supplies. With some luck and the help of friends we should be "rolling the presses" sometime this summer.

Our summers are centered around a great number of activities at our summer home in the Snowy Range Mountains west of Laramie, Wyoming. With the help of friends and family we built a "second home" ourselves from our own design, incorporating our art work and making available a place to pursue our creative interests. To our pleasant surprise, we discovered Ken Ferguson, former resident potter at the Archie Bray Foundation, had build his summer home and pottery studio within a few miles of our location.

The creative arts have been an integral part of our lives. We have enjoyed being creative together, from the beginning simple art lessons and class routines to more matured levels of our present work. We have encountered no great conflict in our interest in the arts, enjoying each other's pursuit of expression. Working together provides us with an added plane of enjoyment that has continued to grow through the years and takes a major part in our activities. We are probably each other's most severe critic, but the criticism has been stimulating, sometimes frustrating, but always helpful.

Virginia and E.H. Loeffler, Billings, 1972

Peter Meloy

In collaboration with his brother Henry Meloy, formerly instructor of painting at Columbia University, Pete has made pottery that is now in museum collections.

Peter Meloy has been mistaken on several occasions for a judge, a congressman, a detective.· He enjoys relating the story of his trip to the Negro section of Ossining, N.Y., one night with his sister to help a Negro maid who was in trouble. On arrival, all persons present denied even knowing the woman and his efforts to help were futile because he resembled the traditional officer of the law, stocky and authoritative. In his pottery clothes, however, he seems more like an easy-going inventor — which he is. Professionally he is a lawyer. In art circles, he is considered one of the best potters in the Northwest.

His first attempts at pottery began on the farm near Townsend, where he was born; and in his typical way of making the best of everything, he claims the depression years were the best beginning possible. In his own words, "There was never anything to do. No crops. The land was bad. So we spent our time putting on plays in the barn and I fooled around trying to fire some little pinch pots in an old iron barrel. They were really funny." This, then, was the germination of his activity in ceramic art, which has since become the most significant craft in our region.

During the 1940's his potting began in earnest. Near his garage a workshop was built with a kiln room and glazing space. Hank Meloy returned each summer from New York to help with the decorating. These were good years. Together they made handmade sculptured horses, large plates, small bowls with calligraphic animals, pots of all sizes — some of them so funny they'd make you laugh, but all warm, simple and charming. In the Portland Museum they were listed as "Contemporary American."

Pete's achievements as a potter are well known, but too few people are aware of his prodigious efforts in behalf of other craftsmen. The reason for this is that he prefers to help them anonymously when possible.

In 1951 he sat down with Archie Bray and drew up the Articles of Incorporation for the Archie Bray Foundation. Every night that summer he met Archie, Voulkos, Autio, and Kelly Wong at the brickyard and the five of them carried mud and laid brick until the sun went down. They constructed the kiln and built the stack. With the last brick in place and the pottery built, Pete became a trustee and the Foundation's legal advisor.

In 1952, when it became a certainty that Bernard Leach, Hamada, and

Dr. Yanagi would tour the United States, Pete helped Branson Stevenson to arrange for their stay at the Foundation for a week's workshop. A printed discussion of ceramics by Dr. Yanagi (which was completely sold out) was published by Pete at his personal expense. Because of the large number of people who attended that workshop, he arranged another which was held by Marguerite Widenhain internationally known potter from California.

As Art Director of the State Historical Museum, he has carried out an extensive program considering that he accepted this post without salary. To some extent, it is because he is a collector himself, but undoubtedly the best reason is his enormous curiosity about the effect certain exhibitions will have on thousands of tourists who go through the museum each year.

For all Montanans who wish to show, he rations out time and space, managing to mix them up with outside shows to keep the public exposed to art in all fields. Amateur cowboy artists must certainly have been inspired to better draftsmanship by the two fine pictorial shows of the early west: George Catlin and Carl Bodmer. On the other hand, Pete has gone out of his way to find buyers for the work of a contemporary nature in an effort to encourage painters and craftsmen working in this vein.

Considering limited funds, the shows have been good. Small, wonderfully carved figures and animals by Alaskan Indians, Navajo rugs, syndicated cartoon strips (by a Montanan), oils by young New Yorkers, an Old Masters show of originals (Veronese, Correggio, Corbet, Innes, Vezanne, etc.), Japanese ink drawings, the American Advertising Annual, school exhibits — high school and college, the MIA Travelling Show.

Acting with his authority as Director, Pete has sent slides and write-ups of Montana artists to the Western Museum Directors' meetings for selection in traveling shows on the west coast. He has obtained work at the Museum for more than one artist, painting, modeling and hanging shows.

After his brother's death in 1950, Pete collected Hank's voluminous paintings, drawings, and notes and built a cement block building to house them safely. A retrospective show of Hank's work was hung in the Historical Museum in 1953, which included brochures containing four very fine reproductions. Pete sent these to museums and galleries throughout the country to keep Hank's name and work in circulation. That same year he visited galleries in New York to show some of the drawings and sold several pieces to their permanent collections.

He has stimulated interest among his friends, sometimes with success, sometimes without, in various handicrafts. After seeing an expert making paper in New York, he talked several people into making handmade paper (it did not turn out with a fine rag content for it eventually became a mixture of toilet paper and weeds — and a little absorbent to write on). He renovated an old printing press which he discovered in a ghost town newspaper office. Several of his five children have used it to print cards — which they sell for spending money. Some interesting welded iron sculptures have come out of his welding shop, also swings, beds and tables. One whole summer was spent teaching his friends to play the guitar. With the addition of a few more pieces, they have had some of the loudest if not the best jam sessions in Helena.

This year Pete began and completed construction of a gas kiln. A complex burner (made in his welding shop) fires this kiln to stoneware temperature (2400· F.) in the amazing time of six hours.

Most important of all to us is that no problem is ever unsolvable to Pete. He has kept many teetering factions from toppling. With his downfarm humor and a few words of meditation when needed, he's been our mainstay. Even anonymous benefactors must be found out sooner or later.

Lela Autio, Missola, 1956

HISTORIAN

A Search for Scribner

A statement in old records that a messenger had been paid $64 to carry the 1873 election returns from Scribner to Missoula evoked the question, "Where is Scribner?"

Local historians said they had never heard of the place — early journals and history books did not mention it; maps in the University Library and the Helena Historical Library did not show any settlement of that name; nor was there any Scribner Peak or Creek on Forest Service maps.

Since the messengers from known places were paid approximately 50 cents per mile, it appeared that Scribner must be at least a hundred miles distant from the courthouse at Missoula, Missoula County in those days including all western Montana. But was it a hundred miles to the south, west or north?

So many people had traveled through the Bitterroot Valley in the preceding decades that it seemed impossible any settlement at the southern tip of the county could have escaped written notice.

Although there were a number of short-lived mining towns along both the Cedar Creek and Clark Fork rivers to the west, messengers from

91

election precincts in that area were paid much less than the man from Scribner. This meant that the only place Scribner could be was somewhere north of the Indian Reservation, but was it near Dayton, or at the head of the Flathead Lake, or in Tobacco Plains?

When gold was found on the Kootenai River in Canada in the early sixties, Missoula was one of the closest places where supplies could be bought. Many pack trains of flour and other goods traveled along the western shore of Flathead Lake from Missoula and the Bitterroot Valley to the Canadian mines. Of course, many prospectors also rushed to the Wild Horse Creek and spread out hopefully along all the streams flowing into the Kootenai.

There were a number of traders in Tobacco Plains, on both sides of the border, and there were cattle herders, too, wherever the grass bunched thick in the meadows north and west of Flathead Lake. It would have been natural for some of the traders to build cabins, particularly during the winter when prospecting was difficult and cattle needed shelter.

In the early years of the county, whenever a dozen or more men congregated near a trading-post or mining prospect, there was a demand for an election precinct. Many such precincts lasted only a few years. A search of courthouse records showed that a precinct was created at Scribner in June 1872. Elections were at "Cohn's store" in '72, '73, '74, and '75; at an unspecified polling place in '76; and at "Romain's" in '78, the precinct being abolished in September 1880.

The election judges for each year were named as well as the messengers who carried the returns to Missoula. There were lists of Scribner taxpayers for 1875 and 1876, and a record of the road supervisors for the district north of the Reservation from Dayton to the British Line. The names of all these men were checked in the ranch, water rights and mining books in the hope that if any of them had filed a claim during this decade its location might give a clue. But none filed any claims until the eighties, and then they were widely scattered over most of western Montana.

However, Isidore Cohn was mentioned in a book about the Flathead Valley (*The Fabulous Flathead*) that stated he was the first postmaster at St. Ignatius in 1872, the same year in which Scribner's elections were at his store. How could he have been simultaneously postmaster at St. Ignatious and storekeeper at Scribner, unless the store were on the Reservation near the Mission? This seemed unlikely, because the Indian Commissioner had decreed that all whites must leave the Reservation in 1871 except the Jesuits at the Mission and the men working for the Indian Agency. The Hudson's Bay Post at Fort Connah was closed and presumably no other store would have been permitted to continue.

The next step consisted of getting photostats of postoffice records from the Washington, D.C. archives. They showed that the same day Isidore Cohn was appointed postmaster at St. Ignatius, Angus McLeod, a Hudson's Bay trader, was appointed postmaster at Scribner. This confirmed the guess that Scribner could not have been on the Reservation, because it was known that McLeod was trading north of the Reservation. But it left unsolved the problem of why the Scribner elections were held at the store of a man (Cohn) who was apparently postmaster of another town. Why weren't they held somewhere in Scribner, as for example at the home of its postmaster McLeod?

Further study of the archival records suggested a solution, because a new postmaster was assigned to St. Ignatius the year after Isidore Cohn was appointed. If Cohn had left town shortly after his appointment, he could have been the first postmaster at St. Ignatius in February and the storekeeper at Scribner the following August when elections were held.

The postoffice records also stated that Scribner PO was renamed Flathead Lake PO the year after it was established. This eliminated Tobacco Plains as a possible location and narrowed the search to the vicinities of Dayton and Kalispell.

Since a Scribner taxpayer had been appointed the first supervisor for the road district between the Reservation and the British Line, the petitions for new roads during that decade were next studied. It was learned that the northern district has been created in response to a request in 1873 for a county road to be built "from Flathead Lake to Dayton's Creek." Upon first reading, this petition is confusing. The creek empties into the lake: how could there be a road between the two? But if the words "Flathead Lake" referred to the community around the Flathead Lake postoffice rather than to the body of water itself, then the petition makes sense and implies that the Scribner-Flathead Lake settlement was at a distance from Dayton, perhaps near present-day Somers or even Kalispell.

A trip was soon made to the Kalispell Public Library to consult the ten-volume set of reminiscences that Sam E. Johns had collected after interviewing all the early settlers he could find. This proved that Scribner was indeed north of the lake because it included a story about the killing of a man in 1875 "at a place called Scribner below Demersville." (Demersville was several miles south of Kalispell.)

Again a problem arose. Scribner was established in 1872, yet all the accounts in John's collection agreed that the first settlement north of the Lake was called Selish. However, one oldtimer told Johns that Dooley's store "had belonged to a Jew who went back to Russia with the intention of getting a colony of Jews to come out from Russia and colonize the valley here; that the Jew met and married an heiress and never returned."

Isadore Cohn was listed on the assessment rolls as owning real estate in 1875 but not in 1876. 1875 was also the last year that the Scribner elections were held at his store, as well as the year that the Flathead Lake postoffice was discontinued.

This suggests that Scribner preceded Selish at the same place, a suggestion that is further supported by the fact that Casimir and Henry Romain were listed as Scribner taxpayers in 1875; the 1878 Scribner election was held at "Romain's" with Henry as one of the judges, and the first Selish election in 1882 was held at Dooley's store with Henry Romain again as one of the judges. Although these coincidences apparently resolve the question of Scribner's location, they did not explain the origin of the name.

Sometimes petitioners for a postoffice called it after a man associated with the neighborhood, as for example, Victor, Stevensville, Thompson Falls. But no Scribner was mentioned in any of the official lists of men north of the lake during that decade.

In fact, there appeared to be only two reports in books and public records about a man named Scribner anywhere in western Montana. Leeson's *History of Montana: 1739-1885* stated that "W.S. Scribner was post trader at Jocko Agency in the spring and summer of 1871," while mortgage records showed he became a partner in the Missoula Pioneer newspaper the following November.

If W.S. Scribner were the Wiley S. Scribner who was territorial secretary in 1869-70, he would have been knowledgeable enough about governmental procedures to have initiated the petitions for the postoffices at Jocko, St. Ignatius and Scribner that were all established the same day by Congress. Yet it would have taken considerable nerve for a man living in Missoula to insist that a postoffice a hundred miles or more away be named after him.

At this point in the search, the *MIA Quarterly* published a note asking readers for further information about Scribner. A librarian responded that collections of early newspapers from a variety of sources were being microfilmed and could soon be obtained in local libraries or through interlibrary loans. By skimming copies of Deer Lodge and Missoula papers after they became available, it was possible to confirm both Scribner's location and the fact that it was indeed named after the territorial secretary. Specifically, the papers reported that Wiley S. Scribner left the Missoula Pioneer for the north in the spring of 1872, after wintering in

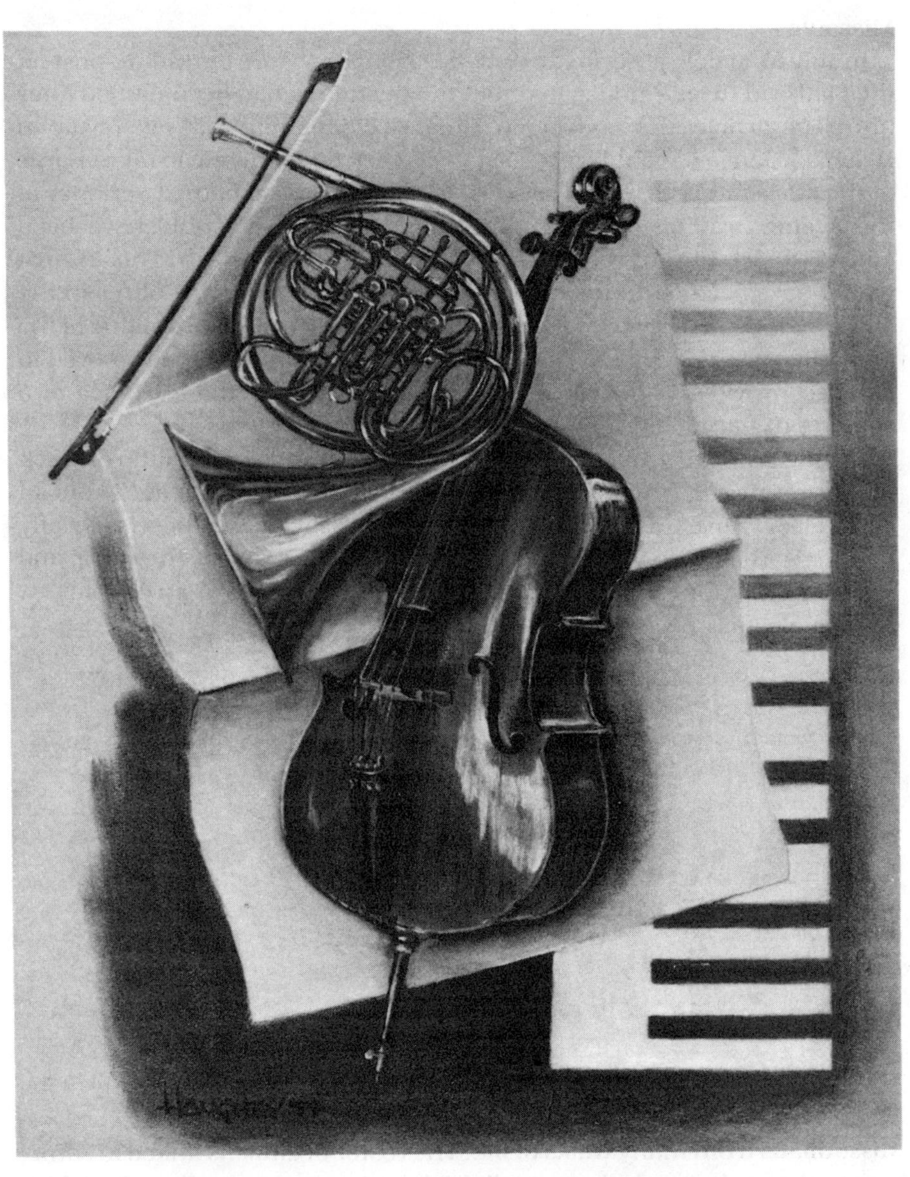

Charcoal drawing, James M. Haughey, 1958

Missoula.

In July an article described a visit to Scribner's "store or trading-post on the Flathead River," and stated that the postoffice had been named after him. The article also commented that Scribner himself was "away in Helena." Hence it would have been necessary for someone to take charge of the store in his absence. Because Isidore Cohn had helped Scribner at the Agency trading post the preceding summer, it would have been natural to ask him to run the store at the head of the lake. This in turn would have accounted for the store's being referred to as Cohn's in the election notice rather than Scribner's. Lastly, the fact that the name of the postoffice was changed to Flathead Lake in 1873 when Scribner moved to Chicago provides a plausible explanation as to why the existence of a settlement named Scribner was forgotten so quickly.

During the sixties and seventies there was a shifting population of stock herders and traders who generally referred to their location as "Flathead county" or "Head of the Lake." Apparently Scribner was there so briefly that his name was never adopted by the people living near the store, and remained alive only in the Missoula courthouse records as an official title for the election precinct.

Audra Browman, Missoula, 1973

Editor's note: Research, the basis for historical writing, is tedious work and demands perseverence, as Mrs. Browman has demonstrated.

MUSICIAN

Eugene Andrie — A Success Story

Missoula boasts one of the finest symphony orchestras of any city of its size anywhere, thanks to a truly community-wide effort that involves Missoulians from many walks of life. The roster of citizens linked in some way to the orchestra lacks a candlestick maker and an Indian chief, but doctors, lawyers, merchants, clergymen and others serve on the board of directors of the Missoula Civic Symphony Association, which administers the Orchestra and Chorale. The energetic women's committee performs yeoman service for both the orchestra and the chorale and contributes much to the cultural life of Missoula generally. Hundreds of Missoulians

96

hold membership in the association as benefactors, patrons and sustaining members.

The orchestra is, of course, dependent in important ways upon the behind-the-scenes work of the association, but it takes the artistry of the conductor to raise performance from the competent to the inspired. Art can be supported and abetted by committees but it cannot be created by them. Under Eugene Andrie's direction the orchestra attracts ever more enthusiastic audiences each season by offering a happy balance between traditional and contemporary music and by presenting outstanding guest artists, including, fittingly, a fair share of Montana artists. Obviously, the Missoula Symphony Orchestra, now in its fourteenth season (1968), owes its success to a great many persons, not least of whom are some eighty performers who make the music.

Eugene Andrie, music director of the association and conductor of the orchestra since its inception, would be the first to acknowledge the orchestra's debt to all these people. They in turn will tell you that the one person above all others who is responsible for having molded the orchestra into a superb instrument is Eugene Andrie.

Missoula's symphony, along with community orchestras in Billings, Butte, Great Falls and Helena, is one of the state's most valuable cultural resources. In a particularly felicitous exercise of its function to promote the arts, the Montana Arts Council awarded grants to these five organizations this year. Some of the Missoula orchestra's grant goes toward the concertmaster Marie Runberg's salary; the rest of it has enabled the orchestra to engage a professional bass viol player, Frank Diliberto, who has been a member of the Houston and other professional orchestras.

Andrie has been a member of the University of Montana faculty since 1946. He is director of the University Symphonette and a founding member of the Montana String Quartet. The latter, a resident faculty ensemble, performs every year for thousands of grade school children as a Young Audiences, Inc. touring unit. As first violinist of the quartet and as a clinician and festival adjudicator Andrie is a dedicated worker in music education programs for youth.

Andrie made his debut as a violinist at the age of fifteen with the Grand Rapids, Michigan, Symphony Orchestra. In 1940 he won the New Artist Award for violin virtuosity and in 1954 he was selected by the American Symphony Orchestra League to participate in a conductor training program under George Szell of the Cleveland Orchestra.

Andrie's wife, Lorraine, is an accomplished musician. Their daughter Karen is a graduate of the Eastman School of Music and has studied abroad on a Fulbright Scholarship. She won international recognition as a

97

cellist when she was awarded first place in the Ecole Normale Lycense du Concert in 1966. She made her Paris debut in May 1967 under the patronage of the Ecole Normale.

Adapted from an article by
Maribeth Dwyer, Missoula, 1968

PAINTERS

MIA Artist of the Year: James E. Dew

MIA Artist of the Year is James Dew, Chairman of the Art Department at the University of Montana. Jim is a painter, printmaker, and craftsman, who received his training, A.B. and A.M. degrees, from Oberlin College. He has exhibited widely and has been accepted in many competitive shows. He is currently listed in *Who's Who in American Art* and *Who's Who in the West.* He has also been MIA vice-president, Fine Arts chairman, member of the Advisory Council and Art Editor of the *MIA Quarterly.*

When Jim first came to Montana he was fresh out of Oberlin. His paintings reflected his immediate past training: sound draughtsmanship, carefully considered pictorial organization, careful craftsmanship, and some reflection of the academic habits of some of his teachers. Building upon this disciplined type of training, he developed rapidly as both a painter and as a teacher. He has always been exploring new approaches, new concepts, new technics. He still does. All of the resulting "know how" is utilized in his teaching and shows up in his creative work.

Many members of MIA can recall examples of some of his more memorable experiments and explorations: encaustic paintings, the use of the ancient wax-painting method, spray-paintings (dimestore or otherwise) using natural forms or contrived ones, acrylic paintings, also fine works in colored paper, oil and watercolor — works ranging from the fairly representational to the completely non-objective and abstract expressionism.

He is inventive, he respects his medium, he is a good craftsman, he is a good colorist, he has a developed sense of what is appropriate. Above all, I believe, he is most concerned with quality. And although he has broad tolerance and appreciation, he is least friendly toward the slipshod and the haphazard. He is committed to high standards and their advancement.

Aden Arnold, Missoula, 1967

98

James M. Haughey

James Haughey of Billings, who is held in great admiration and awe by state watercolorists, was scheduled to conduct the Fine Arts workshop at this year's Festival, 1967, and appeared Saturday morning all ready to look over our shoulders in the well-known struggle between water and color known as watercolor.

In spite of the fact that Haughey is an attorney of some note, and a legislator accustomed to some strategy and maneuvering, events took a sudden turn that caused Haughey to find himself on the bottom step of the Student Union building, Rocky Mountain College campus, with twenty-eight people looking over *his* shoulder, onto *his* drawing board. There expertise took over and Haughey took out a thumbnail sketch and was in full command from then on.

According to Fred Mass, it went something like this: First of all, Haughey dabbed indifferently at his clean paper with some bright red and some blue. Then he grabbed a wet sponge and soaked his paper all over and then attacked it with ultramarine much darker than we all thought advisable at that point. (It dried just right.) Next he laid in his chimney in warm stone colors, and immediately mixed a dark blue-green and began surrounding his wet chimney with dark tree forms. We were all sure the colors would bleed together as he edged closer and closer on the unpredictable wet paper. (They didn't.) Suddenly, although there was no indication on the thumbnail sketch, he quicky erected some trees on the left side of his paper, twisting the trunks, gnarling the branches, and curling the twigs with deft strokes of his brush. Finally, with a knife, he began to delineate branch and twig forms from the dark blue-green area of tree forms. As every watercolorist knows, if this is done when the paper is too wet, the lines fill in and get black; if the paper is too dry, it scratches the surface off, which is unattractive. (It was just right.) James Haughey turned out another of his masterly and distinctive water colors, and the Fine Arts group was delighted with the opportunity to see how easy the whole thing was. The whole secret is being James Haughey.

Jeanne Rhodes, Deer Lodge, 1967

Isabelle Johnson

There are some good people and some good painters, and the excitement surrounding one's knowledge about them is electric when both meet. Such was my first encounter with Isabelle Johnson and her work in early 1965. Miss Johnson has a rich Montana heritage which has been enhanced over the years by encounters with painters and institutions throughout the United States. Born in Absorkee, Montana, attending public schools in Billings, she took her BA degree from the University of Montana. Later study included an AM degree from Columbia University, the Los Angeles Museum School, the University of Southern California, the Colorado Springs Fine Arts Center, the Art Students League, and a year's travel in Europe. Her selection by Henry Varnum Poor in 1946 as one of the twenty-five students for the experimental school in Skowhegen, Maine, left her with a lifetime essence-impression of that encounter. Poor's enquiring and inventive experimentations affected and continue to affect the painting attitudes of Isabelle Johnson's work. She later taught in the Billings Public Schools and then at Eastern Montana College, from 1949 to 1961.

Isabelle returned in 1961 to the Johnson "home ranch." To say that she was a well-schooled painter who ranched might have only a slight edge over a well-informed rancher who painted. Therein lies the real essence of Isabelle Johnson's work. Her drawings and paintings are essences of Absorkee, the home ranch and the magnificant Stillwater County of southern Montana. Her pictures are totalities of fragments of that great country: smells of cattle, grassland, sheep and river, sounds of the North Wind and the Chinook, documents expressive and factual of living, growing things, knowing all is tempered by the coming of the winter of the land but never the winter of the spirit.

Essences are the heart, the spirit of the life process, and rarely does one have the good fortune to encounter and to learn from these essences so explicitly. To experience this transcends all talk of art, of pictures, of quality — all those things geared to the superficial aspects of man.

This retrospective exhibit is a tribute to the painterly and graphic poetry and the encounter with the woman, the rancher, the artist . . . Isabelle Johnson.

From an article by
Terry Melton, Salem, Oregon, 1971

100

Val Knight

Val Knight is a well-known artist throughout Montana, her popularity beginning to reach outside our state borders. Her work ranges from human interest ideas, expressionistic moods to fine portraits. Her paintings have won prizes. The day I visited Val she was working on pottery in her studio, but I had called to talk about her painting. "How do you select subjects?" I asked. "Well, honestly, they just come to me as I paint. I do make sketches but seldom follow them. Take this picture, for instance." She told me about the boats, water and sky as she had seen them in California, yet, when she did the painting at home she put part of her own mood into it. I was interested in her painting of "Reeder's Alley." It was the superb use of color that brought life into the picture. Finally, I asked when she started to paint. With a steady look in her eyes she said, "When I was a little girl I used to sit on street corners and draw while other children played. To draw and later painting just came natural to me." She told me that she studied advanced drawing in high school, but then marriage and raising a family changed "the way of things" and there was a long time when she did nothing toward her art. "MIA deserves a lot of credit for my starting again," she smiled and said, "The association with other artists kindled my interest and gave me a push."

Val Knight has studied at the College of Great Falls and now gives lessons in painting and pottery to small classes. She has held one-man shows in Great Falls . . . and has exhibited at the MIA Festivals. Her sales have been many, but she doesn't paint primarily for markets. Her work is done both in oil and watercolor. She started out by doing only portrait painting. Her portraits bring out the inner characteristics of a person rather than the outward expression.

My next question was, "Do you ever paint by order?" Val's reply was, "No. I think and change as I paint and sometimes paint only from my imagination. If anyone wants or needs what I have painted I am pleased."

Verna Mae Banta, Great Falls, 1963

Elizabeth Lochrie

Artist Elizabeth Lochrie, a founding member of the Montana Institute of the Arts, was named Montana Mother by the Montana Press Women. Mrs. Lochrie has three children and six grandchildren.

A graduate of Pratt Institute of New York, Elizabeth has had solo exhibits in many of the national galleries in the nation, including the Arthur Newton Gallery in New York, the Walter Goldston in Houston, the Francis Lynch in the Statler Hotel in Los Angeles, the Trigg-Russell in Great Falls, the Montana State in Helena and many others from Seattle to Maine. She has painted twenty-two murals in Montana and other states.

A blood brother of the Blackfeet Indians, into whose tribe she was inducted in 1931, Elizabeth has mothered the Indians. Each year she gives about thirty lectures, using her powers of pursuasion to interest whites in helping the Indian and in being more charitable in judging them, asking that time be given for the Indian to adjust to the complex society of the white man. For her lectures she requests her audience to bring excess clothing and household goods that she may give them to the Indians.

Elizabeth has spent the past thirty-five years on the various reservations of Montana, filling countless notebooks with facts and histories of the Indian and painting their likenesses. The Fish and Game Commission and the Forestry Service give to her confiscated hides, which she has tanned at her own expense for the Indians that they lose not their age-old arts of working in buckskin and beading. She knits garments for them and this past year made nineteen quilts for their use. She helps finance young Indians who desire additional schooling. She has been judge for six years at her own expense at the All-American Indian Day Celebration at Sheridan, Wyoming. She helps Indians to protect their lands, gets better living conditions for them, talks up Indian educational grants in their behalf and tries to find some of them jobs that they can do. Annually she ships tons of clothing to the Montana reservations.

This energetic woman plays an active part in the MIA. She taught art in her home for ten years until the demands for her art work became too great. Montanans express pleasure that she represented the state in New York at the Annual Mothers Convention, held in May of this year at the Waldorf-Astoria Hotel.

Helen Clark, Butte, 1960

Fred Mass, Artist, Sculptor and Forest Ranger

MIA Mass is big in stature, action, personality and ideas. Festival manager and Butte Branch Director of 1956 and 1957, Fred is a soft spoken, affable sort of chap, but don't let that easy-going exterior decoy you. Intolerant of excuse buts in MIA as of flipped butts in his beloved forests, he is the Montana Institute of the Arts number one booster who rides rough-shod over apathy and indifference, with energetic enthusiasm that is contagious.

Fred is a fervent patron of the arts when he is through chasing smoke, scaring appetites from spruce beetles, hunting forest maurauding mustangs, and counting elk herds by airplane.

Here is the forest ranger whose inward eye retains all the inaccessible beauty he encounters deep in the scenic splendor of the Treasure State. Fred gets to walk the trails of wild animals, the Indian, fur trader and pathfinder and he captures the wonder of the primeval, unspoiled loveliness on canvas for those whose feet are riveted to the asphalt jungles.

Fred is particularly interested in color perspectives and all his works have a depth of emotional content that thrills the observer. He is a poet in paint with striking imaginative realism and plenty of humor, too. A forester will tell you the pack horse is the orneriest cabello of them all, for he can shed his saddle bags and harness quicker than a bronc peels his rider. Fred has depicted all the pack horse's sly, slippery manners in his watercolor entitled "The Confounded Top Pack," which qualified for one of the MIA traveling exhibits.

There is plenty of composition, pattern, color and line in other paintings of his, including the famous Rocky Mountain peaks, and forest creatures that come to life under his capable brush and paints. He is equally creative in clay and wood sculptoring. Fred's woodcarving of his dad, a prospector panning for gold, was on exhibition at the Montana Institute of the Arts eighth annual festival in Virginia City, Montana, in addition to his watercolor "Elks and Lodgepole."

In the ninth MIA festival at Bozeman he entered two watercolors. There is realism and humor in "Whoa," which depicts a hunter trying to load a bear on a jumpy mule. The other, entitled "Fair Game," shows deer jumping between the hunters, startling them.

His love of the great outdoors comes from heredity as well as environment. He spent his boyhood at Paradise, Montana, where he finished grade school and high school, working on the family ranch in summer and running a trap line for coyotes after school in winter. The latter is comparable to the city boy's paper route job. Even from boyhood, his activities carried him far into the forest and he started drawing animals and scenes about the same time he learned to write.

As a forest ranger his work leads him into primitive mountain fastnesses that quicken his painting talents. As he states, "These trips are an invigorating change of pace to Forest Management work." In 1927 he started summer employment with the U.S. Forest Service, building trails and chasing smoke on the Big Thompson River. He went into the woods in

June and out in September, continuing seasonal employment with the Forest Service each full summer from 1927 through 1933.

In 1926 to 1930 he attended the University of Montana and received his B.S. Degree in Forestry Engineering. After college, he attended Minneapolis Institute of Fine Arts for three years, studying under Kopeitz Calhoun, George Yphantis, Gustav Krollman, and others, represented the George Yphantis life-drawing painting classes in scholarship events, and acted as parttime assistant instructor. Fred has exhibited in the Minneapolis Institute of Fine Arts, had one-man shows at Montana State University and in Idaho, and has participated in many other exhibitions, including traveling, city and state exhibits in the Montana Institute of the Arts, and served as Butte's Fine Arts Chairman in 1955.

Fred's hobbies include hunting and illustrations, particularly wildlife pictures. His interests, education, outdoor activities and driving personality make him at home in any gathering. He is widely known for the number of unusual displays of forest woods and other products he has designed in the interest of Forest Public Relations.

An exhibit of Montana forest products for the Forest Service which he prepared attracted considerable interest not only in Montana cities but traveled to the Pacific coast and as far south as New Orleans. He speaks frequently on conservation programs. His speeches are never dull, for he illustrates his talks with blackboard crayons and chalk sketches of animals, birds, and trees.

Adapted from an article by
Mary McCourt Anderson, Butte, 1957

The Master in Masterson

Jim Masterson, portrait painter and sculptor, when asked how he achieves the elusive freshness, brilliance, contemporary look in his paintings, says, "Forget about the house, barn, trees, all you want is *color*. You must have *color*." He continued, "I often use a stretch of canvas for a palette finding that it builds into patterns and these can be worked into different kinds of painting. Paints applied on paint are more brilliant when applied on canvas, because the canvas absorbs certain of the colors. I like working with a palette knife instead of a brush, which has a tendency to drag colors together, producing what is not intended, while the knife gives the direct and more brilliant result." He squinted his eyes at another brilliant painting. "Of course one cannot bring out infinite detail that way, but who wants detail taking the place of wonderful color?"

"My first attempt at drawing which I remember," chuckled Masterson, "was a cartoon. A high school principal was my typical subject . . . . I had always wanted to paint." He was sitting in his two-story studio, located a few rods back of his pleasant Miles City home. He was surrounded by his brilliant, eye-catching paintings, sketches and sculpture.

The trail by which Masterson has reached his enviable position is long, rough and varied. He also worked as a clerk in the CMSt.P railroad company. "Finally," he says, "I saved $55 and off to Chicago to study art." Tuition to the Academy of Fine Arts absorbed most of his savings, so he resorted to a number of jobs to supply the necessary cash . . . . After three years of study at the Academy and one year at the Art Institute Masterson and two buddies started their commercial art studio as the road to oil painting . . . . In cartoon work Masterson won several awards.

At the Academy, Jim Masterson had become interested in Montana while listening to a glowing verbal description by a fellow student, E.W. (Bill) Gollings. Jim was also attracted to an ad which pictured "a farmer in Montana ploughing the land, the plough turning up not only rich alluvial soil but dollars, dollars, dollars, just crowding each other to get out. So, Montana it was." He smiled ruefully. He had decided that farming might be the answer to financing his longed-for career in painting . . . ." After years in which the visionary dollars turned into grasshoppers, dry years, and hard winters I moved to Miles City, where I secured work with the State Land Department and traveled extensively throughout Montana." During this time he gathered material for his book *It Happened in Montana*, subtitled, *Anything Can Happen, Most Everything Has*. Later he landed a job with the Internal Revenue Service, helping to take it away from those who had it.

After several years spent in ranching he was spending more and more of his time painting. During the last fifteen years he has devoted all of his time to art. He has visited and painted in Mexico and Canada as well as Hawaii. He has also studied under Leonard Richmond of the Royal Academy, England, and Marcus Reitzel of Santa Cruz, California. He recalled that the highlight of his art life occurred when he was informed that he had won a Huntington Hartford Fellowship Award in California in 1962.

Jim Mastersn's favorite artist is the Russian, Nicolay Feechin, who "just slapped it on with a palette knife and the paint looks as though it was put on with a trowel." As his eyes rested upon his "Fighting Stallions" sculpture he continued, "Lately I have been doing some sculpture. I start with metal, wire, netting or anything that will assume the rough form I want to sculpt; then I take the clay and do the real modeling; after that hardens I cover it with metal. There is a new metal called Sculpt-metal, and it comes in the consistency of putty. You can apply that onto your clay and in the matter of a few hours it becomes real hard. As a result you have bronzed sculpture. I have made one of Robert Frost.". . . .

Masterson's paintings may be seen at the Academy of Fine Arts, Chicago; at the First Security Bank, Carnegie Library, High School, Holy Rosary Hospital, Milligan Hotel, Industrial School, all in Miles City; in the Schellinger Studio, Livingston; at the Brown Barn, Billings; and in many homes throughout Montana, the United States, Canada and Mexico.

From an article by
Myrtle Mockel, Billings, 1967

J.K. Ralston, Artist of Western History

Kenneth (J.K.) Ralston of Billings says, "My interest in history and the West goes as far back as I can remember. I was raised on it and I find a great satisfaction and enjoyment in trying to keep some of these early events alive on canvas." Ken's keen interest in history and his great talent for transferring significant happenings to canvas have made him famous for painting authentic Western Americans.

Ralston's commissions to do historical paintings usually come from organizations or individuals familiar with his work. After an agreement to do a painting has been made, Ken checks source material to make sure history will be depicted accurately in the finished picture. Ken and Mrs. Ralston have a good library which includes books by Larpenteur, Chittenden, Denig, Kunz, Washington Irving, Stuart and Russell, as well as other authors of Western history. He has access to the publications and books in public and private collections.

Ken's research sometimes includes a trip to the scene where the historical event took place so that he can paint the terrain with correct detail. As an example, in his current work on "Into the Unknown," he and Mrs. Ralston have made two trips to the spot where the Lewis and Clark party met the Shoshone Indians on the Beaverhead River near Armstead, Montana. The place was named Camp Fortunate on August 17, 1805, by Lewis and Clark.

"Into the Unknown," commissioned by the United States Park Service, will preserve on canvas the historical event that occurred there long after the water of a dam will cover it. This mural will hang in the Jefferson

106

National Expansion Memorial in St. Louis, Missouri.

Ken's procedure with "Into the Unknown" is similar to that used for all his murals. He first makes a scale-model oil sketch on canvas. "I do my sketches in oil because I enjoy working in oil more than with pencil or charcoal," he says. When the sketch is complete Ken sends it to the buyer for approval. If there are no changes at this stage he proceeds with the larger picture. He makes a graph on the model by stringing thread on tacks. This leaves his model unmarred. He projects a blow-up image of the sketch on the mural canvas and sketches an outline from that.

Ralston prefers to work in his convenient home studio when doing a painting or a mural, for it has an atmosphere conducive to producing Western art. He is surrounded with items such as flintlock and cap-and-ball guns, as well as Indian regalia to be used as models for his work. The flintlock rifles used by Lewis and Clark will show in "Into the Unknown."

Ken's murals are painted on canvas to be mounted permanently at the exhibit space. "The difference between a mural and a painting is that a mural is permanently attached to a wall while a painting is mounted on a stretcher and framed," Ken explained. Mounted murals done on canvas can be moved if the job is properly done.

Exciting things are happening to some of Ken's paintings. The "Fetterman Fight," owned by Don Foote, is being reproduced and sold by the Sheridan, Wyoming, Chamber of Commerce. The painting is reproduced with a colored photograph in a 29" x 36" size which is framed in a gold leaf frame imported from Belgium. There is also a postcard size reproduction. The profit from the sale of these pictures will go to help support a memorial park which will probably include the site of the Fetterman Fight, the Wagon-box Fight and Fort Phil Kearny.

"After the Battle," also owned by Don Foote, is now on display at the Custer Battlefield Memorial near Hardin, Montana. It will go on the Montana Centennial Train to the 1964 World Fair in New York City. The painting depicts 39 separate authenticated incidents of the aftermath of the Custer Battle.

The United States Park Service has contracted with Ralston for the official painting for the Custer Battlefield Memorial. The painting, "Last of the Defense," will depict the final grouping of the stragglers on the hill where the Custer Battle took place.

"Prelude to Tragedy," another painting dealing with the Custer subject, has been reproduced by the Montana Historical Society in Helena. The original belongs to Denzil Wilson, in Surrey, England.

Ken recently did a painting with the Big Horn Mountains in the background for Robert Taylor, the movie star. Another work, still in Ken's studio, was done for Harold Ruth of Billings. It shows a jerkline freight outfit in an Alkali Creek setting which is opposite the Ruth residence. In 1957 the sketch for the mural on the wall of the Logan Field Airport went to William Lambrecht in a drawing at the time the mural was unveiled. Later, Harold Ruth bought the sketch and still has it.

Ken Ralston has no idea how many paintings he has done. He attended the Art Institute in Chicago in 1917 and, after World War I service, again in 1920. He has lost track of some of his first pictures, but in the last ten years his policy has been to have a photograph taken of each new painting before it is sent from his studio. Then Mrs. Ralston puts the picture of the painting in a scrapbook of his work.

Ken says he will never part with one painting in his studio: "Cowboy in the Rain." It shows a cowboy on his horse, dressed in a yellow slicker, with a bunch of longhorn steers. Ken himself is the cowboy.

From an article by
Nancy Olson, Billings, 1963

Note: A more detailed, intimate account is in Vol. 21, No. 3, 1969.

Cowboy Artist "Moquea Stumick": Irving Shope

Untiring MIA worker artist Irwin (Shorty) Shope of Helena brings enthusiasm to the classes he instructs in art under MIA sponsorship. Shorty's field is Western Americana, and his canvasses glorify the range, the cowboy, the cowhorse and the original American, the Indian, and his counterpart the buffalo and wild game on the plains.

A friend to the Indian, Shorty was made a blood brother of the Blackfeet in 1937 when he was christened *Moquea Stumick* (Wolf Bull, or translated into white terminology, Man the Size of Wolf with Heart Big Like Buffalo).

Shorty was born in the Boulder Valley and grew up performing ranch chores. He spent years in the saddle punching cattle around Miles City and the Pahsimeroi Valley in Idaho. The knowledge he brings to his canvasses is first-hand, won from experience on the range.

Shope has illustrated numerous western books, such as Davis' *The Bells Woke Me*, Ely's *The Lost Dutchman Mine*, Bernado's *The Men and the Mountains*, Ferris' *Life in the Rocky Mountains*, Howard's *Strange Empire* and *Montana: High, Wide and Handsome*. He also painted several covers for books, such as Fisher's *Passions Spin the Plot*.

Included along with his painting Shope has constructed dioramas, making three for the Veterans and Pioneers Memorial Building at Helena. Murals by him dress the walls of the Montana State Highway Department, Helena, and the University of Montana School of Forestry at Missoula. His oil paintings have been exhibited and sold in galleries in New York City, Chicago and St. Louis.

A graduate of the University of Montana, Shorty has studied also at the Portland School of Art (Oregon), at Minneapolis, at New York Grand Central School of Art under Harvey Dunn, outstanding outdoor illustrator. He and his work have been featured in several magazines; an article about him accompanied by illustrations of his paintings appeared in *The Western Horseman.* Shorty has also served as commercial illustrator for the Montana Power Company and the Montana State Highway Department.

Each member of the Shope family, wife Eva and the four children, owns a horse, and Shorty has painted a picture of each astride his or her favorite animal. Their backyard houses not only a stable but in summer an Indian tepee. All persons who visit he instructs in the ways of the West, lauding the best traits of cowboy and Indian.

Shope's generosity in all matters — in training others in use of the brush and oil or in schooling the tenderfoot in outdoor lore — is sung by those whose trails cross his. The Indians named him well when they said of him, Heart big like buffalo.

Helen Clark, Butte, 1958

Jessie Wilber

A retrospective exhibit honoring Jessie Wilber's thirty-one years as a teacher in the School of Art of Montana State University filled the first floor galleries of the Ketterer Art Center in Bozeman from April 30 to May 24.

The pieces ranged from a tiny lithograph of mountain sheep, "Bighorns," dated 1940, to a large and technically complex silk screen, "Girls from Guthrie," completed just before the show opened. Included were oil and gouache paintings, woodblock, lithograph and silk screen prints. The Exhibition opened in a snowstorm, but the rich and subtle color characterizing her work brought spring to the gallery. The subject matter — landscape, horses, cats, children, musicians, flowers, birds — is treated with obvious affection but without sentimentality. The carefully preserved awkwardness of the first quick sketch keeps the tension of life and feeling of spontaniety through the many steps of an elaborate color print.

A series of fifteen silk screens based upon sketches made during a trip to Africa filled one gallery; in a hallway a four-foot long woodblock,"The River: Don't Dam It," commemorated a trip down the Missouri after the MIA Festival at Havre; "Slide," an oil painting dated 1960, followed a trip to Yellowstone Park after the 1959 earthquake, but most of the inspiration is closer to home. "Spring Creek Valley," a silk screen, is the view from her living-room window. "Owl," "Cats in the Garden," "Puppies," "Huns," also celebrate the immediate scene.

Frances Senska, Bozeman, 1972

PHOTOGRAPHER

Rudi Dietrich: A Close-up

Rudi Dietrich of Bozeman is MIA's new photography chairman. He brings to MIA a rich and varied background in the U.S. and Europe. From his birthplace in Bludenz, Austria, where he graduated from the Gymnasium he went to Salzburg to attend the University. After receiving his master's degree in photography he operated a studio and also served as chairman of the masters' examining committee for photographers. He recalls with a rueful smile that this committee gave a week's testing of techniques in every phase of art, which provided a traumatic experience for the aspiring cameraman. "Master photographers in Europe," he says, "must be proficient in other skills, such as business law and bookkeeping."

It was in Salzburg that the young Austrian met the slim American girl who became his wife. Carol was attending the music academy. Their mutual interest in music now extends to a family quintet.

On a student flight to the U.S. Rudi and Carol visited in New York and California — "But we don't like the life style in either place," explains Rudi. They came to Bozeman to visit Carol's family. The Dietrichs are now happily settled in a big frame house in Bozeman. "We value the quality of life here and cherish the friendships we have made."

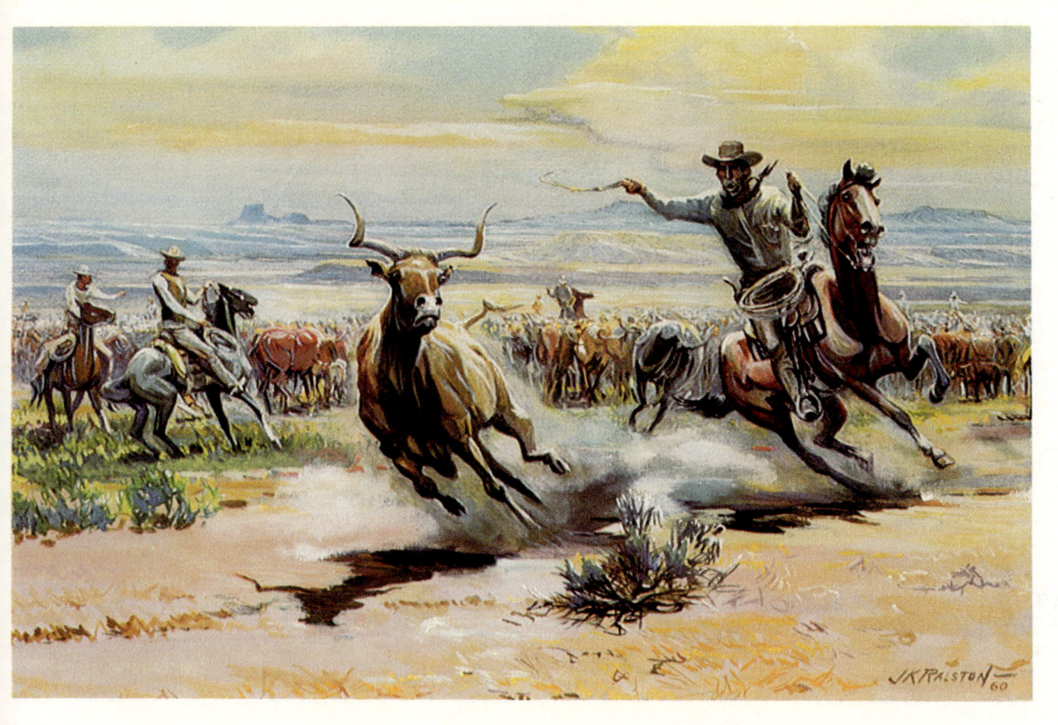

Cutting Out the Big One, J.K. Ralston

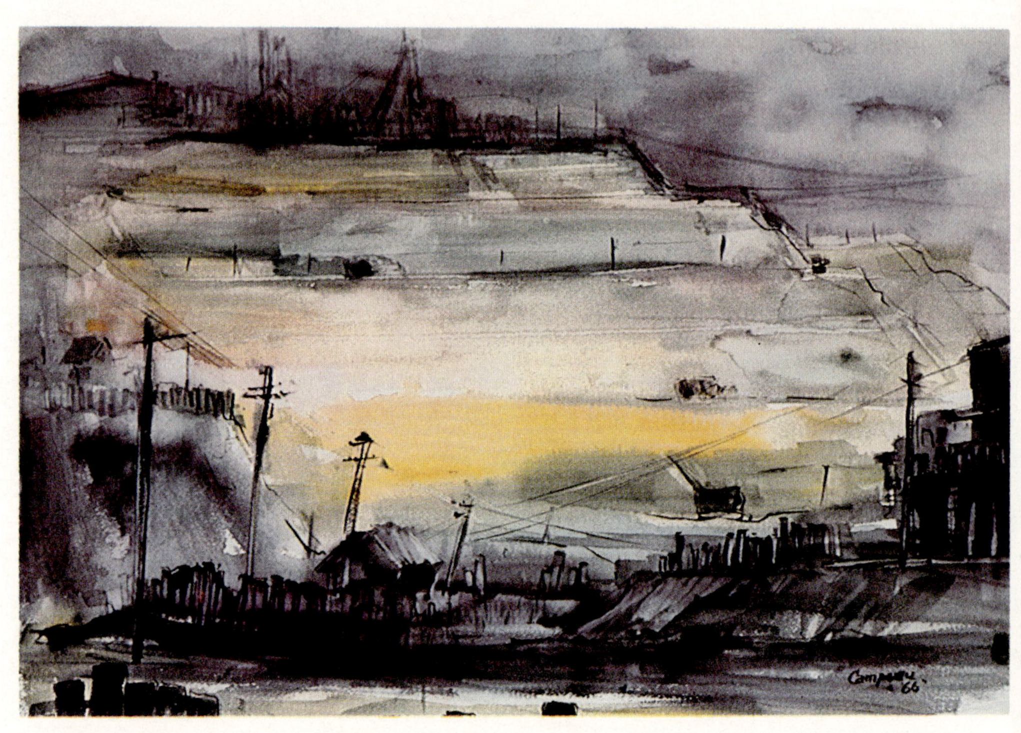

The Pit, Raymond Campeau

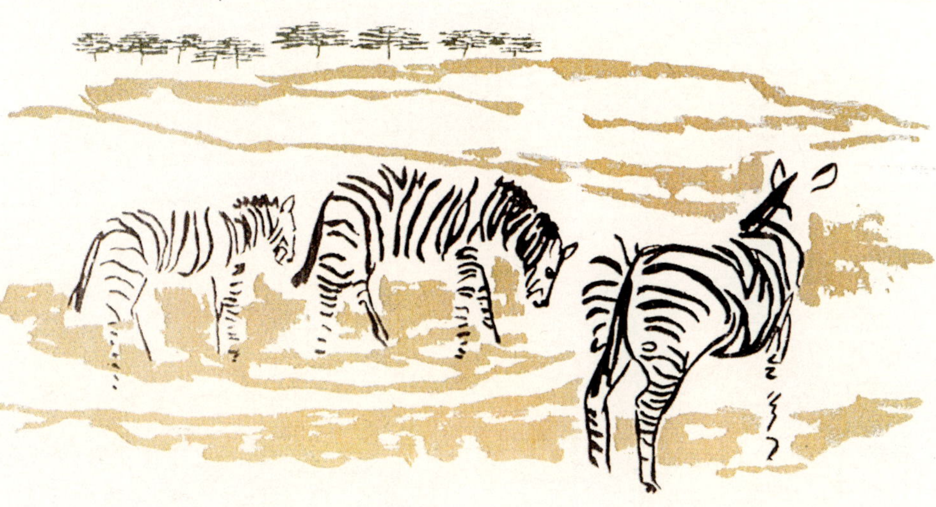

Zebras, Jessie Wilber

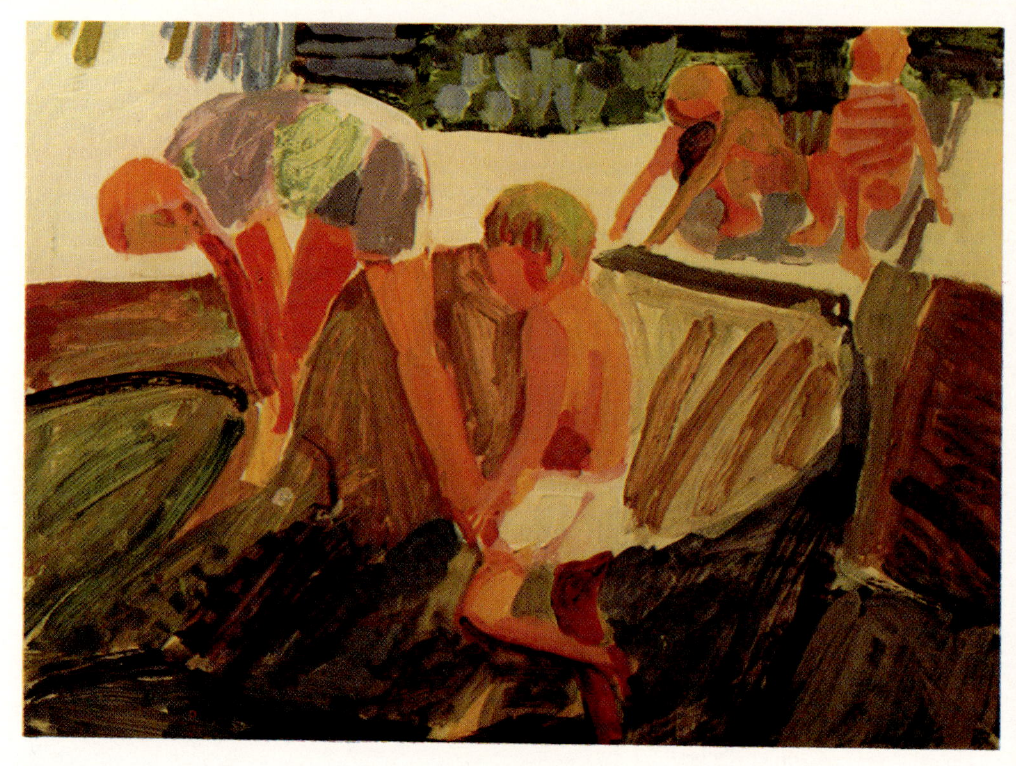

August, Lela Autio

The energetic Austrian earned his bachelor's degree in film and his master's in philosophy while instructing photography classes at the State University. He has been a member of the faculty in the film and television department since 1969. He is working on his citizenship papers and will be taking tests instead of giving them.

Fresh from Shelby's MIA Festival, 1974, and full of plans for the coming year Rudi Dietrich hopes to concentrate on get-togethers and workshops to maintain enthusiasm generated at the Festival.

Peggy Todd, Ennis, 1974

SCULPTORS

Lyndon Pomeroy, A Profile

"'Es a stranger, 'eave arf a brick at 'im." These often quoted words said to have been made by new settlers in the Old West, indicated their attitude toward those who came after they did, embody the philosophy of Lyndon Pomeroy. Were it not for his cordiality, his conviviality, his great humor, such a philosophy would make him something less than the generous, outgoing person that he is.

Born at Sidney, he lived alternately at Turner, Ferdig, and Kevin before moving to Havre, where he grew to manhood. During his years as pilot in Uncle Sam's Air Corps his many flights to faraway regions made him realize that he was of Montana and the Great Plains region. Montana was where he would develop his future, where he would hope to live his entire life.

During the years he was a student in the Art department at Montana State College he spent his summers as a "grasshopper" pilot flying through eastern and northern Montana. His career as a pilot terminated the summer he received his degree at Montana State College, when the plane he was to fly while "grasshoppering" was damaged in landing at the Havre airport. Lyndon already had been offered a position in the Art department at Northern Montana College. He then started his career as a teacher.

The five years he taught at Northern Montana College were busy years. Besides developing his teaching areas, he spent a summer of study at Syracuse University, a summer at the Archie Bray Foundation, and earned a Master's degree in Art at Montana State College. While at Havre he created the Max P. Kuhn Memorial Sculptured unit as a means of solving

111

the problem of water for use on the campus at Northern Montana College. This involved a fountain, a pool for irrigation of the campus and an area for meditation. As a contribution both practical and esthetic it became a memorial to Lyndon Pomeroy as well as to the civic leader who was being commemorated. After the five years he resigned his position and moved to Missoula where he intended establishing his own pottery.

At Missoula he missed the open country and the big blue sky. Despite the beauty and the majesty of the mountains he found them too confining and welcomed an invitation to become a member of the faculty at Eastern Montana College of Education at Billings, there to develop an area of ceramics and sculpture within the Department of Art. Lyndon worked intensively for two years — setting up a kiln, building equipment, experimenting with local clays. When everything was ready to go he became aware that in an academic department within a college of education he had neither the breadth nor freedom necessary for the development of his concept or philosophy of real art. He resigned his position. At Eastern as at Northern he left a memorial to his name, for in the time he had designed and executed an imposing entrance to the campus. This entrance consisted of an incoming-outgoing roadway, a landscaped island with a large metal sculptured sign.

Lyndon Pomeroy liked the Billings area and the people of Billings and elected to keep his residence there. He had no kiln of the type necessary for firing his ceramic experiments. He did have a welding unit and a cutting torch. With characteristic courage and resourcefulness he started using these as never before. The Fates must have thought wisely of his decision to become a solo craftsman, for today Pomeroy fountains, metal doorways and screens, sculptured animals and religious pieces grace many homes, public squares, churches and office buildings in Washington, D.C., Minneapolis, Detroit and cities throughout the west. One need not mention the many works completed within Billings and throughout Montana.

His workshop is no longer his garage or backyard but a rural studio where he has ample space, not alone for developing the ideas from which he creates, but room in which to expound his philosophy and exchange ideas with those individuals who come to see him. Lyndon's coffeepot is always on, his brew is strong, his mugs generous. And Lyndon has many callers, for he likes people as much as people like him. His folksiness contradicts the remark "'es a stranger, 'eave 'arf a brick at 'im.''

And yet it was Lyndon, often given to brash statement, who said, as he read the quoted remark, "Why only half a brick? Why not heave the whole brick at him?" Such thought and feelings emanate from his love of the

Great Plains area. His is not a sentimental attachment but a studied and deep-rooted affection. Appreciative of the nurture and education he received in Montana, he has studied her topography, her flora and fauna, her history and ecology. His conclusion, felt increasingly, is that an inflow of population into Montana will not only despoil Montana but will destroy the individuals who migrate here. Land, oil and mining booms illustrate his premise. His ideas and ideals have become one with the feeling of sparseness which is his Montana. As a result, his purpose in life through his art is to arrive at an art form that will embody the spirit and the strength of this broad and difficult land.

At a time when many young people see no future in Montana and are seeking opportunity elsewhere, Lyndon Pomeroy is both a fortunate and a happy man — fortunate in his consciousness of that toward which he strives, happy in that his aspirations are as one with his native habitat. Montana and The Montana Institute of the Arts are fortunate in being able to count as citizen and member an individual whom nature seems to have endowed with the ideals and objectives which they represent.

Isabelle Johnson, Absarokee, 1963

Robert Scriver: He Knows His Subject

Some artists portray cowboys because they like the romance of the subject and some artists do it because they like the healthy sales appeal. Bob Scriver sculptures cowboys because that's one of the subjects he knows best. Since his birth at Browning, Montana, he has known horses and cows as well as he has known people. Ole Rock, who pulled the delivery wagon for the Browning Mercantile, Bob's father's store, and Jack, Mr. Stone's massive Percheron stud on the horse ranch where Bob spent his summers, were early friends and he's never had a better one than Banjo, his first horse. Jim Stone picked Banjo, a five-year-old blood bay stallion, especially for Bob, from a wild horse band that ranged near what later became Glacier National Park. Bob broke his own horse and from then on the two were inseparable.

When Bob Scriver was a boy, the cowboys weren't like Roy Rogers or even Matt Dillon. They were short, bandy-legged and sometimes smelly; but they stuck to horses like burrs and could tell what a cow was thinking as far as they could see it. They wore hair chaps, leather cuffs, and vests, and they did more fence-mending than gun-slinging.

In Bob's quiet moments he painted, drew, and made models of

stagecoaches out of wood and little statuettes of horses and riders out of river bank clay. They were fun and satisfying, but he never considered that they could become a career. Instead, he learned to play the cornet and taught high school band in Browning and Malta.

But somehow, music, rewarding as it was, didn't fill the spot he thought a lifework ought to and slowly he began to feel his way back to art through taxidermy. It was an ideal transition. He was learning anatomy from the inside out; he was exploring business methods; he was accumulating enough capital to finance the casting of bronzes; he was learning the complicated crafts of mold making and plaster work. In 1950 when Bob began making curio figurines there were few of the miracle materials that simplify an artist's work now. Also, the taxidermy shop and the adjoining Museum of Montana Wildlife that Bob built were an ideal introduction to the many fine artists who visited the area in search of material and who were generous with their knowledge.

At first Scriver figurines were North American big game and he insisted that animals were all he would ever do. Inevitably images of horses and riders formed in his mind and he couldn't resist giving them shape in clay. Soon Scriver felt he needed to know more about horse anatomy and movement and he began looking for a horse to ride and to use as a model.

He found Playboy, a neat little sorrel with mostly outer horse breeding and a complicated relationship to Descent, the famous cowboy bucking horse. Bob wanted him because he was so beautiful and because he had a smooth, almost gliding walk. As time went on, Scriver needed a different kind of horse — more of a character. Then he found Gunsmoke, a white gold-flecked half-Arabian. Bit headed, bony and broke for bulldogging, Gunnysack, as he soon became known, was remarkably versatile.

Since being chosen to do a heroic portrait of Bill Linderman, the world champion cowboy, Scriver has met a whole new kind of cowboy, only to realize that they are fast disappearing. The traditional rough-and-tough lone-wolf professional rodeo cowboy is a special breed being replaced by air-borne athletes who step onto their first horse while attending college. Even the rodeo stock has changed since Bob was a boy.

This summer Bob kept a Mexican bull-dogging steer and a Brangus calf in his driveway to use as models. They were excellent watchdogs but the calf developed a habit of butting the side of the house about 4 A.M. when she ran out of hay.

Both animals, along with Gunsmoke, Playboy, and other horses belonging to the artist and his friends, will appear in a new series of large dynamic rodeo sculptures, one for each event plus some smaller studies. These are currently being cast in Bob's own foundry and will be seen for the first time next summer at the newly built million dollar Whitney Gallery of Western Art in Cody, Wyoming.

Bob Scriver is just a sincere guy who has special feelings about animals and some kinds of people and who puts his feelings into a permanent form that other people can appreciate. His bronzes are direct expressions of first-hand experience, disciplined by realism and a sensitive and sophisticated knowledge of compostition, design and artistic technique.

Adapted from an article by
Mary Schriver, Browning, 1969

Jack Weaver: The Sculptor As Workman

Wherever the machine has not been able to come between man and the material of which he makes the world, there is the workshop and studio where the master's vision can take form under his hand. Here there is a sameness in all ages, and when one turns up the alley off the busy Butte street, through the unpainted door, up the worn stairs, he might as well be in the time of Vasari, as the present. There are special tools, the dark bottles, the stained palette on the wall, debris of material everywhere, a stove and a scuttle of coal in a corner. A reclining nude in wood lies under some heavy cloth; a fantastic allegorical painting hangs on the wall made partly of old signs. In the center are the work tables with figures now in progress.

But this is not a Hollywood ideal of Bohemia, and Jack Weaver, the husky, good-looking young man who works there is not an ivory tower dreamer. Now in his early thirties, he is a hard-working craftsman and artist with an enviable record of accomplishment.

The Weavers are an old Butte family and like the artistic families of the Renaissance, they are a family where art is a way of life passed on from father to son.

Jack Weaver learned his basic art at home. He started modeling early, and the few pieces he has from his school days show the energy and vitality that he has refined and brought under control in his more mature work.

At the Art Institute in Chicago, where his father had studied also, Jack won an Albert B. Kuppenheimer Scholarship in 1941, class awards in sculpture, figure drawing, anatomy, and architecture. He was graduated from the Institute in 1946.

In 1944, civic groups in Butte made plans for a plaque and statue

115

memorial to Butte's servicemen of the Second World War. Weaver was given the commission, and the work, with the exception of the supporting block under the statue, was carried out under his hand and as he had planned it. The figure of the soldier, which dominates the monument, is eight feet high, made of cast stone. It is not a naturalistic figure and is purposely ambiguous in clothing.   Massive and solid, it is suggestive of calm determination and alertness.

Like most artists, Jack is not completely satisfied with his earlier work. "There are a few things I would do differently," he said. "But when you get a chance at a commission like this, you don't just say 'Come back in five or six years'."

Another work, also begun while he was in Chicago, probably brought him more praise and critical attention than anythng else he has done. In 1946, St. Luke's Church at River Forest, Illinois, commissioned a creche designed by Frederick Doyle. Installed in the chapel of Christ the King, the prize-winning creche had in it first only the holy family with some shepherds and animals, eleven figures in all. The background was painted by the sculptor's father. Three years later, Weaver was commissioned to add three wisemen, a camel and a camel driver.

The plaster figures of this group are half life size, painted. For some, perhaps, they are a little romanticized, but their appeal is undeniable. Tender and strong at once, they capture the awe and beauty of the moment, at once sad and joyful, in a way that counters any charge of sentimentality and mere prettiness. This is a sculpture suited to a purpose, and it serves that purpose very well.

For a few years, Weaver was a teacher at the Layton Art School in Milwaukee, Wisconsin. While here, he did the remaining figures for the St. Luke's creche and two remarkable seven-foot abstractions in concrete and lucite for the College Inn in Chicago's Hotel Sherman. The abstractions were titled "Music" and "Dancing."

In 1951, he did more commercial work of this type in making sculptured reliefs for the Fox-Bay theater in Wisconsin. The reliefs, one of water with boats and seagulls, the other of trees and flying ducks, were each about thirty-two feet long. They were built, says the artist, "like suspension bridges."

About this time, he also designed and built in Wisconsin a "solar" type concrete house for himself, which without heat reached about 80 degrees on winter days.

During these years, he was also exhibiting. His works have been seen at the Seattle Northwest Artists Show, 1944; Chicago Renaissance Society at the University of Chicago, 1948; Chicago Art Institute, 1948; Denver Art

116

Museum, 1948; Springfield, Illinois, 1947, the Wisconsin Salon of Art, Madison, 1950.

He has had one-man shows: Butte Art Center, 1942; Layton Art Gallery, Milwaukee, 1948; WTMJ-TV 1948; Milwaukee Women's Club, 1950; Milwaukee Art Institute, 1951; Montana Power Company Lobby, Butte, 1954; a three-man show with the works of his father and grandfather, Historical Museum, Helena, 1954.

At these exhibitions he has displayed a surprising variety of sculptures. Versatile, he can work in many materials and styles.

One often exhibited work is his "Madonna and Child," which has appeared in Chicago twice and in Denver. This is a wood sculpture, of walnut, 45" high. His creche figures were also exhibited before being permanently placed.

Other work consists of a number of figure studies, in marble, wood, and plaster, including some vigorous sculptures of miners and workers and outstanding portrait heads. He has done a few abstractions, like his commercial work for the Hotel Sherman, but he prefers to work with the human figure. He excels in the portrayal of strong, powerful character, and has a distinct feeling for the dramatic. He reveals this in his religious sculpture as well as in his works like his "Wounded Soldier with Maternal Figure," which portrays the tragic side of war, in contrast to the heroic spirit caught in his Butte monument.

His most recent work and the work perhaps most interesting to Montanans is his diorama for the Historical Museum in Helena and two dioramas for a planned permanent display in Butte. The Helena diorama is for the downstairs gallery. For Butte he has done a group of drillers and another of Indians.

These dioramas reflect the careful skill of this sculptor, his scholarly and sound approach to his practical problems. Unlike a monument, says Weaver, the diorama does not require fitting to an environment. This leaves the sculptor free to work within it.

Weaver points out that the figures in a diorama, however brilliantly conceived or executed, would not be exhibited as art in most museums in the United States. But this does not mean that good diorama figures are not art in a very real sense.

Art, as Weaver sees it, is for people; it is a part of life. If the rules of critics, which come usually after the art work, are productive in turn of work which people do not like, then the criticism is probably wrong and not very meaningful.

This does not mean, however, that there is no disputing tastes or that one thing is as good as another. Weaver's discussion of abstract art brings this out. A man who has done a few abstractions himself, he does not particularly favor them. "There is not the warmth of human appeal in abstract sculpture that can be achieved in more realistic work. Not that I discount abstract art. But after all, good sculpture, whether abstract or realistic, must have the same qualities of sensibility, form, shape, and balance." The last qualities are the concern of the artist and the good diorama will have them as well as "pure" sculpture.

The work of the professional sculptor, Weaver explains, is to him the work of providing the person who commissions a work that he wants while at the same time giving it those qualities that only the professional artist can give it. In one sense, there is little difference between a good sculptor and a good plumber. A good plumber will make a satisfactory drainage system. A good sculptor will make a good statue for a church or a portrait head. He is an artist, but he is even more a craftsman, an artisan.

Although he professedly gives those who commission him what they want — like the small figures he is now turning out for the Rocky Mountain Studios of Butte — Jack Weaver has done some impressive work, and no one who has seen the variety and range of it would find him limited or lacking in power and vitality. A worker in a wide variety of materials — plaster, marble, wood, cast stone, ceramics, plastic — he can likewise command a range of styles and moods without losing a fundamental individuality that is after all the difference between the real artist and the faceless hack.

Robert T. Taylor, Butte, 1955

WEAVERS

Margaret Burlew

Mrs. Margaret Burlew of Charlo, Montana, will be the artist weaver at the Twenty-fifth MIA Anniversary Festival in Great Falls. The Handweavers Guild of America wrote of her, "Mrs. E.P. Burlew, president of the HGA, is currently a member of the Alpine Weavers Guild of Montana. As she has moved throughout the country during past years she has belonged to guilds in Oakland and Southern California, Chicago, Milwaukee, Philadelphia, and Richmond, Virginia. she has taught at Stockton Junior College and Virginia Commonwealth University. Her textiles have been shown at the Museum of Contemporary Crafts, N.Y., in Seattle, Washington, with Designer-Craftsman USA, 1960, Fabrics International, Craftsmen of the

118

Eastern States (Smithsonian Institution) and the USIA Traveling Exhibit of American Crafts in Europe. Margaret Burlew is also a three-time winner of the Kathryn Wellman Award given by the Piladelphia Guild of Handweavers." She has conducted several workshops in Montana cities and towns.

Ethel E. Nelson, Belt, 1973

Marion Brockmann

Weaving first entered my consciousness in 1941 when my husband and I were driving through the Kentucky mountain area and had stopped briefly at the roadside craft shop. There to my delight a young girl was weaving finger-tip towels at what appeared to be a mile-a-minute, completely relaxed and at ease with a group of tourists watching her. I had never seen a loom before or realized patterns were woven in. About three years later at the University of Wisconsin summer school I had a choice between a mathematics course and weaving and chose the latter as, after all, it was vacation time. Miss Helen Allen . . . . gave a comprehensive course with just a bit of actual weaving experience. But that was all I needed to get started on a continuing new adventure in the craft field. After summer school she left on her vacation but kindly let me weave on one of her leftover warps . . . . Bozeman welcomed a new weaver that fall and after weaving on a loom borrowed from Harriet Douglas (Tidball) I bought a table loom, which I soon outgrew and yearned for a big floor loom so that I could weave like Lois Blankenhorn at Bozeman. Lois' husband John took pity on me and offered to make me one like hers. I was thrilled with my new 36-inch, eight harness handmade oak floor loom with twelve treadles plus a spool rack for rapid warping. My living room drapes were turned out in zip-time at the rate of one a week . . . .

Moving to Havre presented a new problem, as there were no weaver friends there. I found it necessary to teach a few others so that we could all enjoy our hobby together . . . . This eventually led to a year's study at the University of Oregon, culminating in the M.F.A. degree and a renewed courage to continue in the design field . . . . Now, as I struggle to establish a small weaving studio in our home at Fullerton, California, I find myself divided between Montana and California, with six looms in Glacier Park and three here, a wealth of yarn and equipment in both places . . . . I have discovered a new way of life, namely, creative living, in which one enjoys and profits from each new experience . . . .

From an article by
Marion Brockmann, Fullerton, California, 1964

Hilda Cunningham

Hilda Cunningham, who lives in Simms, writes that she is teaching children in grade school how to weave the simpler patterns. She has offered this service for more than ten years, until her retirement, and still extends help one afternoon a week. "It seems," she writes, "that should be the greatest contribution for the future. The children have woven and though they never weave again they have an appreciation of the art that otherwise they would never have had. Boys as well as girls weave and boys, it appears, have a better concept of weaving. Should the day ever come when time hangs heavily on their hands they may turn to weaving again. Some have done outstanding work."

Hilda, during the two years when Marion Brockmann was state chairman of weaving, acted as North Central district chairman, then followed as state chairman herself. The Great Falls group asked her to represent them on TV and many weavers from all parts of the state sent their weaving to help make the program the success it was. Hilda was an assistant to Marion when she held workshops for four successive years at the Montana House in Glacier Park.

Margaret Berlien, Great Falls, 1964

The Maloneys: Weaving a Life Together

John and Marguerite Maloney of Helena are, without a doubt, one of the most, if not the most, colorful and durable of the several husband and wife artist teams in the State of Montana. Most members of the MIA who regularly attend the Annual Festival wherever it may be will remember seeing this couple there with a beautiful array of original hand woven items and some original appurtenances as well.

The Maloney home is filled with looms, all different styles and sizes with weaving in the process, surrounded by handwoven baskets that hold the yarn and tools with which they work plus books and books and books.

Mrs. Maloney came to Montana in 1889, the year of Statehood, and lived

in Missoula near the present site of the University of Montana. She and
her husband moved to Helena in 1923. It was not until 1938 that she began
to get interested in weaving. She decided if she was going to weave she
should have some lessons and so she took *two*. The first instruction was
with Eleanor Ropes and the second with Mary Atwater. From there she
launched forth on her own, encouraged by the fact that one of the
instructors said she would be a *weaver* because her edges were always
even and good. She admitted that both she and her husband are perfec-
tionists.

She gives much credit for her weaving to her husband. He always sets
up her loom. She explained that his process is termed "threading, or
warping the loom." This entails accuracy. This is Mr. Maloney's forte.
Each time she decides to work on a new design and a new item he must
figure out how many threads will be in an inch of that design and calculate
setting metal heddles that will raise and lower the thread as she weaves.

The weaver takes the shuttle in hand and proceeds to weave the thread
back and forth to achieve the "weft" or the back and forth design. And the
Maloney shuttles! They are beautiful wooden creations made by Mr.
Maloney, every one of them, and they have them all over the place. It is
doubtful if they have any idea how many they have — many different
sizes, styles, designs and woods, all beautifully carved and polished and
smooth. Mr. Maloney said he has always made things out of wood. Mrs.
Maloney added that she has shuttles made of many kinds of wood,
including one of sandalwood.

Mrs. Maloney recalls one time when she missed getting a blue ribbon
on some of her weaving because the judge thought it was so perfect that
people would think it was machine made. This, incidentally, was a plaid
scarf designed by Mr. Maloney and when they said it was a Maloney plaid
the judges said, "Who ever heard of an *Irish* plaid?"

This sparkling, enthusiastic couple suggested that we might "put in a
little squib" that they are in their late eighties and they are proud of their
age. Mr. Maloney had gone fishing on this wintry day in February when
this interview was conducted and when he returned home he was as fresh
and smiling as the wintry day.

The two big thick scrapbooks on their table would probably divulge a
right interesting history of weaving, as well as some of the MIA and some
important people, artisans of all kinds.

Ruth Beem, Helena, 1972

Will James

Success came to Will James long before he started writing. Among his personal effects is an oval medal on which is inscribed "Will James, World's Champion Rough Rider, Cheyenne, Frontier Days Rodeo, 1914." Before and after his First World War service he followed the rodeo from Mexico, north to Calgary and east to Madison Square Garden. His interest in the rodeo was greater than that of the itinerant performer out to acquire glory and cash. Of bucking he said, "It is a true-born art like it has to be with the painter or singer in order to be good at it." He often spoke of the twisting, sunfishing and side-stepping necessary to a good bucking broncho, and the rider was not a good rider unless he felt these various movements coming intuitively. The horse and rider must be one. His interest in the rodeo was but one phase of his interest in the horse. Long after he ceased to be a performer he followed the rodeo as illustrator and journalist.

During these early years, when not active in the rodeo James was working on the range with some cattle outfit or trapping wild horses. After he became a full-time writer and illustrator he bought 8,000 acres of "Dead Indian" land in the range country in order to establish a ranch where he might continue practise in riding and roping. He felt it necessary to keep in contact with the changes in the life about which he wrote.

When Will James was twenty-eight (in 1910) he was injured by a "bad pony." While recuperating at Lake Tahoe he started doing serious sketches and sent them to various magazines. He was beginning to be discouraged when a mining man gave him a letter of introduction to Charles Fiske, editor of *Sunset*. After two months of struggle for the magazine he was paid $25 for his first illustration. Momentarily there was a demand for his work from other magazines. When this demand ceased as quickly as it had started, James enrolled in drawing classes at the California School of Arts and Crafts. There he put forth all of his knowledge and effort in portraying animals of the West in interesting situations and with dramatic action. His instructors recognized his carefree style and his outstanding ability in delineating the life of the mountains and the deserts of the west. But they were disheartened in the hope that he might learn to draw the human figure. Always on his easel was an abandoned study of the model, surrounded if not covered by many sketches of horses, coyotes, bears and other western animals.

Within four years from the time he entered art school in California he had made his way to New York. There he painted magazine covers. He sold idea drawings to the old *Life* magazine. By 1923 he had returned to the West, for he was not making ends meet. A friend encouraged him to try writing for his drawings. His first article, entitled "Bucking Horses and Bucking Riders," was accepted by *Scribners*. *Scribners* published his first full-length story, and in 1926 *Smoky* appeared. During the next sixteen years he published twenty full-length books.

James not only wrote about animals but on how to write about animals and about writing books. He was also a reviewer of western fiction for *The Bookman*. During the life of *Youth's Companion* he was a regular contributor. By 1929 he had become one of the most popular authors for high school students. *Smoky* brought fame of a different nature when it was selected for the annual Newberry Award as the best book of children's literature written in the year 1927. The book, now termed as a classic, received the award because "it tells of a phase of American life to boys and girls nine to sixteen. Alive with action the book tells of cowboys, ranches and the West." The quotes are from those who selected James as the award winner. They continue, saying that the book is filled with real convincing humor, truth and observation. Now, thirty years old (1958) *Smoky* maintains a medium popularity. The book is accepted as a genuine contribution to American literature.

In 1933 Will James came to Otis Art Institute in Los Angeles to talk with the students on "Colt's Knees." I was surprised as were the other students at his knowledge of the structure of the horse. He made complete sketches of the colt in action, the colt in relation to the horse, the bony structure of the knees, its muscular structure, using anatomically correct terminology.

While we think of James primarily as a writer of western stories he was not that in the usual sense. As early as 1928 in writing of one western story he said, "There's everything in it that will please them that don't know the West." He had an antipathy for the so-called Western and for the "dude." To him both were phony. In 1932 he provided the ironic formula for the creation of the Western: two dozen cowboys, four dozen guns, six tepeeful Indians, three bad mugs, one mortgage, one hero, brave, one girl, sweet.

Will James recognized his West as a fast disappearing West. Most of his stories were of the horse in relation to that West. In the foreword of *Smoky* we read: "To me the horse is man's greatest, most useful, most peaceful friend." A New York *Times* writer said: "Will James has a sixth sense insofar as his knowledge of horses is concerned plus an ingenious lariat and a tophand brush."

To his activities as rodeo performer, illustrator, author and lecturer

James added movies. Two of his books have been made into movies and he was in Hollywood supervising the production of a third when death took him in 1942. Only two months before his death we find mention of his yet retaining that "bashful, quiet dignity that was real. Wherever he is or whoever he is with James is always the unaffected and unspoiled self."

Excerpts from an article by
Isabel Johnson, Absarokee, 1958

The Mankers

One says The Mankers as one does The Tudors or The Rothchilds. The appellation connotes more than a man and wife — it is an institution. My first visit to the Mankers was back in the thirties when they had been married only a short time. After exhausting the topic of weather and crops on the ranch I looked about the room. At my back stood a bookcase covering most of the wall and reaching from floor to ceiling. I got down on my knees examining what these people were reading stuck out here (in Broadus) miles from nowhere. My hands passed lovingly over familiar titles. I looked up at Don. His eyes were twinkling. "Oh," he said, "We sort of run a neighborhood library." He did not say that he wrote poetry; nevertheless, I could see that he had a deep appreciation. There were books of poetry and the best on sociology, philosophy, history and biographies.

From that moment a long and interesting correspondence developed between the Mankers and me which has lasted throughout the years. Gilberta usually does the writing with Don perhaps adding a postscript. Always in a Gilberta letter there is a day-by-day account of the poems Don has written, where sent and where accepted. There was a great day of celebration when the hundredth poem was sold; now there are more than 200 published and Gilberta is aiming at a hardbacked anthology of Don's poems.

Almost as soon as Gilberta arrived at the ranch after their marriage she began finding poems stuffed into every cranny. "What are you doing with them?" she asked Don. "Nothing," he replied. Right then she took over the job of agent and personal relations person. Soon his poems began to appear in the Sunday sections of nearby papers. That was just a starter. The poems were good. Gilberta began studying the markets. Before long the slicks were accepting poems. She struggled on and before long poems were entered in national and international contests, and won. Yet through

124

it all Don was first a rancher and proud of it and she a home-maker and wife and equally proud of her part.

Quietly, without fanfare, the Mankers started an MIA Branch in Broadus. It was probably the most unorthodox Branch in Montana. Yet it brought results. We now have several budding poets in the area. Further, all who live there are enriched by new vistas that have been opened. In the early sixties, after repeated invitations, the Bozeman Poetry Group decided to hold one of its meetings at the Mankers'. As it turned out only four of us could go, yet with the Mankers we had a good meeting. It did not take many minutes to find out that Don was more than a poet — he is an excellent teacher and critic. He always came up with just the right word or phrase to give what we were trying to say a deeper meaning. He was so gentle when giving suggestions only the most egotistical or sensitive person could possibly take offense. We could not believe it when the clock struck midnight.

The upshot of this visit was that we felt the Mankers must become better known on a state-wide basis. They were too valuable to be prized by the Bozeman group alone. Thus when we had a state-wide writers' workshop in 1966 in Bozeman we persuaded the Mankers to chair the poetry part. They accepted. The first afternoon and evening were general for both poetry and prose writers. Many in attendance found Don's comments usable and practical. Sunday morning was the highlight of the workshop. Prose writers and poets broke into separate sections. The time was devoted to the reading and criticism of the different members' poems. While various members gave valuable contributions, it was easy to see that we all turned to Don as final authority. At this meeting the Mankers shone as a team, Gilberta offering her ideas of where a certain poem could be marketed and why. She knows her markets and most of the poetry editors. The workshop was really the beginning of state-wide acceptance of the House of Manker by all state poets. Don has repeatedly judged poetry contests and headed workshops in poetry at MIA State Festivals.

It was while they were my houseguests in Bozeman that Gilberta shyly brought out some of her original black-and-white paintings. Was she being overly ambitious to work on them? I should say not. It was interesting to find that she also had a creative streak. Her black-and-whites have been hung at MIA Festivals. Right now she is to have a one-man show at the Ketterer Gallery here in Bozeman.

You ask, what does the House of Manker do when fall plowing and seeding has been done and the animals cared for? They read. It does not matter that roads frequently become choked with snowdrifts so that the postman cannot even make the rounds. They stoke up with worthwhile books as some ranchers think only of flour and sugar to see them through.

Don's poems are certainly not Pollyannaish. He has lived close to stark reality and yet he sees beauty and hope in every living crisis.

We salute the House of Manker.

Adapted from an article by
Harriette Cushman, Bozeman, 1972

Meet These Writers

Bozeman has a number of well-known writers and an active and productive writing group. One of its successful members is Margaret Kraenzel. She wrote for school papers and magazines from grade school through college, but selling her work did not arrive until considerably later. After her marriage she continued to write poetry. When her children were in school she wrote children's stories. After joining MIA in 1948 and the resulting foundation of the Bozeman MIA writers group she "wrote madly," she has said, "at anything I could think of. The local writers' workshop was the first good criticism since college." Presently, she has another children's book almost completed, is working on a teen-age novel for girls, also a suspense novel and has completed an adult novel. Although she has been most successful with children's books she prefers to write the short story, because it necessitates telling the story in, as she states, "the shortest and clearest way and choosing only what is necessary to give the reader the character and setting without interrupting the flow of the narrative. A long novel has its charms, too — the author can wander at ease." Margaret gets a character in mind, puts him in an interesting situation and scene, plunges into the action and lives it through him as the story progresses, knowing where she wants to arrive at the end.

The Great Falls writers do many types of writing. Verna May Banta prefers to write stories and articles about, as she has said, "simple, down-to earth people and things . . . ." She and Carl Kolter have finished a book, *Air Force Diary*, and are working on its sequel. She is preparing an article on Mexico and working on a book, *The Small Grains*. About MIA she says, "I cannot find words to say enough about the help I've got from

126

belonging.''

Some persons write for the enjoyment of it or because they can't seem to stop writing. Payment for what they sell means little to them. Elsie Kolashinski admits to being such a writer — a ''sort of Sunday writer.'' If she feels deeply enough about a story, article or poem it nearly always hits print. She began writing when a child.

Alice Schumaker likes all types of writing, preferring humor first and poetry last. During this winter, 1963, she has written and sold, under contract, twelve different series on various subjects. Her present projects include a weekly series, under contract, of full-page features; freelance efforts with short stories and books, including a figure-skating junior novel to be dedicated to the U.S. Skating Team killed in a Belgian plane crash; a book in the science field and a biography of ''the father of amateur radio.'' She says, ''A writer must extend himself beyond his creations, be a salesman and a promoter, enter contests, interview people, dig into legends, strange facts, use his own experiences, study markets, keep up to the minute.''

Archie Joscelyn of Missoula is one of Montana's most prolific and successful writers. He began writing as a child and never quit. ''After I took it up in a more serious vein I made a few sales within the first half-year; after that the disease was incurable.'' Archie does many types of writing — articles, general fiction, detective novels, many Westerns, historical novels and juveniles. He writes in the morning and devotes the rest of the day to ''thinking, reading, planning, research.'' Although ''the best stories result when they spring from a character, I tend more to situation and plot.'' Joscelyn writes under the pen name of Al Cody as well as his own name. Two books were published this year under the former name and one under the latter. *The Crown,* an historical novel, was issued under his own name. As a professional writer he says that one must be attuned to the constant and swift changes in the field and be ready to accept them. Joscelyn knows well the things of which he speaks because he has lived by his pen (typewriter) for many years, a successful and personable man.

Another type of writing is done by an editor and appears as staff written. Such a writer is Fay Kuhlman of Billings, assistant editor of *The Dude Rancher.* She has also written and sold feature stories about ghost towns, the boy next door, a grizzly attack on a park employee, a trail-blazing engineer and others. Research is the key to her success. It has led her into productive fields and rare experiences. Sources of help have been stiff criticism from editors and from others in writing groups. ''MIA has been inspirational through workshops, contests and continued interest in writers of Montana.''

May Vontver's short story "The Kiskis," first published in *The Frontier* (March, 1929), has had an almost unrivalled circulation; it has been reprinted in eleven textbooks. J.K. Howard reprinted it in *Montana Margins;* it was published in Sweden in *The Swedish Journal* and in U.S. publication, *The Senior Citizen,* and this year (1963) is to be printed in braille.

May Vontver has achieved remarkable things since coming to the United States at twelve years of age. She completed grammar school in Sweden and high school in Nebraska. After some teaching she attended the Normal College in that state, Western Montana College of Education and the University of Montana, from which she obtained her degree. In Swedish she wrote *Emigrants to Nebraska* in 1960, going to Sweden to read proof on the book. It went into a second printing last year and is included in a series of ten outstanding books called "The Green Books," a collection that includes works by Robert Louis Stevenson, Jules Verne, Viktor Rydberg. Recently, May received word that her book is being published in the United States in Swedish. To her the greatest reward is the satisfaction that her literary efforts are of lasting worth.

Extracts from an article by
Mildred DeCrosse, Billings, 1963

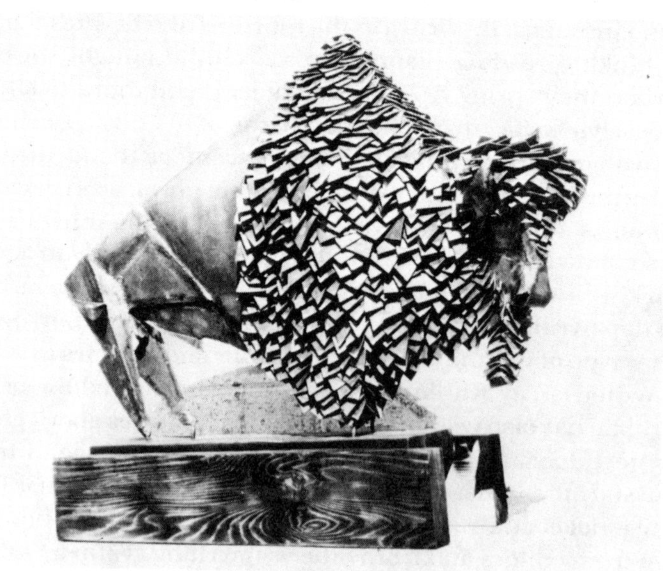

Welded steel scupture, Lyndon F. Pomeroy

128

Section III

THE VARIOUS
ART FIELDS

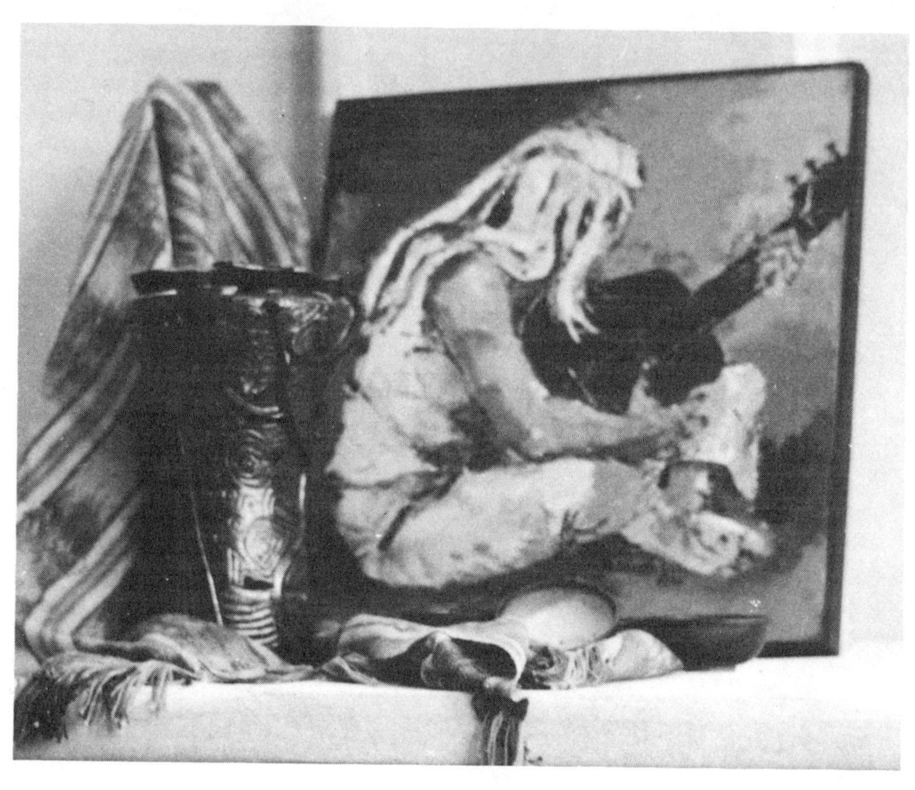

Painting, Donna Loos

Stoneware vase, Peg Valeton, 1971

130

ARCHITECTURE

Partners in Design

Some architects in Montana were asked, "What part do you expect artists and craftsmen to contribute to the esthetic as well as practical aspect of a building's design? Does the art created today lend itself to better use of space and material? What state artist's work have you used in your building designs?" Their answers would show there are still frontiers in the Big Sky Country.

"I hope," says R. Terry Johnson of Page-Werner & Partners of Great Falls, "the artist in Montana will find his way into the decision-making process of architectural problems. Not so much his talents in media but his ability to recognize artistic order and influence others to do the same." He continues: "The use of art in architecture in the past was considered more of a problem of what to do with art. The problem was usually solved by using art as adornment — a little here and a little there because 'here' and 'there' were not being claimed for any other specific use. By utilizing art in this manner the artist could retain his identity as the contributor to the artistic enlightenment on 'such-and-such' project and the architect could feel a sense of accomplishment in having brought the artist into his camp. In the past art and architecture seemed to prevail as separate disciplines forced to combine in building design.

"Now that new disciplines are entering into architectural decision-making the construction picture should include the artist as a consultant to the overall effort. Buildings are becoming more sculptural in concept and color is being accepted as an integral part of the architectural milieu."

Hoiland and Zucconi, also of Great Falls, report they have used the works of Rudi Autio, Lyndon Pomeroy and Walter Graham and say they *expect* artists and craftsmen to become a part of the design-build team to the point of influencing the entire design, perhaps.

An architect himself, Herbert L. Jacobson, present President of Montana Institute of the Arts, says that he believes building design and other art work such as painting and sculpture can be compatible and separately identified. His firm has used the art forms of Jack Weaver and Irwin Shope.

F. Edward Jones, CTA Architects, Engineers, Planners of Billings, used the word "environment" often in his statement. "Environment is the basic unit of planning and design today, so that environments are man-oriented rather than object-oriented. Architecture is evaluated by the quality of life it permits and encourages. Good fit becomes the important measure of design for the human environment. Opportunities for designs or artists and craftsmen have greatly expanded." CTA has worked with Lyndon Pomeroy, coordinating their building design and his sculpture.

R. Terry Johnson throws out a challenge to Montana artists in all media: "I truly sense a need for a more meaningful dialog between artist and architect and would welcome such an opportunity." Some Montana artists and craftsmen have met this challenge and the profession is waiting for others.

Dorothy Larson, Billings, 1970

CARVING

Wood Carving

Wood carving is an art which has been handed down through the ages. The abundance of wood in nature, its usefulness in natural form, its wide variety of texture, its beauty and warmth of grain and its inherent strength have made it an extremely versatile and widely used medium. It has been intimately associated with man's esthetic and physical welfare.

Opportunities in wood carving challenge the carver's skill and imagination. As in many other skills, a high level of proficiency can be developed by learning a few simple techniques and practising persistently. The objective in carving is to study a piece of wood, and to apply the carver's skill to produce a work that employs good design and utilizes the natural inherent qualities of the wood to a high degree.

Carvings can be classified broadly into three kinds: bas-relief, chip and sculptured or round relief. Bas-relief carvings are made in low relief and they may be purely decorative, symbolic, or realistic representation. Chip carving is an interesting technique based upon simply executed geometric designs. It is carved by removing shallow chips from the wood surface. The many angular faces created catch the light and shadows thereby accentuating the design. They can be simple or intricate in design depending upon the carver's taste and desires and they are chiefly decorative. Sculpturing or carving in round relief is considered by some people as the acme of wood carving. Opportunities to produce pleasing works in sculptured wood range from purely abstract form to life-like representation.

Anybody can carve if he so desires. Unlike many other art forms it does not require a large outlay for expensive equipment and materials. Many

132

fine carvings have been produced with no more than a jackknife and a piece of wood. The desire to create works with hands and mind is prerequisite. The serious carver will desire a few basic tools, such as a straight chisel, a small gouge, a skewed chisel, and a v-shaped chisel. Additional tools may be added at the carver's discretion as his skill develops. Tools should be selected for quality steel rather than appearance. Those made of poor steel do not hold an edge well and they are not only difficult to work with but they are unsafe. A dull tool can slip off the work much more easily than a sharp tool and cause injury to the carver. Many carvers enjoy fashioning their own tools. Old files, springs or other pieces of steel found in the scrap pile often provide excellent material for making carving tools. My favorite skew chisel is made from an old worn-out six-inch mill bastard file.

Design is the starting-point in carving. Beginning carvers would do well to select or develop simple designs. Intricate patterns are not only difficult to execute in wood but the uninitiated carver may become discouraged before he acquires the necessary skill. Often simple formalized lines are most effective for achieving the desired effects and they are easy to execute.

Design should make use of special traits of wood. Often in wood with contrasting grain the contour of the wood can be shaped to bring out grain and thus emphasize certain features in the finished carving. This is one place where the carver's imagination comes into play.

Selecting the right kind of woods is an important step. Many writers advise the beginning carver to start with soft textured woods such as white pine or basswood. This may be sound advice, but as the carver's skill increases he will most certainly want to branch out and explore special woods. Therefore, he should study all the woods and their technical characteristics.

Many native Montana woods show excellent qualities for wood carving and they present an impressive array of desirable traits with which the carver should become acquainted. The characteristics considered imperative in wood for carving are grain, texture and strength along the grain. Grain is defined as the arrangement of wood fibres. Trees grow by adding a layer of wood each year on the surface beneath the bark. This is known as an annual ring. The fibres or elongated cells developed in early or spring growth are thin-walled, light-colored cells, whereas the fibres formed in late or summer growth are thick-walled, hard, and usually dark cells. Wood is made up of many layers of alternating early and late wood. Low contrast results in a uniform wood with little or no figure in the grain, but high contrast gives rise to highly figured grain with variegated colors.

Some woods have cells with large openings or pores. These woods show open or coarse grain, as exemplified by the oaks. Other woods may be characterized as having closed grain where the cell openings are small and uniform in size giving rise to a smooth uniform surface, as illustrated by maple or pine. Texture relates to the uniformity and hardness of the wood. Maple is an example of uniform hard texture with closed grain. Strength along the grain is important in carvings where it is necessary to shape very small projections at a right angle to the grain. Woods with low strength along the grain will split easily in such circumstances.

Cross-grained wood can be troublesome to the carver. It is characterized by bands of grain that change direction alternately across or through the piece. Undetected directional changes in the grain can cause uncontrolled splitting or chapping of the wood and may damage the work. Working such wood requires extra care and attention to grain detail. When grain changes direction it is necessary to alter the cutting strokes to follow the grain. Grain is often distorted in the vicinity of knots and this condition also requires special attention.

Intricate carvings usually require a dense, closed-grain wood that is not too hard to carve but at the same time is strong enough to hold together without splitting along the grain. Hardwoods generally have enough resistance to enable the carver's knife to make a smooth cut across the grain. Soft wood is often brash and unless the tools are razorsharp it is difficult to make a smooth, clean cut across the grain because the fibres tear, break or collapse, causing a rough surface.

When the wood is selected and a design is obtained, the next step is to transfer the design to the wood. The design can be sketched on the wood freehand, or it can be traced over carbon paper placed on the wood. Orient the design so that thin or small long parts parallel the grain rather than cross it.

After the design is in place on the wood the next step is to remove the larger quantities of unwanted wood. This is usually necessary in bas relief or sculptured carvings. A large carpenter's chisel serves this purpose well. In round relief the work is roughed conveniently with a jig, band or coping saw. Rough cuts should be made as close as possible to the outline. Roughing out the block as much as possible in this way permits the carver to spend more of his time on the actual job of sculpturing. After the work is roughed out the most interesting part of the task starts. With sharp tools the carver shapes the features of the carving and, finally, completes the surface in either a smooth or roughened texture, dependent upon the effect he wishes to achieve. Veiners or small gouges are well adapted to attain texural surfaces. The carver will want to experiment with various

134

tools and textures to achieve the desired result.

In the process of carving, the pattern on the wood is lost because it is carved away; therefore, it is essential that the carver visualize how the completed piece will look. It is well to have a sketch in front of him to refer to as he carves.

The carving is now ready for the final step, finishing. In many carvings made from carefully selected wood no finish is necessary. It is desirable to rub the carving with boiled linseed oil or wax on some hardwoods, while others may be varnished or lacquered. Here too, the carver should experiment to achieve the finish which harmonizes best with the nature and mood of the carving. Above all, he should try to obtain a natural finish and permit the beauty of the wood to contribute to the esthetic quality of the completed article.

Part of an article by
A.L. Roe, Missoula, 1964

Out of the Woods

Great Falls is very fortunate in the quality of artists living in the area. Among the best are wood-crafters Ken Brobeck, Ron Ronning and Ray Steele. They have similarities in their feelings for wood but express them in widely varied and individual ways.

They prefer to design and make their own pieces but all have collaborated on occasion. Ken made the frame for a hammock while the macrame swing for it was knotted by Ruth Franklin. Ron's wife, Anita, designed some light fixtures for their den and he constructed them. Ray collaborates with Korell and Iverson, architects, on building interiors.

All three men have art related vocations. Ken is an art teacher at East Junior High School, Ron is a woodshop instructor at Paris Gibson Junior High School and Ray is director of the C.M. Russell Museum. All find time to create handsome pieces clearly marked with their personalities.

In talking to Ken, he commented, "I have a great desire and need to create — create using natural materials: clay, wood, leather, metal. I like to create functional sculptured furniture. Designs come internally over a period of time, and are then sketched. Only glue and dowels are used to lock the pieces together, no screws." He signs his work with a branding iron by burning his name into each piece of furniture as it is finished.

A music stand of Ken's took first place in sculpture in 1973 MIA state juried show in Great Falls and a drop leaf table of oak placed in the show this spring. His clay pieces frequent juried shows, too. His last remark was, "Wood is a beautiful material to work with, beautiful to look at, and to me, it is most beautiful to feel."

Ron feels that working with wood includes not only professional involvement but personal expression as well. "Wood has a responsiveness not found in metals for me," he said. The contrasting textures of cedar and oak, the smooth hand-rubbed feeling of a carefully worked walnut surface are found repeatedly in his work. Several pieces are presently in the designing stage. Ron prefers to have things well thought out and underway before planning show participation. Created objects have varied from a laminated walnut container to an oak sink stand which features a stoneware sink and fixtures by Billings potter Chanson Ching.

When asked about his feeling for working in wood, Ron commented, "Wood has a warmth and character that no other material has, never constant, always changing its character and personality." He finds that wood is compatible with other materials, whether metallic or ceramic. Ray feels he has been strongly influenced by the simplicity and function of Shaker design. Asked about the difference between wood sculpture and furniture, Ray replied, "All furniture is sculptural, the functional qualities make the difference." He likes to use wood in newer ways, such as door locks and hardware, towel racks and chandeliers. He has placed first in juried shows in sculpture and crafts and topped it off with a "Best of Show."

A final comment from Ron sums up what seems to be the general feeling for all three: "Wood is Wonderful."

Betty McDonald, Great Falls, 1975

ENAMELING

Copper Enameling Is Fun

Enameling on copper is like eating popcorn — once you start it's hard to stop. As a craft it is a logical digression for either metalworker or potter. Essentially, it is the process of applying glaze (potter) to a formed piece of copper (metalworker). It entails more work and expense than copper work but less than pottery. It has the advantage over pottery of taking relatively little time from original conception to finished piece, and the advantage over both pottery and metalwork of colorfulness — the bright, shiny colors that appeal to us all but do not seem compatible with pottery, are perfectly at home on the hard metallic surface of copper or silver or gold, if you can afford it.

The basic equipment necessary for enameling consists first of the various mallets, hammers, stakes or sandbags necessary for forming the metal and second the emery cloth, steelwool and acid used to clean the surface preparatory to applying the enamel. A brush, a small spatula, a small sieve and a little gum, either tragacanth or arabic, seem to be all that is absolutely necessary for applying the enamels, although one tends to add other tools to suit one's own technique. The main item is, of course, the kiln. Unless one plans to enamel dinner plates, a small kiln of inside dimensions approximately 9 by 9 inches by 5 is perfectly adequate. A satisfactory kiln can be made easily from insulating bricks and Nichrome wire elements. Since enameling does not require temperatures over 1400 F., the Zonolite bricks from Great Falls could be used; Nichrome wire can be purchased, already coiled, from the Denver Fire Clay Co.

This article intends merely to give some idea of what one is getting into before he leaps. The cost should not be prohibitive for an individual or a small group of craftsmen. It is possible to have a lot of fun with enamels by going ahead with no instruction and experimenting freely. However, there are some good books which may save some errors and give ideas for further investigation.

At present there are relatively few either serious craftsmen or hobbyists doing enamels in this country as compared to the thousands working in some phase of pottery. It is an open field and an enchanting one. There is nothing so fascinating as watching the enamels melt in the kiln and then, when the piece is out, watching the colors develop from the glow of the kiln to the final cool state. Changes can be made and the piece developed as one wishes. A completed piece can be turned out in one evening's work.

Adapted from an article by
Frances Senska, Bozeman, 1952

What is Good Enameling?

The answer to this question, which was posed to me as my subject, may seem easy, and, from a technical point of view, it is. From a broader point of view it is much the same as trying the answer the question, "What is art?"

Technically, good enameling consists of a coat of enamel of such thickness in relation to the metal on which it rests that it will neither burn off in dark spots because it is too thin nor crack or chip because it is too thick. The technical aspects of enameling, especially the Limoges type most popular today, are quite simple and can be mastered by anyone willing to take a reasonable amount of care about cleanliness and precision.

Artistically, good enameling is quite another thing, and rather difficult to define, and its appreciation depends on the experience and taste of the beholder. In my opinion, a good enamel, like any other work of art, is, in the first place, a personal and individual expression of the creative imagination of the artist. In the second place, the technique must be competently enough handled and well enough suited to the design that a consideration of technique is subordinate to the appreciation of the artistic whole.

There has been a strong tendency since enameling has become a popular as well as a professional craft for the amateur enamelist to buy prepared, commercially spun blanks; and not only prepared and commercially ground enamels, but also enamels which have been made into threads and beads and crawling slushes and other readymade elements of design. Along with this is a tendency to lift the design itself from other objects, or from a book of examples of designs. I suppose one could say that this approach to the craft is an expression of an individual personality. I don't believe that most of us, if we stop to think about it, wish to say the thing that this approach implies about ourselves.

I would not preclude the use of commercially spun or stamped blanks for the artist-enameler, but I feel that carrying the whole object through from forming the base for the enamel to the final polishing tends to give a personal quality and unity of concept not so apt to be present when the enamelist allows himself to become merely one station on an assembly line.

Another point at which the enamelist abdicates his prerogatives as an artist is in the use of threads, beads, and other readymades. These devices are good methods for the commercial producer whose speed of production is essential to this economic survival, and they do have a certain place in the vocabulary of the artist, but habitual use of them is as limiting to creativity as occasional use may be stimulating. A thorough artist can control these devices and subordinate them to his intent. In the hands of the beginner the result is likely to look commercial in a cheap sense rather than truly professional.

I should like to toss in the idea that a certain difficulty to be overcome is of value in any art, and the mark of the true artist is that he makes the

138

difficult look easy. The earlier types of enamels — cloisonne, champleve, plique-a-jour, basse-taille — are neglected today in favor ofthe late-comer Limoges, the painted-on (sifted-on) technique using a smooth ground, probably because they are more difficult and involve the preparation of the ground from the beginning, the ground being part of the design. They involve a thoroughly thoughtout design disciplined by the nature of the technique, and allow a much wider chance for failure. Their difficulty runs counter to the basic culture-philosophy of our time and country: we buy food mostly prepared, cooking is no longer a valued personal art; we not only accept but cherish the accidental, the found object, in painting and sculpture; our instructions to educators are that every child must be a success in something and no one must fail. Please do not imagine that I do not find our culture convenient and comfortable; I do. But I don't think buying one's art experiences in a kit — I don't think refusing the discipline of difficulty and insisting on easy success leads to personal greatness or to memorable works of art in enameling.

Craftsmen in the past were willing to work on one object for a long time, and their scarce products were highly valued by a discriminating, if small, public. Now we have an economy of abundance, or mass production, where there is enough of every sort of machine-made object for everyone, which objects are used but not appreciated by this large and often undis-criminating public. In this industrial culture, an important value of the product of the artist-craftsman is that it is unique, and when the indi-vidual accepts commercial shortcuts he loses some of this quality and relates his product to the mass rather than to the class.

Of course, there are many shades of expression between the mass factory product and the unique individual masterpiece. For persons for whom the mechanics of a craft hold a fascination, and the struggle to create does not, a good place would be in a group of craftsmen working with a designer — the sort of thing the State Planning Board would like to see developed to supply the tourist trade. There must be enough individu-ality that the tourist does not see the same object at every stop across the country, but enough uniformity of design and technique and sufficient quantity that a retailer can depend on his supply. The enamels of Jade Snow Wong, which have been very popular, come in this category. She designed them and a group of craftsmen did the enameling.

For those who prefer to consider enameling an art and wish to explore beyond the familiar sift-and-sgrafitto or dip-and-swirl, there are several books explaining the more demanding techniques. When enameling first started to take hold as a popular rather than a professional craft, few texts were available, of which Herbert Maryon, *Metalwork and Enameling,* and

Greta Pack, *Jewelry and Enamelling,* are still good. More recent and popular books are: Kenneth F. Bates, *Enameling, Principles and Practices,* a classic text by one of the leading enamelists in the country and instructor at the Cleveland Art Institute, an oustanding school in this field; Oppi Untracht, *Enameling on Metal,* by an excellent craftsman and writer who regularly has articles on this and other crafts in *Craft Horizons and Ceramic Monthly* and its handbook, *Copper Enameling,* a collection of articles by Jean O'Hara and Jo Revert.

When we come to the design aspect of enameling, which to me seems rather more important than the technical, even though the two really cannot be separated, any more than we can make a truly valid distinction between fine art and applied art, there are no books I can recommend — not that there are not many compiled, but that I think they have little value for the artist. Design is something that must evolve individually from the native sensitivity and accumulated experience of the artist. By the time someone has worked out a system of design cut-and-dried enough to be put in a book, it becomes dry bones, and the illustrations appearing in such books invariably seem overworked, overfamiliar, cliche-ridden and dull. Most books, or the usual chapters on the subject in books on technique, which purport to tell us how to design end up giving a pretty good picture of how not to design. So for design I recommend studying nature, not with the idea of copying it, but to become sensitive to its forms and patterns of growth. And I recommend studying art — any aspects of the visual arts, not just enamels, and art history — not with the idea of copying any particular style or artist, but of becoming sensitive to the responses artists have made to nature and the forms they have evolved. Perhaps in the process of this study we may be led to individual insight which, in conjunction with technical proficiency, may lead us to "good enameling."

Frances Senska, Bozeman, 1961

CERAMICS

Mining Camp Glazing with Kay

A Butte ceramist, Mrs. Larry Smith, makes her own glazes, using mineral-rich clay taken from raw ore-laden clays found in the Mountain Con, Skryme Pit, Travonia and Anselmo mines. The original and unusual effects achieved through mine glazes have caused Kay to abandon the commercial ones, as she feels beauty has been lost in refining. Her mineral-laden glazes, complete with their impurities, capture a rare loveliness impossible with commercial glazes.

The Mountain Con yields a clay heavy in copper, manganese and iron which achieves a tan, tweedy result. The overshot of mineral in Skryme Pit clay contains an enormous overload of copper, lead, manganese, zinc and iron resulting in a striking ebony glaze.

Although Kay describes her work as "guess and by gosh," the Kharauba award for her Rice Bottle with particular commendation for its distinctive glaze states otherwise. Her pottery continues to gain distinction in exhibits here in the United States as well as in Canada. The Rice Bottle clay came from clay dug in the Bert Carlson mine near Basin. Totally different colors are obtained through her methods of application. The most unique glaze of all is one she labels Alligator.

Any ceramist will tell you there are almost inexhaustible minerals in the Treasure State. Mrs. Smith has gathered clays from Nisler Junction, Missoula, Georgetown Lake, Ruby Valley, Flint Creek, Alta Gulch Mine near Basin and many others, not to mention sacks of clay sent by friends and unknown admirers and boxes of clay left on her doorstep while she is down in the basement pottering around.

A sheepherder, who prospected too, sent Kay a small package of clay stating in his little note that if she could use it he would supply loads of it very cheap. The only things he failed to include were his name and address. This happens with many donated batches of clay, which she is reluctant to use because, as she states, if the results were lovely it would be heartbreaking not to know where to obtain more of the same kind.

Although we do not question the ways of refining mud pies many others do. Roadside trips for clay by Mrs. Smith and her friends have caused no end of wonder to passing motorists bewildered by ladies busily making mud pies with their clay and water bottles testing the clays to see if they are sufficiently plastic to work satisfactorily.

Knowing I was following a very ingenious person to the basement, I still was unprepared for what it contained. In one room was a loom on which Kay weaves mats for her pottery. On the walls were her paintings. All around I noted various jars, vases, bowls, heads, pitchers in many stages of progression. One bench contained her lapidary tools for gem cutting. Creating art work, useful and lovely, is a satisfying experience with Kay.

She showed me three wheels, one electric and two foot-pedalled. There was a kiln she was building and another one she had completed. An old washing machine was used to mix her clays, while wringers were used to hold a jar with pebbles to grind glazes. Underneath a cabinet which she built from old bookcases and pieces of plywood were old beer kegs that held her clays. Rows of shelves had countless jars of original glazes. Hanging in a partition were Christmas bells fired from Missoula clay that really rang in melodious tones, as did the unique dinner bell.

On one wall was her sketching of a ceramist fashioning a cylinder, and I learned that six inches tall took the potter out of the primary class while ten inches was good. Kay has done some measuring twenty-two inches. On another wall was a skillfully lettered saying: "Do Not Scoff At The Potter's Clay For It Too Was Once A Man."

From an article by
Mary McCourt Anderson, Butte, 1955

Rudy Autio's Architectural Ceramics

Rudy Autio is one of the individuals in Montana who is doing things in and for the state. His projects in architectural ceramics are quite new and different not only for Montana but in the United States. They are not only new as ceramics but show a forward trend on the part of state architects. Someone suggested that I as Fine Arts chairman "do a story" on Rudy as part of my annual report. The notes he sent me were so complete that I submit them as he sent them.

First Lutheran Church, Anaconda, Hugo Eck, Bozeman, Architect

The First Lutheran Church relief will be made of carved brick or a variation of this method and will measure 24 feet by 7 feet in size. The carving was done directly on soft green clay, on blocks made on the extrusion machinery at the Western Clay Brickyard at Helena. These blocks were made by removing several cutting wires on the cutting machine at the plant which produces a mud block equivalent to four uncut bricks in size. The blocks were then assembled on large easels and carved into intaglio, or low relief.

The design represents The Last Supper, showing Christ and the disciples around the table. The carved block wall will be located on the exterior near the main entrance to the church. Clerestory windows will be above the relief carving. The wall will be freestanding.

After the blocks have dried thoroughly they will be reassembled on large easels and color, glaze or iron, will be applied to the surface by rubbing. This will enrich the tone, produce variations on the surface and itensify the modeling. The bricks will then be fired in the brick kilns at the brickyard. After firing, the blocks will be taken to the job and assembled. Each block has a number to indicate its position on the wall.

Glacier County Library Relief

This will be a glazed bas-relief sculpture in ceramics that will be installed on the outside of the newly erected library at Cut Bank. The relief will measure 12 by 4 feet. The colors will be in light blues and whites along with natural clay tones which will contrast with the glazed areas. The subject consists of three animals — a bison, a horse and an ox. Each of these three animals depicts a period in the developing of the country. The bison represents the primitive or undeveloped period, the horse symbolizes discovery and exploration, and the ox represents settlement, cultivation and permanency. Decorated suns appear in each panel to indicate the passage of time and are used as chronological symbols.

The animals and suns are in high relief and are modeled initially on large easels. From the models plaster casts were made and impressions cast into clay that is blended partly from Whitehall clay and Blosberg clay, both native clays. The plaster casts were made larger than the final piece to allow for shrinkage during the drying and firing. The relief decoration will be sectional and will be assembled on the job. The individual sections will weigh from twenty to fifty pounds each. The entire composition will fit accurately together like a jigsaw puzzle.

This relief is being presented to the library in memory of Bill Linder from the Oilfield Lumber Company. The architectural firm of Page and Werner of Great Falls are the designers of the building.

Many other architectural commissions have been completed by Rudy Autio. On the Liberal Arts Hall on the University of Montana campus is a circular highly glazed terra cotta relief symbolizing or depicting writing — Indian writing on skins. The relief is 8 feet in diameter. Of this one Rudy says it made him realize how much he had to learn. Gus Link of Butte designed the building. A series of nursery plaques above the fireplaces of two schools in Havre followed. The buildings had been designed by Van Teylingen, Knight and Van Teylingen of Great Falls. Rudy executed a series of four plaques according to the specifications of Bishop Gilmore near the main entrance on the north face of Anaconda Central High School portraying the four evangelists. Designers of the building was Fox and Ballas of Missoula.

In Great Falls Rudy did two of his largest works. The first is located on the north wall of the Methodist Church in that city and is similar to the one he is working on for his Lutheran Church design. The Sermon on the Mount measures 10 by 30 feet, is a large block relief composed partly in relief and in part in incised line with iron rubbed into the surface to intensify the modeling and enrich the surface. The subject is Christ speaking to the multitude. Hoiland and Lund designed the building. His other work in Great Falls is a wall of the C.M. Russell Gallery, designed by MacIver, Hess and Hausjaa. It is a repeat pattern done on structural clay tiles, measuring 12 by 12 inches. Motif for this design was derived from Indian pictograph writing. The design is repeated over a series of eight tiles with the writing incised and superimposed on natural clay tones and black areas.

Rudy's work at Chinook was a part of the church which was adjudged the First Award winner in the 1956 Professional Competition for Catholic churches. This is St. Gabriel's Church, designed by Bordelau-Pannell and Amundsen, Great Falls architects. The fourteen Stations of the Cross are done in partly glazed stoneware. Each station measures 12 by 16 inches. The corpus of Christ located on the cross behind the altar was executed in the same manner.

Isabelle Johnson, Absarokee, 1957

Waxing Eloquent With Wax Resist

When I read in *Time* magazine in the early part of 1950 that Bernard Leach, the famous English potter, would visit the United States and hold seminars on potting in various places, I felt justified as a long-time *Time* subscriber to write and ask if they would try to put me in touch with him. By and by I received a note from Leach telling me his schedule of appearances and I was enabled to catch up with him at the one he held at the St. Paul Gallery and School of Art. This meeting and subsequent correspondence in 1952 resulted in Leach coming to the Archie Bray Foundation at Helena accompanied by Shoji Hamada and the late Soetsu Yanagi, in 1952.

During the session at St. Paul, Leach demonstrated the wax-resist glaze decorative method, using the paraffin wax in the time-honored form of melting it and rapidly brushing the design on the unglazed pottery piece with the hot fluid wax. Of course, the wax chilled and solidified immediately upon contact with the cold pot.

The following day I brought to Leach a gallon of an emulsion wax that can be thinned out without heating by merely diluting with water, and can be readily and easily brushed on the cold pot without hardening immediately. It does harden when the water dilute evaporates and the design is left in pure wax. This wax, known under the brand name of Mobilcer A (formerly called Ceremul A) is a product of Socony Mobil Oil Company.

144

Leach was delighted with its use in place of the cumbersome and fire-hazardous melted wax method and, of course, found it ideally suited to brush decoration because it applied fluidly without congealing, just like painting with oil or water color, unlike the melted wax, which congealed the moment the hot fluid contacted the cold pot. This emulsion wax presented a definite improvement over the wax resist decorative process Leach described in his excellent work, *A Potter's Book.*

A letter to me dated September 14, 1950, from Leach, after he returned to St. Ives, Cornwall, England, indicated that he "fell in love" with this product. Leach had developed and made effective designs using the hot, melted wax-resist process and this new wax emulsion enabled him to further exploit his genius in that direction. He advised me in this letter that he had run out of the supply I had given him in St. Paul and was sending me an urgent plea to have some more sent to him, as it was apparently unobtainable at that time in England.

Before furnishing the sample to Leach I had been the first to use it in the wax-resist decorative process, as suggested in Leach's book, and I also had furnished some of it to the Montana State College Art Department in Bozeman, where Peter Voulkos, now an internationally famous potter, was then a student. Voulkos' first prize-winning pottery in the Syracuse National show was decorated by wax-resist, using the Ceremul in a manner developed by him which would be next to impossible to do with the melted wax method. I believe Voulkos brushed wax over the entire outside of the unfired pottery piece, then sgraffitoed through the wax exposing the clay as his design. Then using an iron oxide, aqueous slip he brushed over the entire pot and the water diluted slip adhered to the clay in the sgraffitoed lines, and refused to adhere to the wax covered areas. Since those early experiments and uses of the emulsion wax, word has spread about and it has become quite extensively used by potters everywhere.

For decorative process a quart of "Ceresist" will last the average studio potter a very long time, as it is generally diluted 50/50 with water before using. The emulsion wax is beneficial as an additive in small quantities (about 4 to 10%) to glaze batches to improve their adhesive and cohesive qualities, and prevent crawling of the fired glazes.

Many uses are being found by artists for this wax other than for pottery decoration. It has been found by users to be superior to tousche and less expensive, for silk screen work. Another suggested use is for batik, both for designing by direct painting with the wax emulsion on the fabric and also for waxing the fabric before tying and dyeing. It has advantages, too, I have found, for watercolor painting, to use in place of straight.water — to dilute the water medium with a small percentage of wax so that when the

pigment applied to the paper has dried the color is invested in a wax —
and subsequent background or other washes will not mix with the previously painted areas and cloud or sully them. Before the emulsion wax
watercolors dry, however, other colors can be flushed or washed into
them, when desirable.

Leach, Hamada and the late Dr. Yanagi visited the Archie Bray Foundation during a week in December of 1952 and the following year introduced
the use of this emulsion wax to potters in Japan. It has become an
increasingly popular means of pottery decoration since its first use in
Montana for that purpose.

Branson G. Stevenson, Great Falls, 1964

HISTORY

Meagher County Centennial Year

This year Meagher County pridefully points to its officially recorded
beginnings dated from 1867, and is announcing its one hundredth anniversary. In the courthouse the old records from Diamond City days
which have been kept in the vaults have been brought out, studied by
history buffs, and are presently being microfilmed at the library of Montana State University, Bozeman. These books are the Commissioners'
Proceedings from 1865-67 and files on mining claims.

In a time when there was little organization, with every man for himself
in his frantic search for gold, it is commendable that these people in
Diamond City took the time to keep records and maintain a form of
government. It is more commendable that these documents have been
saved. Paper work of any kind was somewhat rare, as one can believe
when history tells us how Thomas Francis Meagher became acting-
governor: he arrived at Bannock by stage, having accepted the position of
military secretary of the Montana Territory; he was met by Governor
Edgerton himself, told that he was immediately being installed as acting-
governor, and, on the spot, given all the gubernatorial papers. These he
tucked into his pocket, mounted a horse and set out for Virginia City.
Edgerton left on the next stage.

Territorial legislature divided all of Montana between two counties,
Meagher and Choteau. Diamond City was the County Seat of Meagher
County until the gold camp died and was moved to White Sulphur Springs

146

in 1881. It is small wonder that vigilante justice moved in.

Diamond City seems very distant from the slopes of the Highwoods, St. Peter's Mission on the Missouri, the outlaw hideouts in the Judith Basin and the Indian infested Gallatin border. In 1885 Fergus County was taken off of Meagher, and in succession, Musselshell, Wheatland, Golden Valley. In the slicing what was once Diamond City became a part of Broadwater County.

Meagher County, because it encompassed so large an area, has an interesting history. Most of it was well recorded by the early day newspaper editors, the Sutherlin Brothers. Their *Rocky Mountain Husbandman,* published at Diamond City and later at White Sulphur Springs, was one of the first of the Territorial newspapers. The first year's edition, 1866-67, is complete and bound, and can be read at the Historical Library in Helena.

Choosing some of the historic names found in the county and placing them in proper sequence, one has a vignette of the history of Montana. Jammison Trail belongs to the first phase, when great herds of buffalo grazed on the grassy plains. Jammison was a big-game hunter from England. Castle and Copperopolis are ghost towns of the mining era. Fort Logan brings to mind the days of the Indian scares and many of the old ranches bear the names of the men who made history — the Dave Folsom place, the Charlie Cook ranch, the Moore Ranch.

In the noting of the one hundredth year of Meagher County, some special events are planned for the summer. A great interest has been revived to open the Stone Castle Museum that sits atop one of the hills of White Sulphur Springs. This ornate Victorian mansion was owned by Michael Donahoe and his heirs for some fifty years and has been given to the Meagher County Historical Association for a museum. The original owner was B.R. Sherman, who came to Montana in 1864 and ran a grist mill at Fort Owen. He came to Meagher County in 1869.

Theresa Buckingham, White Sulphur Springs, 1967

Steamboating to Fort Benton: 1860

July 2, 1960, was the 100th anniversary of the arrival of the first steamboat at Fort Benton, Montana. The boat was the *Chippewa,* which blew up on its return trip in 1861. This year the citizens put on a three-day celebration of the Centennial and produced a pageant of the history of the town and its pioneers (under the direction of Professor Bert Hansen of the

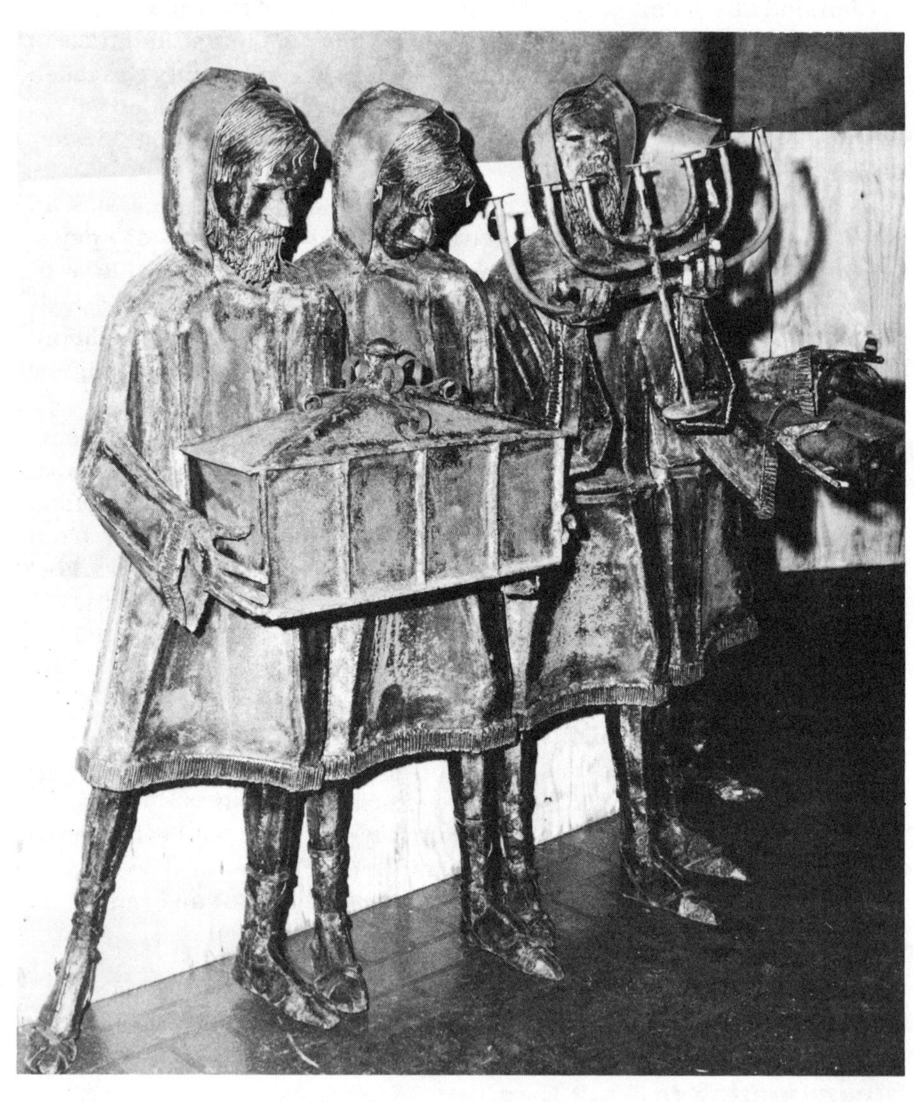

Covenant, a welded steel sculpture, Leo Olson, 1975

148

University of Montana). A party of five cars from Chinook arrived in Fort Benton in time to have a picnic lunch in the Old Fort Park.

The parade was led by a Sheriff's posse mounted on fine horses. These were followed by Shetland ponies ridden by kids proud to be in the parade. Then came Tin Lizzies of 1910 vintage with brassbound radiators. Many other old cars were there. An old steam engine moved ahead well but was hard to stop, the crowd scattering fast before the driver got it under control — though he might have been bluffing. A man representing Abraham Lincoln marched with a bunch of kids around him.

The Old Fort Park, with a wonderful lawn, is so large that it accomodated the large crowd. We found the paved streets of Fort Benton to be wonderful for any town. Sidewalks and curbing were near perfect. In 1908 the high water ran over the flooring of the bridge, but you would have to see that to believe it, as it is a long way to the water when the flow is normal. We drove around and saw some of the old buildings, some of which have early day signs, "I.G. Baker," for instance.

We got good seats for the pageant. The large *Chippewa* was just to our left. She blew a real steamboat whistle and some power inside moved her right along the dock. In this episode the main characters shown were Major Culbertson, who built the fort in 1850 and named the site Fort Benton; Lieutenant Mullan who had just finished the surveying of the trail from Fort Benton and later built the Mullan Road; Granville Stuart, who with his brother James had first discovered gold in Montana.

Presentation of the Baker Massacre on January 23, 1870, was realistic. When the soldiers started firing and the Indians ran out of the tepees quite a few papooses almost stole the show, for when they were killed they fell hard and seemed really dead.

The first election in Fort Benton, April 4, 1883, was lively but with little competition, for all candidates were elected. The arrival of the *Helena*, first boat of the season of 1885, was more lively, the women aboard going to Helena saw to that. They did not think much of the Missouri River water for drinking and thought much less of Montana whiskey. The last steamboat to arrive at Fort Benton, on July 16, 1908, was the *Mandan*, which was a government boat that was supposed to clear the river for navigation. At this time there was a welcome home for Congressman Pray and wife on their return from Washington. [Celebration of] Brother Van's birthday, March 22, 1918, was very interesting. However, just as he started to cut the cake a big wind came up and blew down some of the scenery and a big dust storm struck us; then the rain began to fall and we hit for the cars on the doublequick. We had to drive slow because of the mud on the windshield. However, a fresh rain washed it clear. We had a wonderful time and relived some of the past.

Extracted from an article by
J. Lee Sedgwick, Fort Benton, 1961

Trouble With Town Names

It is nothing new for Montanans to wonder where their mail went, and why it took so long for it to arrive, if it did. Back in Territorial times, prompt and reliable delivery of letters was something which did not happen. Several factors contributed to this, a few related to climate, distance and terrain, others to human behavior.

One of these was the pioneer habit of naming settlements without waiting for formalities like establishment of a post office, or clearing with some agency to see if that name had not been pre-empted elsewhere. A well-known case involved Virginia City, whose mail might go to Nevada while the other town's sack came to Alder Gulch. On a less continental scale, postal matter went adrift wherever there were duplicated or nearly identical names in the Territory. Occasionally there were three of a kind. Multiple use of the same words for different places led the editor of an early newspaper to suggest action by the legislature to put the assignment of names under some kind of control. This never happened, of course, and there continued to be originals and carbons of such favorites as Boulder, Elkhorn and Beaver Creek, besides less likely pairs such as Marysvilles, Park Cities, Ophirs, Finns and Carrolls. There were several Junctions, and altogether the editors as well as the mail sorters had to do some guessing.

Of course the Post Office Department did not establish offices with duplicate names within the Territory, and often required changes whenever words looked too much alike. Gwendale had to change to Morristown to avoid confusion with Glendale, not many miles distant. Also, they maintained a register where name changes were recorded, and tried to keep their people informed on the best handling of letters addressed to discontinued offices. But some troubles were beyond reach of these remedies. People in the Territory frequently supplied their correspondents with addresses which were not served by postoffices, and brought on further difficulties by careless writing and erratic spelling. Some of this, of course, could occur at either end of the line. For a while, all mail for Montana came to Virginia City, and if the clerks there had any clue, they would pass the item on to the office which might serve that patron or where he might be known.

There are stories of informal delivery systems which flourished (or limped along) parallel to those operated by the Government. An obliging postmaster would send a sack of mail to some outlying camp which had no office, relying on the residents there to distribute it. A common procedure was to dump the sack in a public location (floors of saloons seem to have been deemed especially public), there to be sorted out by the assembled citizenry. The fate of anything unclaimd had to be left to conjecture.

Some miraculous deliveries are recorded. An envelope originating in Europe arrived with this address:

        Rev. Catholic Clergy
        The City of Blackfoot
        Montana Territory, California
        South America

Nevertheless it reached Deerlodge, and was reported safely in the sack going the last few miles to the gold camp of Blackfoot.

Less successful was an attempt by the Helena postmaster in 1881 to find a customer for a letter addressed to "The Biggest Fool in Montana." Deciding that it was not for himself, he attempted delivery at the Legislature, then in session, but was rebuffed there. No better results came from offering it among local businessmen and the postmaster was left holding it, and he advertized for "anyone claiming the essential qualification."

Possibly mail was delayed sometimes by doubts, in the minds of those who sorted it along the way, as to whether there really were such places, even in Montana. Should one take seriously the labels on that cluster of camps strung out along Indian Creek, featuring Hog 'em and Rob 'em? It was no easier to believe the names found in the gulch above Bear's Mouth (itself bad enough), where they had Snatch 'em, Scratch Awl, and Got 'em Sure. A mail clerk may well have faltered when he picked up something addressed to Royal Hell, Montana. And into which sack should he throw an item directed to Somewhere, Montana? (This one would be delivered if it got as far as Butte or Helena, where it would be recognized as a suburb of Jefferson City.)

To digress for a moment of whimsy, what a shame it is that none of those settlements survived into the era of high school athletic teams and cheerleaders. Think what could be done with team names for squads from Lop Ear and Tar Head. What cheers could be built around Royal Hell and Snitch 'em, Sheep Dip and Bird Tail.

But what would Chambers of Commerce have done to promote growth and trade in these centers? Could they urge people to do their banking at Rob 'em, or Bilk Gulch? Or their shopping at Cheat 'em? Buy your new spring outfit at Ragtown?

Most places died of their own ailments before any such problems arose, but a few did try to soften their names, hoping to attract settlers. Ross' Hole bid for a postoffice as Rossvale, but had to settle for Sula. That flat below Helena once put on airs by shifting from Prickly Pear to just plain Pear Valley, believed to sound more attractive to timid eastern dudes. The pears continued to stick, but the name did not.

It may not be a coincidence that no town with a ridiculous or frightening name ever grew into a metropolis. Missoula did better after it shook of the Hell Gate image, Last Chance Gulch might have made it that way, but became Helena at once, so we'll never know. There have been places called Trouble and Discord, neither of which ever enjoyed a great boom. We have a couple of Dry Creeks, doomed to precarious existence and small populations: here on the edge of the desert, we flinch from Dry Creeks or Dry Anything-else. But fanciful names haven't proved attractive either — Clear Creek, Gardenland, Progress, Abundance and Sunnyside, were all expected to attract people, but none have.

We seem to prefer names which don't promise anything special — Billings, Butte, Great Falls and Missoula, all may come to mean whatever the hearer wants them to. He would not have this option with Hungry Horse or Muddy. Nor Trouble. Nor Discord.

Stanley R. Davison, Dillon, 1974

The Writer's West

The writers and their critics have been saying much about "westerns." Our Robert Taylor dealt briefly but forcefully with the subject in the 1967 MIA *Quarterly;* Owen Ulph of Reed College recently wrote "Literature and the American West" in the *American West Review;* Wallace Stegner of Stanford University discussed "History, Myth and the Western Writer" in the *American West Magazine.* These are but samples of the considerable attention currently directed at the subject of regional literature, especially that of the West. The mingling of history and writing as fields in MIA is plainly seen here. The historian hardly becomes such until he writes (not necessarily for publication) and the writer of regional literature can scarcely escape contact with the history of his area.

The problem in both fields is this: how to retain the important and distinctive elements of life in the West without sinking into the falsely romantic. It is generally agreed that few writers of either fiction or history completely solve this difficulty. When the first fictioneers tackled the West the field was theirs and no one can accuse them of stereotyping when they

152

created the characters (later to become stock) of cowboys, eastern girls, horse thieves and bandits, nor when they glamorized the land with colorful descriptions of the terrain. However, they did this so thoroughly and with such later assistance from movies and TV that it has become difficult to use a western setting for any kind of story without identifying the piece with all westerns that have gone before. One hardly dares to use words like mesa, roundup, stagecoach or cayuse, knowing that the reader will understandably brace himself for a familiar plot with the usual violence and heroics.

Mr. Taylor challenges us to improve upon all this, but his remedy is to give up utilizing the past and turn to the West of the present. This may well be worth doing, but even so I doubt that anyone will find it easy to set up a western background without slipping over into the conventional picture. Anyway, historians can't avail themselves of the suggested escape unless they confine themselves to the recent and modern, where they would feel somewhat cramped.

Stress on the colorful and picturesque has spoiled many kinds of writing on western themes, including much that qualifies as history. Even textbooks suffer. Authors who write quite calmly about other times and topics will dissolve into romantic drivel the minute their story takes them west of the Mississippi River. Violent terms, cowboy slang and fancied western vernacular replace the usually accepted diction of school books. All winds become gales, all streams torrents, all snowstorms blizzards and few wildernesses are non-howling. Cows are critters, horses are broncs and people appear desperately regional, coarse and obnoxious. One even expects to find the list of review questions at the end of the chapter will be headed "Draw, pardner!"

Similarly, outside of textbooks there is a scarcity of material about the normal activities of the frontier. Regional and state histories are strong on mention of individuals whose preeminence comes from something irregular or illegal. Far harder to find are accounts of early-day business and professional men and the achievements of artisans and builders. School children easily learn the names of Plummer's gang, but who knows about the carpenters, blacksmiths, road contractors and architects who really built the West?

Those of us who work in local history can help writers and the students by bringing to light all we can about these more worthy people and by allowing the gun-slingers and broncbusters to ride away into the sunset, with no one interested in heading them off at the pass.

Stanley Davison, Dillon, 1968

MUSIC

Montana's Community Orchestras: A Survey

Every week in seven Montana communities some 345 musicians meet to play music together. Of these fewer than 70 are professional musicians or musicians with degrees in music. The rest are strictly amateurs — people who play mostly for love . . . . The purposes of these orchestras are at least three: (1) to provide live music in a state where one may grow to maturity without ever hearing a real orchestra or even a violinist other than a purposely flat "cowboy" fiddler; (2) to provide pleasure and practice to musicians who might otherwise not get full enjoyment from their instruments; and (3) to educate, to develop the musical tastes of the community.

The Billings Symphony . . . now totaling 65 members and with the best balance of strings, wind and percussion draws its members from at least six neighboring communities. Each year five concerts are given. Its programs are varied and intelligently selected. Bozeman has two orchestras, one entirely of Montana State College people, the other extending out to include townspeople as well. The orchestra connected with the College has been in existence since the founding of the school in 1893. Programs have been drawn mostly from standard classics and light music. The orchestra in Butte . . . was organized in 1950 and has grown from a chamber group of about ten members to forty . . . . For several years it has been giving free concerts in Butte, Anaconda and at the state hospital in Warm Springs. The programs have generally been light, with a few symphonies by Mozart, Haydn and Schubert, music from stage productions, and light novelty numbers. The Flathead Symphony Orchestra in Kalispell was organized in 1952 and includes musicians from Columbia Falls, Big Fork, Eureka, Lakeside, Creston and Kalispell itself . . . . Programs have included movements from symphonies . . . operatic airs, lighter numbers. The Great Falls orchestra . . . has existed since the winter of 1947-48 . . . . It draws members from Great Falls, from Ryan Dam and Malmstrom Air Base. The Helena Symphony Orchestra was organized in 1955 under the Helena Symphony Society . . . . Four or five concerts a year are given . . . . The Missoula Civic Symphony Orchestra, founded in 1954, has played three concerts this year. Its programs have been of unusually high quality, offering major standard works and some seldom played works of quality, like the symphony in F Major by Carl von Dittersdor . . . . Since all of Montana's civic orchestras are so young it is difficult to assess their value or place in the cultural life of Montana, but their record is an encouraging one.

Adapted from the article by
Robert T. Taylor, Butte, 1956

Bravo Montana

Big Sky . . . huge state . . . not many people . . . a few moderate-sized cities. How much music can a population equaling that of Columbus, Ohio, produce in a geographic area that covers almost one hundred and fifty thousand square miles? Folks might live so far apart that they couldn't afford the time or gas necessary to get together to make music.

Some of our most exciting musical moments have come in the past two years since our arrival in Missoula — school groups, young performers, civic or community orchestras and choruses, returning native sons and daughters who have "made it" in the concert world. Obviously, there was much happening, musically, in Montana, and there had to have been for some long time, to produce the enthusiasm and quality present today all across the state. How proud we all were to hear the groups from Billings, Great Falls, Missoula and the University of Montana at the recent northwest MENC conference in Spokane, Washington, bearing out what we had been realizing all along. Not only is there a tremendous amount of musical activity and participation under the Big Sky — it is good!

How could it be otherwise when there was an orchestra active in Missoula as early as 1903? The ancestor of the Missoula Civic Symphony, it was presenting concerts when the state was still in its infancy.

Of the symphony orchestras active today, four — Butte, Billings, Helena and Missoula — were active twenty to twenty-five years ago. Great Falls symphony began in 1959 and Bozeman entered the scene in 1968.

All six orchestras have companion choruses which appear with the orchestras both in combined works or in straight choral performances. All are comprised of a combination of professional, adult amateur and student performance — city and area residents. Support sources also seem to fall into similar categories — local businesses, series subscriptions, ticket sales and the Montana Arts Council. (The Montana Arts Council also aided in gathering representatives from all the orchestras for a fruitful meeting last year.) For the most part, the orchestras have been formed, as have their choruses, as much to provide an opportunity for musical expression for the performers as to add to the cultural life of the

155

community. More likely, that addition has only been the fulfillment of a realized need for music. Steady growth has been the pattern in size of group, in the kind of local support, and in the type of music performed.

Youth activities figure in the programming of several of the orchestras. Billings and Missoula have young artist competitions, with winners appearing as soloists with the orchestras. School concert programs or special ticket prices for school groups are sponsored by Billings, Great Falls and Missoula. Great Falls, Helena, and Missoula have scholarship programs for young performers.

One could go on pointing out similarities in the activities and growth of these groups, but individual recognition is truly called for, and I'll close this portion of the article with one final observation. After several of the orchestras had been in existence for some time, a logical outgrowth seemed to be chamber music activities for some of the performers. Billings now has a Renaissance Ensemble, which performs under the aegis of Young Audiences, Inc. The Montana State University Adult Chamber Music Festival, a summer activity, was begun in 1971 and draws fifty to seventy-five players from the region. In 1973 the Montana Chamber Orchestra was formed under the sponsorship of the University of Montana. Other chamber groups include the University of Montana Woodwind Quintet and the String Quartet, who also form the core of the first-chair players in the Missoula orchestra, and the Montana Voice Quartet.

And we're not through yet, obviously! Youth programs, in addition to the many fine public school music programs, have burgeoned over the years. The Red Lodge Music Festival was well described in a recent *Montana Arts* article by Mary Hauf; The Montana State University Chamber Music Festival for young people has been in existence since 1957; and the University of Montana Fine Arts Camp since 1936, although recent trends have resulted in a temporary revamping of the Fine Arts Camp into the Montana High School Chamber Music Workshop. It was originally a music camp and became a fine arts camp during the mid-sixties.

High school students, mainly from Montana, but also from other states, comprise the personnel for these programs. While some of the students end up attending the university where they attend "camp," not all do. However, these experiences have provided grounds for the decision by many young musicians to seriously pursue music, because of the intense exposure to what a life of music might be. Conversely, it has aided some students to realize that music is important to them as an avocation only.

At Bozeman, the program is directed by department chairman Creech

Reynolds, Montana State University faculty members and guest artists, for a group which has grown from thirty-five to seventy-five. The guests serve as coaches for small chamber groups. The festival began with strings and piano only and has since added wind players and a choral group. Financial support has come from registration fees, the Montana State University Department of Music, and the Montana Arts Council.

The University of Montana Fine Arts Music Camp is directed by the University of Montana Faculty members and guest artists. Offerings have included academic courses and performances in the visual arts, dance, drama and music (band, chorus, orchestra, vocal and instrumental chamber groups). Financial support has come from registration fees, the University of Montana School of Fine Arts and the Montana Arts Council. Registration for the camp has varied between one hundred and two hundred.

When one stops to consider the number of private music teachers necessary to help to prepare young students to become performing musicians, in addition to the many school music directors, not to mention the obstacles presented to a rancher's youngster in seeking private music instruction, the Montana music scene is staggering in yet another light.

Music is obviously a vital part of the life of Montanans. To recapitulate the original theme: "Bravo Montana!"

Extracts from an article by
Patricia K. Simmons, Missoula, 1975

Montana Composers of Music

The Montana Composers' Forum, the musical part of the 1957 MIA Festival, proved to be a very successful venture. Ten Montana composers presented some of their work for the enjoyment of Montanans genuinely interested in music as a field of creative expression. Ranging from the secular to the sacred and from the simple to the complex, the compositions were evidence that creativity in music is a real entity among Montana musicians.

The ten Montana composers whose works were presented were: Mrs. Madge B. Peck and Mr. John Lassilla of Great Falls; Mr. Robert Beers, Mr. Malcolm W. Lewis, Mr. John Schwarzkopf, Mrs. Irene McPherson and Mr. John Selleck of Billings; Mrs. Dora Athearn of Butte; Mr. Eugene Weigel and Mr. Lawrence Coloff of Missoula. These composers were assisted by Mrs. Hugo Kenck, soprano of Butte; Miss Joan Bergland, reader, of Billings; the University of Montana Trio of Missoula — Mr. Eugene Andrie, violinist, Miss Florence Reynolds, cellist, Mr. Rudolf Wendt, pianist, assisted by Mr. Eugene Weigel, violinist, and Mr. Justin Gray, clarinetist.

Of all the music activities in Montana it is believed that this kind of program is of vital importance inasmuch as it provides an opportunity for Montana composers to get a hearing for their efforts in music. It is analogous to an art show in which painters have the chance to hang their paintings regardless of technical development or style of painting used. An opportunity for music composers to "hang their pictures" is equally important.

A pre-Festival which might be well emulated by other Montana communities occurred in Billings. Radio Station KOOK presented three of the Billings composers in a performance of some of their compositions in a half-hour broadcast. Mr. Cliff Ewing, KOOK Program Director, engineered and directed the broadcast from the home of Mr. Robert Beers, one of the composers, the others being Mrs. McPherson and Mr. Lewis. The program was of an informal nature in which conversation was interspersed with musical numbers. Mrs. McPherson performed her vocal composition, "Interlude," a musical setting of a poem by Carol Myers, and her piano composition, "Aurora Borealis"; Mr. Lewis played a recording of his "String Quartet, with Oboe and Piano"; Mr. Beers played his composition, "Rain Forest," written for the rare, antique instrument the psaltery, as well as his "Scherzo Antique," a composition for violin, for which the accompaniment was played by Miss Lorene Bates, also of Billings. Mrs. Evelyn Beers sang an arrangement of a Spanish folk tune by Mrs. Beers. All these compositions and others were presented at the MIA Festival program.

Adapted from an account by
Alfred W. Humphreys, Helena, 1957

Red Lodge Music Festival

The growth of the Red Lodge Music Festival is attributed to the national reputation the Festival has earned. Professional artists and music teachers from the four corners of the United States inspire and teach students from the cities and rural communities of Montana, a well as from other states.

The 1974 Festival enjoyed more than a twenty-five percent increase in

attendance, a total of 127 students participated. During the 1973 Tenth
Anniversary Year 94 students participated. Five students for every teacher
make superior instruction possible.

Instructors for the 1975 Festival faculty will be Arthur Tollefson, pianist
at the University of Maryland, who has concertized with the Severence
Quartet of the Cleveland Symphony; William Steck, violinist and concertmaster of the Atlanta Symphony; Noel Collins, brass specialist and
graduate of Rocky Mountain College, whose band, composed of youth
from Carbon, Yellowstone and Stillwater Counties, won an invitation to
perform at the Expo in Spokane; James Ogle, clarinetist, conductor and
prize-winning participant in an international competition in
Copenhagen.

Mary Hauf, Billings, 1975

PAINTING

About Painting

We all know, of course, that painting is only one of the arts. To the
painter, its particular fascination is this: No other art form has such an
immediate concentration of the elements that go into any art — shape,
color, space, scale and movement.

The painter's adventure can grow out of his response to a particular bit
of nature (the "real," more or less abstracted), and it can also grow out of
painting itself ("non-objective," or no recognizable object whatsoever).

No matter the stimulus or what "style" it is labeled, adventure itself is
the ingredient that lives and has sustained the painter and thus works its
way out of the painting and into a receptive, and also adventurous,
spectator. When this happens, the painting exists as a fact in itself, not as a
substitute for a kodachrome of a subject or as a tasteful accent of the
interior decoration, but as itself. It has become a highly utilitarian object
to the spirit.

A working painter often turns his work upside down so he can see "it".
Such an act mystifies the layman, but to the painter the subject often
raises its many possibilities all at once and, worst of all, in one small area,
and so it must be suppressed and held in check until one of its many facets
loses its identity and becomes a color shape to fit the whole visual idea.
This is nothng new, not a trick of "modern" art. A story is told of Courbet,

159

a French painter of the last century, a "realist," (when that was new), who was calmly observing his painting (right side up) from a distance when a friend asked him what the object was in the lower left. Courbet didn't recall, though it was quite realistically painted. He had to walk up and identify it as a bunch of sticks. He didn't know what it was, but he knew it was brownish, so big, and going this way.

The layman looks at paintings and judges in his own terms. A carpenter calls wood birch, maple or pine, not color shape; a horticulturist looks for zinnia, evergreen, and buffalo grass, not color shape; (but there is also a legend that a painter lost his life beneath a traffic signal looking at red, yellow and green instead of stop, caution and go!)

Non-objective painting, the prevalent international style of our time, strips itself of all reference to nature in its very intention and purpose. It is often led out of this seeming wilderness by the spectator who joyfully or woefully plunges into his encyclopedic task of identification.

We have all enjoyed the lazy sport of gazing at the clouds and seeing great ships, fish, and pretty girls. The layman feels no offence when he is gently reminded that they are, after all, just clouds. But before a painting of pure shape and color, the shift to *its* reality is tremendous. Is it because a pure paint shape, identifying nothing else, has no seeming utility? After all we know what clouds are for.

Painting is difficult for the layman to evaluate, but the painter's purpose is not that of pleasing the public. To be honest, he must deal with his own visual sensations and thoughts, not those of others. The penetration of his own thought and feeling is not a social activity. He may be willing to share the results, but he won't trade his eye for yours.

Robert K. DeWeese, Bozeman, 1954

The Observer and Modern Art

It is common knowledge that the majority of people will react favorably to factual paintings, paintings which are close copies of nature. However, if we begin with the idea that art is a copy of nature and is created with the single purpose of decorating a livingroom, we are using a false premise. Pictures should be observed as entities, things in themselves.

In order to appreciate modern art it is necessary to see a great many originals. Montanans are at a disadvantage in the field of art because of the few opportunities to see paintings. There is not a museum in the state that

160

has a permanent collection of good examples of modern art (1951). Unless a person has the chance to see exhibits in some of the larger museums in the country, he is handicapped in appreciating many contemporary paintings. Good reproductions, prints and slides are substitutes for originals; they may differ greatly in color and are never accurate in paint quality.

Everyone enjoys listening to some type of music, but the percentage preferring the classical is a small one. How much is music the imitation of natural sounds? Is it not abstract form which we hear? Music is created from elements and worked into order or composition in a way not unlike painting. I am not able to explain why visual abstraction should be any different from aural.

An historical background and an explanation of a few terms will aid in the appreciation of modern art. "Modern" has been used as a classification for most contemporary paintings that are not objectively naturalistic or realistic. "Naturalism" and "realism" are two terms often confused. Naturalism is applied to paintings that are photographic in quality, the particular; realism is the universal in the particular. It may be a tree without being a particular tree.

In 1874 the French school of Impression caused a great stir in the art world by presenting to the public paintings handled in a manner different from the conventional. This group of artists employed a technique of painting which used subject matter under various conditions of light. In other words, they attempted to paint light and air on the canvas. Traditional colors and application of colors were changed. Shadows were no longer brown, edges were fused, and the use of broken color and juxtaposition of color were practiced. Today impressionism is misused in describing modern art in general; it should be confined almost entirely to the style of painting just explained. Critics denounced these men as poor draftsmen and extremists, but today one does not think of this type of painting as modern or extreme.

Toward the end of the century other artists felt that the Impressionists were losing form in landscapes, figures, and still lifes. The use of color was becoming scientific rather than expressive. This later group has since been labeled Post-Impressionists, although the term Expressionists has also been added. At one time expressionism was used in reference to the German school of subjective expressionism, which was strictly a strong emotional type of painting. Now expressionism is generalized into the strong use of form, texture, line, and color, regardless of subject-matter, but the paintings may still be emotional. Cezanne, Gaugin, and Van Gogh were masters of the Post-Impressionism period.

Other strong influences in the art world came about with the discovery in 1879 of prehistoric cave painting and of primitive negro sculpture at the beginning of the twentieth century. These discoveries prompted a greater interest in the primitive arts of all periods and countries. Two examples are the Italian primitive painters and archaic Greek sculpture. The use of symbols became an important mode of expression, and recent artists have invented new symbols or new interpretations of universal symbols.

During the last fifty years many changes have come about in modern art. At present we are in a state of flux. Obviously it is not easy to say just what paintings or schools of painting will withstand the test of time. I feel that we are in an exciting period of art history and that it is a great century of notable progress in the fine arts.

With this as background, what should be looked for or what is to be expected from modern painting? First, the observer must accept the fact that the artist may not be trying to reproduce a section of nature. He may have been working away from nature for an abstract effect. There are degrees of abstraction and distortion which are probably not realized by many observers. A line drawing of a figure or a landscape is literally an abstraction, even if it is accurately drawn. The transference of a three-dimensional object to a two-dimensional plane creates a distortion, and the use of line employs an element that does not exist in nature. In drawing a table seen from certain positions only three legs may be visible. Is this necessarily reality, when we know that the table has four legs? An object painted without proper perspective should not be disturbing, because the artist feels at liberty to make any changes he deems necessary in composing his picture. He considers such things as the size and the proportion of the canvas, form, color, line, texture, value, and direction. These are abstract elements which, organized by variable principles, make up a composition.

A painting that has unidentifiable forms or geometric forms is termed non-objective or pure abstraction. The artist may spend as much time in arranging such forms as another artist would in a detailed realistic painting. The ultimate goal is a painting that has the parts composed so as to make a unified total. The changing of one section could throw off the balance. Since a non-objective painting tells no story the observer must regard the work on some other basis. He should look at the color and value relationships, the use of curved or straight lines or the combination of types of lines, harmony of form, and spaces. The space around an object, or negative space, is as important as the object itself. The observer should think of these things as the subject and see if there is a reaction. Individuals will react differently to the same painting, which is as it should

162

be. Life would be dull if all our likes were the same.

Before uttering the phrases, "I don't know much about art, but I know what I like," or "A child could do as well," the observer should stop to think. Similar phrases were written by French critics about Impressionism in the nineteenth century, and the school of painting became an important one. The reason why some paintings look childish is that the artist has striven for the strong, simple emotional experiences of the child, without the ramifications and complications of life. How fantastic it is to hear some of the stories that are a child's imagination. In the growing-up process the world becomes more materialistic, and the wonderful make-believe world fades. There are artists who lack the ability to draw with complete accuracy but who are proficient in forceful expression. Grandma Moses is a leading example of this type. She is classified as a primitive painter because of not having had formal art training. Other painters have fine drawing ability but attempt to express themselves with the vigor of the true primitive. In this style of painting the observer should not be too critical of the drawing without noting the other factors I have mentioned.

A great genius like Pablo Picasso has gone through many periods or styles. His early training was academic, and his first paintings were excellent realistic paintings. Since then he has been experimental and inventive and has been perhaps the strongest leader in modern art. His interpretations were sometimes influenced by previous forms, but his paintings were still innovations. Creating new methods of expression is not a simple process. Picasso has done many paintings with the distortion of human form. A head with two faces can be translated as motion or time lapse, since a front view and a profile are never seen simultaneously. This approach should be considered before a censure of drawing ability is offered.

Without an open-minded attitude or an honest desire to enjoy modern paintings, this source of enrichment of life will never be ours. The process takes time.

Adapted from an article by
James E. Dew, Missoula, 1951

Why Paint Abstract Pictures?

One of the first questions asked any artist is, What is abstract art? and again, Why doesn't an artist paint what he sees? and, What does the picture mean?

The term "abstract" as applied to art is difficult to define, and most artists prefer to have their work called "contemporary." Often two people debating the merits of abstract art begin with premises based on different images, for there are many kinds of abstract art. But while all paintings have many elements of the abstract in them, and the plastic qualities of abstract art are found in all the great art of the past, for the purpose of this discussion the term "abstract" may be used as a description of paintings and sculpture in which there is little reference to nature. Abstract artists are experimenting with space, form and color, all more or less removed from any associations outside of the picture frame. The forms and colors should have a life of their own, should exist in their own right. The "modern" artist addresses himself to this severe and difficult program of creation.

It is not generally realized that abstract art is not new. In the arts of primitive peoples all kinds of abstract designs are common, and some abstraction is present in Greek ornament, Flemish and German painters of the fifteenth and sixteenth centuries, in the work of Renaissance artists when ideal not realistic faces and colors were used, and so on. However, not until the twentieth century did abstract art become dominant in the history of Western art.

In this country the 1913 Armory Show in New York gave the first strong impetus toward abstraction. Hutchins Hapgood, writing in the New York *Globe,* commented, "We are living at a most interesting moment in the political, industrial and social development of America." The Armory exhibition contained 1600 pieces of painting and sculpture made up of foreign art and art of a more liberal tendency than was being produced here. The pictures were so "different" that the shock to the public was tremendous — "howls of dismay from academic circles and conservative critics split the heavens."

Here is a quotation from an artist, Macdonald-Wright, written about 1913, "I strive to divest art of all anecdote and illustration, and to purify it to the point where the emotions of the spectator will be wholly esthetic, as when listening to music. Illustrative music is a thing of the past; music has become abstract and purely esthetic, dependent for its effect upon rhythm and form. Painting, certainly, need not lag behind music." At the

164

same time Morgan Russell wrote, "While there will probably always be illustrative pictures, it cannot be denied that this century may be the flowering of a new art of forms and colors alone. Personally, I believe that non-illustrative painting is the purest manner of esthetic expression, and that provided the basic demands of good composition are adhered to, the emotional effect will be even more intense than if there were present the obstacle of representation."

The Gallery of Living Art, New York University, was opened in 1927. Until then no museum of this character had existed in the United States, the most modern of all countries. It was founded by A.E. Gallatin so that the public might have an opportunity to study the newer influences at work in twentieth century painting. In the Introduction to the Gallery catalog an article by James Johnson Sweeney states, "The predominant characteristics of creative work in the plastic arts since the turn of the century has been critical: Creative movements militating against restrictive conventions . . . . Space for 400 years had been represented by linear perspective, conceived from a fixed point of view. Artists came to believe that this conception of space was one-sided. From it no true sense of space as such — that is to say, its extension in all directions — could be had. To provide this it would be necessary for the painter's vision to move about within the picture space, not merely to regard it from the outside. By a depiction of various disparate aspects of the picture-space, which arranged side by side in the canvas would be seen simultaneously, the painter might hope to give the observer a genuine realization of three-dimensionality. But now that the absolute perspective had been abandoned, the logic of natural appearances could no longer be leaned on to give a picture unity. If all logic of natural appearance may be put aside, there is no reason why the artist may not express himself directly, with only a subconscious memory of forms to depend on and with no naturalistic intent."

Irving Kriesberg, a young contemporary artist, says the same, "the objects in my paintings are shown not as taken from a fixed point of view nor at a single instant of time. I see that nature is in motion and change, and that is what I paint." Joseph Glasco, another young artist, agrees, "Painting for me does not consist in something I have seen but in something I am. There is not 'subject matter.' My heads are perhaps landscapes and my landscapes heads. They are interior thoughts that exist in my heart and mind and not in my eyes."

It is possible to give various explanations for the position of contemporary European and American artists. First, the invention of the still and motion-picture camera made obsolete the skill of the artist in copying a scene realistically. Then the artist came to dislike the patronage of wealthy clients of no artistic taste who wished careful copies of nature or flattering portraits. Thirdly, developing scientific ideas seemed to be intuitively sensed by the artist. As far back as 1895, Kandinsky, who was a great modern painter and teacher, was profoundly impressed by new ideas on time and space and the decomposition of nature. He evolved the idea that a solid object is an invention, unconnected with reality. As the philosopher Whitehead says, "We know now that a piece of granite is a raging mass of activity. Whether the change occurs in a minute or in billions of years is merely a matter of human measurement. Two wine glasses stand on a table — the glasses are raging with molecular activity, and if we were not in the habit of measuring time by the ridiculously inadequate yardstick of our consciousness in the human life span, we should remember that those glasses are disintegrating before our very eyes."

In less scientific terms, Kandinsky says, "The threadbare concept of the imitation of nature has blinded us to the spiritual reality underlying appearance." He used color to create space and tension, and he used lines, points and planes to organize the picture plane. Miro, another painter, tells the story of an oil painting, a copy of rocks, grass and mountains, that was placed outdoors on a hill, leaning against a rock. To one going off at a distance and surveying the picture it appeared a ridiculous burlesque of the actual landscape. On the other hand, an "abstract" painting of lines, planes, shapes and colors formed a unity with nature and seemed to express its underlying reality.

Still many people remain confused, resentful and resistant to abstract art. There is still the belief that a picture painted "by hand" in oils is an achievement, that a precise copy of a tree, a sunset, or a person is difficult and wonderul. But suppose the tree *is* copied accurately, its outline, the leaves, the branches, the apples. What is the result? Only an imitation, never as good as the real living tree. What good reason is there for copying it? A color photograph would give an even better likeness.

Gertrude Stein has written at length on how she feels when she looks at an oil painting, and of her dissatisfaction with copies of nature: "Once an oil painting is painted, I can always look at it and it always holds my attention. The painting may be good, it may be bad, medium or very bad, or very good, but anyway I like to look at it. And now, why does the representation of things that being painted do not look at all like the things look to me from which they are painted. Why does such a representation give me pleasure and hold my attention? Ah, yes, well this I do not know and I do not know whether I ever will know this. When I look at a landscape or people or flowers they do not look to me like pictures, no not

166

at all. On the other hand pictures for me do not have to look like flowers or people or landscapes or houses or anything else. Should a picture look like anything or does it, even a Courbet or a Valasquez, or does it make any difference if it does or if it does not as long as it is an oil painting. You see it does get complicated. Gradually I realized, as I had already found out, very often that there is a relation between anything that is painted and the painting of it. And gradually I realized that the relation between the oil painting and the thing painted was really nobody's business.

"But still one always does like a resemblance. Most people think that the annoyance that they feel from an oil painting that annoys them comes from the way the oil painting represents things. But I myself do not think so. I think the annoyance comes from the fact that the oil painting exists by reason of those things the oil painting represents and profoundly it should not do so. Really in everybody's heart there is a feeling of annoyance at the existence of an oil painting in relation to what it has painted — people, objects and landscapes. The oil painting exists as a painting on a flat surface and it has its own life and like it or not there it is."

When the ability to imitate is the essential criterion there can be no creative art. Only the surface appearance of things is copied. Perhaps the evolution of one artist from a conventional viewpoint to a creative experimental one, is illustrated by Moholy-Nagy. He attained world recognition as a painter, photographer, sculptor, art educator, was outstanding in every phase of industrial art. He writes: "I did not begin as an abstract painter. I had no difficulty in 'understanding' the Renaissance painters — Raphael's madonnas, the dignity of Michelangelo. It did not occur to me that beyond the illustration of a mythological and religious story, pictures must have other qualities. I spent much time in drawing and in trying to express something only with lines. I underwent an exciting experience. I used auxiliary lines where no lines would ordinarily be used, and the result was a complicated network of a peculiar spatial quality. The drawings became a rhythmically articulated network of lines, showing not so much objects as excitement about them.   Observing other painters — Van Gogh, Kokoschka, Marc — I discovered that for them nature was only a point of departure. Lines become diagrams of inner forces. I made a drawing; there were no objects, only lines, straight and curved. Wheels and bridges scattered on the sheet were the only shapes derived from nature. I called the drawing 'Build! Build!' I discovered that composition is directly by an unconscious sense of order in regard to the relations of color, shape, position, etc.

"One day I found a sketch for an oil painting did not carry out my intention. Cutting away some parts of the drawing and turning at an angle some of his most complete pictures have been finished in a few sessions. On the other hand, the picture "Exotic Dance" took him weeks of constant painting and repainting. His latest work shows an increasing trend towards abstraction. Color loses its literal relation to form; natural form acts as a springboard for the invention of plastic fantasies. His drawing and line are not an outline of form but a living thing itself, with an abstract beauty of its own. However, he says, "I do not believe in pure abstraction; my work is still linked to reality and human association. Art must keep its roots in the soil of human experience and emotion."

If serious achievement in art demands the total involvement of the artist, how much can the amateur hope to accomplish, the person who can only spend a small part of his time in painting, crafts or other art forms? To quote again from Moholy-Nagy, he believes that anyone has great potentialities for creative expression, if he can liberate himself from the things in the present way of life that crush these impulses. Skills in handcrafts have been mostly superseded by machines, so that for the average person, his goal is not to express himself or to think independently, but to apply his education to the running of machines according to instructions. The "hidden persuaders" are influencing our views of art and science, of how we shall spend our leisure hours. Is there any creative activity in watching TV? In a world of positive thinking, why, just for the fun of it, should a person spend some hours a week painting a picture that does not look like anything when it is done?

It is hard, though, to stifle completely our creative nature. It can't be done completely, and if the part-time artist will start to draw or paint with the freedom from self-consciousness and fear of failure that a little child has, the gain will be a deep sense of satisfaction. Let him believe that a successful creative expression demands the involvement of the person, and that to copy involves him only a little and with an empty result.

It is also richly rewarding to understand and enjoy another artist's picture. The spectator must be involved himself; he cannot be a passive onlooker. Unfortunately, he often is. But, if he cannot see any satisfying order and force, is it the picture's fault? Think of a picture frame not as a window leading the eye into the distance, but as a boundary enclosing an area of canvas, which is an object in its own right. The modern artist is trying to express by means of images the functions beneath the surface of appearances. The spectator must learn to follow the artist into the world of pure creation, to enjoy with him forms, colors, rhythms, for their own sake, apart from any subject.

It is not possible to make any definitive judgement about contemporary art. Much of the abstract art being produced today may look as flat and of 90 degrees I was satisfied. It occured to me that if I could make such changes in a sketch, I could also decide with the same freedom the shapes and colors in my oil painting. I eliminated the perspective in my former paintings. I simplified everything to geometrical shapes, flat unbroken colors.

"This event marked the turning-point in my existence as a painter. I often had the feeling when pasting my collages and painting my abstract pictures that I was throwing a message, sealed in a bottle, into the sea. It might take decades for someone to find and read it. Abstract art, I thought, creates new types of spatial relationships, new inventions of forms, new visual laws as the visual counterpart to a more purposeful co-operative human society.

"My belief is that mathematical harmonious shapes, executed precisely, can be filled with emotional quality, and that they represent the perfect balance between feeling and intellect. I made sculpture from wood, glass, nickel-plated metal, plastics and other material. I made countless experiments in trying to paint with light, translated into color. My stage direction and abstract motion picture work grew out of the same interest. Many of us have departed from the old canons and obsolete conventions to a new space articulation, trying to define intuitively the need of our time for vision in motion."

Not all artists can express themselves as clearly as this, nor do they seem to understand their motivations. But brief statements from various painters show that they are searching. Arthur Dove says, "There was always a search for means of expression that did not depend on representation. It should have order, size, intensity, spirit, nearer to the music of the eye. If one could paint the art that goes to make the spirit of painting and leave out all that just makes tons and tons of art!"

To give an accurate account of present-day painting it is proper to quote some artists who continue to paint in a representational manner. One man, Herbert Katzman, says, "I do not paint abstractly because if I give up the appearance of the world I find I am unable to become involved in it. The subject itself means very much to me," and another, Herman Rose, "I always paint specific scenes and people or situations. For me it is not possible to recreate human emotions and perceptions without the physical shapes of the world that gave these feeling birth."

One more quotation, this one from Max Weber, one of our great living artists. With him, painting is an intensely emotional process. He keeps his canvasses by him and paints on many at the same time. Often on returning to a picture he cannot touch it, or sometimes even bear to look at it, and turns it face to the wall until another day. He is a very fast worker and shallow in a few decades as the average academic work of fifty years ago. The abstract art which survives may be that which is richest in content as well as strongest in form. Critics of modern art may justly find qualities they dislike, but these criticisms cannot possibly apply to the whole of contemporary art. The new art is recognized at first by the relatively few.

Virginia Woolf's observation about current literature applies to contemporary art: "Much of what is best in contemporary work has the appearance of being made under pressure, taken down in a bleak shorthand which preserves with astonishing brilliance the movements and expressions of the fingers as they flash across the screen. But the flash is soon over and there remains with us the profound dissatisfaction. It is an age of fragments."

True, this is an age of violent experimental work, but we may be on the verge of a great age in art. It is more exciting to live in a time of experimental modernism than in a period of decadence or even maturity.

Helen McAuslan, McLeod, 1959

For What Is The Amateur Painter Working?

Santayana has said, "The subject matter of art is life as it actually is; but the function of art is to make life better." Robert Henri has written:

> When the artist is alive in any person, whatever his kind of work may be, he becomes an inventive, searching, daring, selfexpressing creature. He becomes interesting to other people. He disturbs, upsets, enlightens and he opens the way for better understanding. The world would stagnate without him, and the world would be beautiful with him; for he is interesting to himself and he is interesting to others.

Since this discussion regards the objectives of the amateur painter, our entire concern is with him. Who is he? He may be the Sunday or part-time painter. He may be the trained or the untrained. He may be the painter who does not sell or sells to oblige friends rather than for economic gain. He may be that one who paints for emotional enjoyment and release rather than from emotional necessity. One thing we do know: he is neither a dabbler nor dilettante. The amateur is a serious painter.

The Museum of Modern Art has defined the amateur as a layman who does not have special talent, and who works only for his own satisfaction, finding art activity at once gratifying experience and a means toward a

170

better understanding of art, present and past. Who is to say that he does or does not have talent? What is talent? For our purposes let us define the amateur as that individual who paints seriously but does not paint for a living.

Then why does he paint? What is his purpose? Amusement? Never. Pleasure? Yes. One amateur has said, ". . . for sheer enjoyment and to learn what makes good painting." Another has said he paints for release from the pressures of living. Yet another paints for self-expression that will rid him of the frustrations created by today's world.

If the amateur painter's objective is pleasure, self-expression, emotional releases and appreciation, he should become immediately aware of the basic concepts of art: an understanding of line, color, form, texture, space and motion. He should develop an appreciation of the possibilities of various materials and a knowledge of their characteristics. (How he does this is not important.) With a simple text on art it is very easy to study and understand what these fundamentals are. He may choose to learn them by working with a class or group. The end results will be the same. Once he has gotten interested, his natural acquisitiveness will carry him along searching and working for greater understanding of these fundamental concepts.

Why, you ask, should the person who is painting entirely for pleasure bother to study? Why should he expand his knowledge of materials, color relations, elements of form or design, when the charm of amateur painting is in its artlessness — its lack of sophistication? Will this not destroy the very thing for which he is working? Rather it should increase his pleasure by giving him the ability to adventure, to explore, to discover. New ways of seeing, new ways of feeling, new ways of using his materials should awaken him to new and greater delights with paint.

While the joy of amateur painting comes from the freedom, spontaniety, and often naivete of the use of color, the amateur can profit by study of what color is. Learning the qualities of color or color relationships will not confuse or involve. Instead, such learning will free him of prejudices and biases so deeply rooted they seem inherent. Such ideas as that sunset is always orange, flesh is made by adding ochre and cadmium red to white, never put pink and red together, tree trunks are brown. When we know the elementary principles of color, their tonalities and harmonies, we are free to combine them in any way we desire without fearing the results. We learn that color can be lively, restless, positive, bold, cool, heavy, advancing, receding, light, dead. We learn how and how not to create "mud." Color becomes ours to experiment with and try to command.

What is true of color is true of line. The heavy line. The broken line. Recently, in a workshop where a grey-haired lady who was admittedly an amateur was working for an angry line, we watched her slashing her brush vindictively across the page, saying to herself quite audibly, "Just how angry can I get!" Line in itself can become a complete adventure, continuing into the direction line, the contour line, the line of action — in an ever widening circle of knowledge.

All that has been said of line and color may be said of texture. The feeling of bark, of flesh. How to register that feeling with paint.

The creation of mass. Of volume — how to make things feel big, how to make things feel heavy.

Value. The dramatization possible with contrasts of dark and light.

Space. To create the feelings of earth's infinity.

How to organize. To compose the picture plane so that things happen thereon.

Soon the amateur learns that a work of art is a "thing created nearest to the heart's desire." He ceases to think of the postcard, the calendar, the theatrical illustration. He forgets there were ever such things as so-called rules and senses that his work is not a copying of nature but a putting together of elements to create a work of art which responds to its own laws of being rather than to an order imposed by the outer world of our senses.

With this beginning the amateur can go on and on, always remembering that great results only come with great effort. There is no such thing as getting more for something than is put into it.

With constant drawing and painting, with keen observation of surroundings, with the acquisitiveness born of increased knowledge, only form, design, beauty can result. If the desire is to paint realistically, the painter will simplify, clarify, invent new means of making his painting more real. If the desire is to express feeling, the feeling will be greater. If the desire is to express relationships, dynamics, to symbolize, to abstract, to become more contemporary than the latest innovator, the door is open and the amateur may pass through.

Part of an article by
Isabelle Johnson, Absarokee, 1952

Encaustic Painting

Although encaustic painting is one of the oldest painting methods, most people know nothing about it. Until recently it was not a common technique, and the few who experimented were very secretive about their formulas and little was written on the subject. The first book to include the history of the medium and contemporary working methods was *Encaustic,* by Frances Pratt and Becca Fizell, published in 1949.

Encaustic means literally ''burning in'' and is basically a hot-wax painting process. Different types of painting are ordinarily classified by the binder which combines with pigment to cause the adherence to a surface. Examples are casein (milk) for opaque watercolor and lime plaster for fresco painting. Because of the inert quality of wax the oldest examples of encaustic paintings are still in an excellent state of preservation.

The oldest examples are from the Fayyum district in Egypt and date back to the second century A.D. However, the origin is not Egyptian but Greek, even though no examples from Greece are extant. The mummy portraits discovered in the 1880s are attributed to members of a Greek colony which had migrated to Egypt in the Hellenistic period.

Until the present time there has been no individual who has become known in the art field because of this particular painting medium. Perhaps the painter who has been most influential in reviving the process is Karl Zerbe, a teacher at the Boston Museum School. Seeing one of his paintings, a still life of a fish, over twenty years ago was my first experience with the unique surface textures which may be achieved. It was many years before I did any experimenting, because of the lack of available material. When the Pratt-Fizell book was published I was surprised to learn that each one of the contemporary artists had his own recipe, including a number of waxes and resins in varying proportions.

The general formula which I have been using is a mixture of damar resin crystals, pulverized and dissolved in turpentine, which is melted in a double boiler with sunbleached beeswax in about the proportion of one part of resin to four parts wax. The resultant medium has a tough plasticity which the beeswax alone does not have, being quite brittle in its natural state. Next I use the medium with tube oil paints, blended with heat on an electric palette designed especially for encaustic painting. The palette is a recent acquisition. Previously I was using a muffin tin over a hot plate, but I was not pleased with the inconsistency of the heat. At present I am able to have more control of the temperature, which is important. Dry color may be substituted as a means of eliminating all the oil, but this is an added expense and is apparently unnecessary for permanence since many recipes call for oil.

All of my paintings have been on gesso ground masonite panels, which I prepare in quantity. With cold (room temperature) panels the paint sets immediately and does not allow for the freedom of brush work as in oil painting. It is possible to paint on prepared linen canvas, but most painters prefer a more rigid support. I can cite nothing specific from experience about the use of canvas.

Various ways are employed for the burning-in process, but heat lamps and torches are the most common. I use a propane blowtorch and direct the flame onto the surface of the painting without unpleasant effects on the paint or gesso. Edges may be blended in this way or the whole surface may be smoothed as a final effect or as underpainting. The remelting of the wax is supposed to assist in binding the picture to the ground. Interesting textures are obtained by putting one color over another, which can be done almost immediately, and scratching through with a palette knife or razor blade. Sometimes I use a glaze of dark oil paint thinned in turpentine which is rubbed over the surface with a cloth. The dark color goes into the deep cracks in the brush strokes and is scratched off the higher areas when a razor blade is dragged across the surface.

A definite advantage over oil painting is that the oil-wax mixture may be left on the palette for a long period of time and will become usable when reheated. A disadvantage of the medium is the inability to withstand very warm or very cold temperatures. Encaustic paintings are likely to melt under heat and crack with cold exposure. Also, the surface is fairly vulnerable to scratches, so that care must be taken to protect it when storing or shipping.

To me encaustic painting is a very exiciting and versatile technique, and I expect to continue experimenting with it. I do not expect it will become very popular, because it is difficult to manipulate. In the meantime I am working with another rapid dryer, polyvinyl acetate emulsion, which sets in five minutes and requires no heat. My advice is not to attempt encaustic painting or work with some of the plastics without having a great deal of experience with oil painting first.

James E. Dew, Missoula, 1954

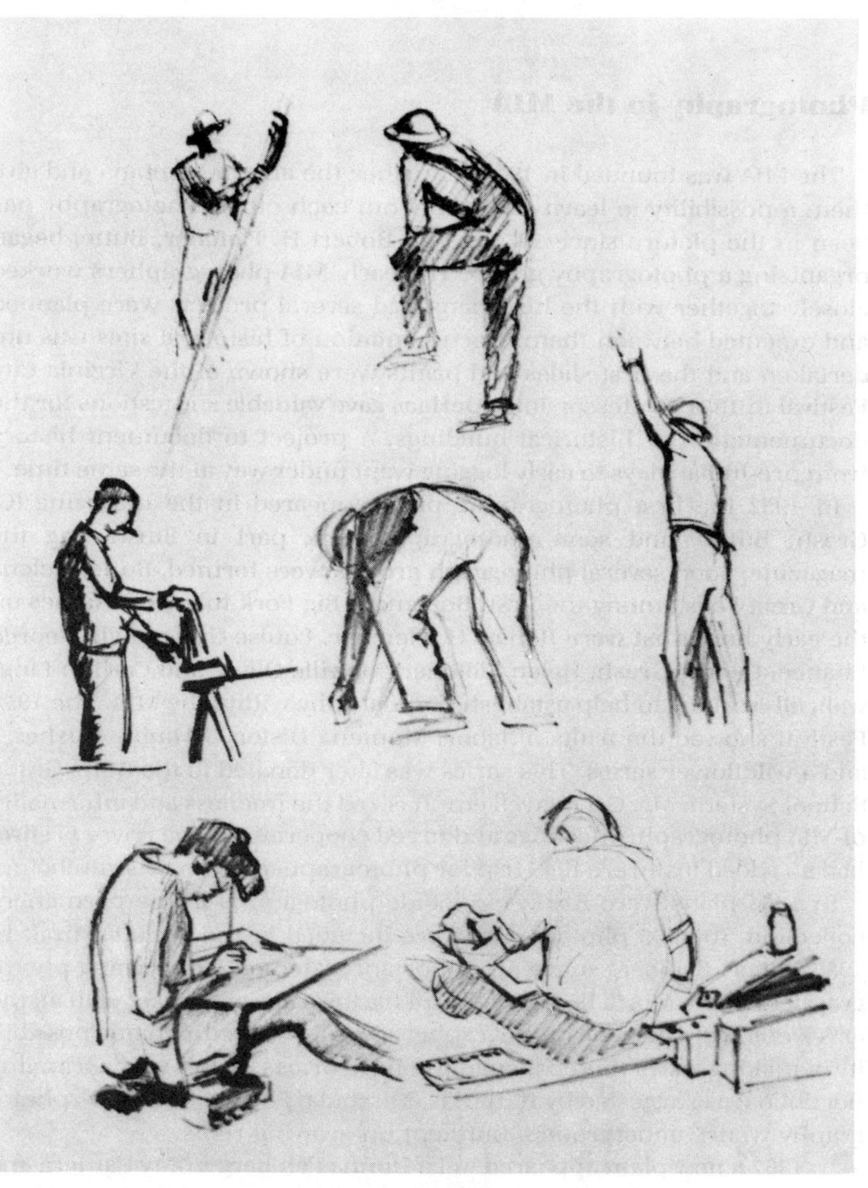

Sketches, James E. Dew

PHOTOGRAPHY

Photography in the MIA

The MIA was founded in 1948 to further the arts in Montana and give them a possibility to learn and gain from each other. Photography has been in the picture since 1950, when Robert H. Fletcher, Butte, began organizing a photography group. The early MIA photographers worked closely together with the historians and several projects were planned and executed between them. Documentation of historical sites was undertaken and the first slides and prints were shown at the Virginia City Festival in 1951. Professor John DeHaas gave valuable suggestions for the documentation of historical buildings. A project to document history from pre-Indian days to early logging went under way at the same time.

In 1952 the first photographic print appeared in the magazine (G. Gresh, Butte), and soon photography took part in illustrating the magazine. Soon several photograph groups were formed, Butte, Helena and Great Falls among the first. Bozeman, Big Fork followed. Names on the early honor list were Robert H. Fletcher, Louise Greenough, George Chance, George Gresh, Helen Fletcher, Melville Oliver and Carlton Lingwall, all working to help establish photography within the MIA. The 1952 Festival showed the fruits of labor; Montana History "Mining Rushes," and a wildflower series. This series was later donated to the Butte Grade School System. Mr. C. Lingwell emphasized the freeness and informality of MIA photography meetings and urged cooperation. The Havre Festival had an added feature, a field trip for photographers to Fort Assinniboine.

In 1954 plans were made to include photographs in the permanent collection. In 1955 photographs were included in the Little Festival. In 1956 Robert Fehlberg made an important statement concerning photographers in the MIA: The possibility of having a closer contact with all the arts would help the true photographer; the MIA offered a unique possibility of making use of this challenging context of arts. In this year a traveling portfolio was suggested by R. Harris, Missoula. For the next years photography went "underground' but kept on growing roots.

In 1967 a new plant appeared in La Donna Fehlberg's "My Camera and I," a regular and valuable feature in the MIA magazine. It showed how personal photography can become. Denes Istvanffy published an essay, "Photography, An Art." In 1968 Robert Miller, Helena, added to the discussion. A new try was made for an exhibit during the Festival in Bozeman. It became a successful venture with over 34 prints exhibited. In 1971 cinematography was added to the MIA and a start was made for the continuous involvement of young film makers in MIA competitions. The Montana Arts Council gave generous help. Fresh work was added in photography by the Sentinel High School Art Club. Leo Olsen, Billings, added a film program to the yearly Festivals. At the Billings Festival a joint workshop for writers and filmmakers was featured with help from the MAC. A guest photographer, Barry Shapiro, held workshops and showed his work.

What are the future hopes for photography? It will grow slowly as a very personal way of expression. Film can be integrated easily with the other arts. Both film and photography need to move out from a passive to an active state and show their leaves and flowers.

Rudi Dietrich, Bozeman, 1975

WEAVING

Summer Greens

Summer is a time of inspiration for the weaver. First and foremost of interest is color in nature. All about are flowers and shrubs of every hue, with a small amount of intense color that subdues it. The green leaves greatly outnumber the flowers — the vibrant hues would be quite too much stimulation without the green. The stars in the sky are set in a field of blue. Both green and blue are kind to the eyes, so that flowers and stars are placed as points of interest. The weaver must remember this. Should too much intense color be used the result would be most uninteresting.

For an experimental lesson in color search for an interesting leaf or rock. Study the composition and balance of colors. The leaf will have many shades of the same color, from deep dark green to delicate light shades that range to blue green or yellow. No color clashes here. Were it not for subtle changes from one shade to another the result would not be so pleasing. Weavers strive for this result constantly. With care and close observation a truly beautiful piece of weaving can be created.

I am reminded of a most unusual mat at the 1962 MIA Festival which was chosen for the Little Festival and called "Glacial Stria." A rock in Glacier Park was the inspiration. The weaver saw and created. Most of us have seen the "Lake McDonald" hanging which our Mrs. Brockmann created; it is truly a painting with thread. Many of her creations were inspired by scenes around her.

In the northern latitudes spring bursts with a riot of colorful blooms after the early green shoots of foliage. In a wheat field the first spears are nearly white; then, as the season advances, the spears change from different greens to ripe yellow.

Consider again the greens of summer. The psychological effect of green is to give a feeling of coolness. Green, however, when mixed with yellow, may express warmth. When different moods are to be portrayed in weaving, these color mixtures must be taken into consideration. Certain tones of green could express envy, jealousy, hardness as in metals, softness as in grass and moss; the grey-green of sage expresses dryness or brittle texture to the point of lifelessness or dust, which is depressing. The yellow greens of spring express gaiety and lightness while the blue greens express quiet and rest.

We go to the mountains or lakes where these green tones abound for a rest and come back refreshed.

Many green tones appear in one single tree. The older growth of the evergreens is darker while the new is light in value. Where shadows appear there are still other effects. The brown and gray branches and trunk make the greens seem different from what they really are by themselves.

The deciduous trees are even more interesting. Their broad leaves reflect the light to the extent that it makes them seem nearly white with light or quite dark when in shadow. The leaves are a study in texture as well as color. Some appear hard and glistening, others soft and velvety. By studying these qualities the weaver may choose yarns which have these characteristics.

Never before has the weaver had such a variety of yarns from which to choose. Almost every day new man-made fibres appear. These, added to the natural ones, make an endless variety in either texture or color from which to choose. Even more variety may be obtained by using vegetable dyes from plants and lichens.

The waters in the lakes and streams, too, are a study for a weaver. Many shades of green appear. Different times of day create many values of green plus the glitter when sun turns waves and ripples to silver. These metallic accents may well be expressed by threads of metallic yarn. Reflections in water may present complete pictures; the shapes and forms may suggest patterns. The soft novelty yarns, some with metallic thread added, might suggest foamy crests of waves, or the firm smooth yarns might suggest quiet water. The waves, ripples and eddies make decided patterns for the weaver to capture on his web.

Next winter when snow covers the earth, may the memory of the beautiful summer greens warm our hearts and reflect in our weaving.

Hilda Cunningham, Simms, 1963

Designing on the Loom

During a recent high wind I noticed that a bird's nest which only recently became visible with the falling of the leaves did not tumble to the ground. It withstood a very severe battering despite its fragile and decorative appearance. At that moment I remembered a statement made some years ago that the birds were probably our first weavers and realized in a deeper sense that somehow weaving is a part of our great heritage as human beings. More and more our linkage with the past becomes evident and a sense of humility and respect pervades our existence, especially as weavers. This does not dull our challenge and feeling of responsibility for the future, but serves as an anchor and as promise of greater developments in this basic art and science.

In its planning, structure, processes and final result weaving is closely related in varying degrees to all the other arts and sciences. Architecture is important in its planning and structural stages, music and dance during the actual weaving, the visual arts during the whole process and final result. Science is related, especially chemistry, in its production of synthetic fabrics and in dyeing yarns; physics in relation to the theory of light and color and the strength of the fabrics; mechanics in the structure and operation of a loom; mathematics as part of the theory of thread manipulation and control; biological sciences in relation to natural fibres and inspiration for textures and design.

Looking back over this impressive list it is no wonder that many weavers feel inadequate and prefer to follow specific instructions to insure a successful product rather than venture out into the vast unknown on their own. All the arts offer a tremendous challenge, but few if any are as complicated as weaving. These widespread relationships coupled with human necessity probably account too for the fact that the textile industry is second in importance to the production of food over the whole wide world today. This, I presume, is measured in value which reflects intrinsic values, as food, clothing and shelters are our basic needs furthering our spiritual existence.

Designing on the loom, then, involves the whole person, his intellectual capacity, his emotions, his background of experience and accumulated knowledge. He has a deep sense of inner direction and urgency to create coupled with a feeling of the magnitude of the task. His idea of plan seems to come to him suddenly from no known source, frequently while engaging in other tasks and even while sleeping. It is essentially a culmination of his concentrated efforts directed toward the solution of a certain problem.

Weavers in their preliminary planning have two quite different processes available to them. One is loom controlled and the other is finger controlled and thus frequently called "free design," as there are few restrictions on this type of design. It is, however, very time-consuming and lacks, accordingly, much of the rhythmical action so pleasing to most weavers. Tapestry, lace and "laid in" patterns are good examples of this type of approach. Sometimes the two processes are combined for the most unusual results. All of nature and past efforts of other civilizations furnish inspiration and background for their present design efforts.

From the very beginning to the end of this project the weaver is closely related to other artists, though he is likely unaware of the fact that each step he goes through relates him to one or more of the arts. First, he sketches his design roughly, getting proportions and general elements into a pleasing pattern; then it must be reduced to scale and details added. This process is identical to design in architecture and other precise crafts. Tracing paper, graph paper and drawing tools are most helpful to facilitate this activity.

Choosing materials and colors is very likely his next step, since decisions must be made on the closeness and number of warp threads before he continues with a threading draft. He has already made a choice structurally whether his textile will be "free standing" or supported. Among recent developments in archectural and industrial fabrics is the stretched skin type of approach, which enables the weaver to discard the old concept of equal tension in both directions. Thus his warp on the frame could become a fabric in itself and additions can be made at will, especially if the frame takes both the horizontal and vertical tensions of the textile.

In any case, choosing the colors and yarn is a tremendously rewarding task, and the weaver feels the challenge of the wide range of yarns and other materials available. He must be aware of how colors combine, what texture and light will do to his design, the fact of a third dimensional quality and the emotional reactions to certain combinations of colors, relationships to the person or room for which the weaving is intended and, of course, the properties and qualities of the various yarns available, both natural and synthetic. Many of these decisions are similar to those made by painters and sculptors and make weaving an art as well as a craft.

The next process, reducing his design to a threading draft, is very complicated, involving a wide and thorough knowledge of interlacing threads. The number of possible combinations of threading on four to eight harnesses is almost unbelievable. It is here that a background of science and mathematics is most helpful, as the draft must be detailed and absolutely accurate. Many feel a relationship to music at this stage, as the draft looks like written music and could actually be interpreted on a musical instrument or by voice. The symbolism is so close that many a weaver has felt he could take a simple muscial score and thread it on his loom. To be sure, many adjustments have to be made at this stage to accommodate actual thread count, type of yarn used and choice of weave desired, but the planning stage has reached a climax and the actual process of threading the loom is at hand.

Threading the loom is a tedious task, but as the warp takes shape, colors falling into line as a result of minute planning, the weaver begins to feel a satisfaction and anticipation beyond all understanding. He may use one of several methods of winding warp, but this is all part of the general knowledge and craftsmanship he has learned. It is the visual aspect of his plan gradually unfolding that truly thrills him. Actually, the warp is only half of his planned fabric, but he reaches a stage of tension that makes it difficult to wait to start weaving.

Tying the treadles is a necessary hurdle at this point unless one is using a very simple loom such as a table loom. This again involves specific knowledge of the operation of the loom and the theory of pattern con-struction. Weavers generally are unwilling to test their own ability at this point and want confirmation and the help of the instructor, but finally all is in order and weaving can begin, providing, of course, no errors have been made. A few trial shots are made to test the accuracy of the threading and to correct errors, and if all is well the weaver is free to try out his idea in relationship to yarn, colors and patterns.

The loom looks inviting as the weaver sits down to try out his design, usually with many misgivings that his plan may be all wrong and will not turn out as he has visualized it. In some cases it may not weave into a usable fabric and frequently is quite different from the original idea. Fortunately, however, the woven fabric is so much richer in quality than the weaver ever anticipated, as his drawing never does justice to the color or texture of the woven piece, that he feels deeply rewarded. He may desire to make changes as he goes through an experimental stage of trying various treadlings, yarns and color combinations, which invariably open his eyes to the endless possibilities that he has set up on the loom in his humble knowledge of weaving theory. There are endless possibilities still which he has not foreseen and in his heart he gives thanks to an unseen power that has guided him in his project.

The actual process of weaving, the rhythmical movement and sound are again like music or dancing and the gradual building up of a fabric thread by thread has a definite feeling of time progressing and unfolding. Time is the distinctive element in poetry, dramatics, music and dance, which is different from an instantaneous visual image produced by painting or sculpture. To be sure, the final piece would have this instantaneous visual quality, but during the weaving part of it rolled up out of sight on the cloth beam during the time that pattern after pattern is being completed. Sections of the reverse side of the fabric are always in view in a changing pattern as the weaver continues adding both confusion and anticipation. Many times, quite unexpectedly, the reverse side produces the better image.

If the fabric is a disappointment, the weaver may change his whole plan as he weaves, since there are always endless possibilities in any warp. A change of weft thread or change of treadling and a completely new fabric results. Knowing this weavers take advantage of the time saved by not rewarping a loom and plan many different projects on one warp. Only experienced individuals are aware of the fact that the warp is the same in many cases.

The real thrill is at hand now in taking the finished piece off the loom. As it is carefully unrolled it is like an unveiling and usually there is a considerable audience to share in this glory of accomplishment and judgment of the individual's piece unaware for the moment that much still needs to be done to bring the fabric into a usable finished work of art. Now the loom looks bare, lonely and forlorn, awaiting the time when once again it becomes an instrument of creation.

The process that has gone on within the person has involved many different angles. His choice at each stage has revolved around such things as utility or function, deep-seated human values as symbolized in colors and forms, stated principles of design which he has learned and tries to apply, relationships to either the person in the case of clothing or the building in case of interior decoration, to his knowledge of endless possibilities in the weaving process itself and the properties of the various yarns used and always, of course, with full appreciation of the limitation of his own equipment and the fact that he is competing with commercial weaving, which is much more versatile than is possible on his simple loom composed of four to eight harnesses. He also realizes he himself is not a machine and cannot produce perfection no matter how hard he tries. Nor does he really want to, because it is this very factor which really labels a fabric "handmade" with all its implications of human frailty as well as of aspirations. He has been truly weaving and designing on "The Loom of Life."

Marion Brockmann, Havre, 1962

Little Lost Lace Loom

My interest in lace making goes back to when I was twelve years old. My mother had an English friend who came to our home to spend the afternoon and have tea. She always brought her lace pillow and made bobbin lace. I promised myself that some day I, too, would make bobbin lace. When I returned in March, 1966, from a weavers convention held in Beaumont, Texas, after having met there a lady eighty-five years old demonstrating bobbin lace techniques, I began a long, tedious search for a lace loom or bolster. After seven months of searching I found a lace loom in Helena. The loom, called "The Princess," was manufactured in St. Louis in 1903. I was able to borrow this loom. I reupholstered it in green velour and repadded the cylinder with green felt. I have since then been able to buy this loom. With the loom were four dozen hand-turned maple bobbins. With it also were twenty-four pricked patterns and a book of instructions for making these laces together with a copy of the *Priscilla Bobbin Lace Book,* published in Boston in 1911. From these books and from Elsie H. Gubser's book, *Bobbin Lace,* I have made some forty samples of laces by the yard.

My ambition was to make a lace coronet for a wedding veil and a wedding handkerchief for my granddaughters. With this in mind I bought a 24-inch mushroom type loom from Holland and am now studying lace making with Henk van der Zanden of Landsmeer, Holland.

Much contemporary interest is being shown in this almost lost art, especially in the East. We have an organization called the National Old Lacers with a membership of 300. Six times a year a ten-page bulletin is published containing patterns, sources of supplies, news of exhibits, articles on laces of all kinds, exchange of ideas and pictures of laces and lace makers. One of the interesting phases of this craft is the collecting, identifying and even exchanging samples of laces of all kinds.

I have been a handweaver since 1954 but like many handweavers I have accepted the challenge of lace making and found it very interesting.

Adapted from an article by
Clista P. Wuerthner, Great Falls, 1968

Whence Came These Lines?

I have written many short pieces which I and others have called "poems." I have been and I am still undecided whether it is better for one first to learn the forms others have used, as sonnet and haiku, whether to learn of meter, rhythm and rhyme, whether to practise metaphor and simile before trying to create a poem. Or is it better simply to write and perhaps to later use a known form or even to develop a new form. On the one hand the constructions of knowing form, meter, etc. may prevent maximum development of a new mind trying to express itself. On the other hand such concepts are examples — they may point the way along which a stumbling mind can go until it can take off into the unknown on its own. Both are interesting and profitable ways to go and both have produced renowned poems. The young today, the avant garde, seem to tend to want to go their own way, unhindered and undirected by the patterns of the past; the staid are sticking to the established rules.

I have not decided how to go myself — in abandon and utter freedom, or with as much knowledge as I can accumulate from others. There are security and comfort in the known and the tried, exhilaration in the strange and the unknown. I seem to want a little of both. I've written sonnets that can be counted in fourteen lines abba cddc effe gg rhyme and perfect iambic pentameter. I have written pieces that obey no rules that I know of except to try to tell the story. Perhaps a good description of how I write poetry is to say that I discover my way along until I've said something I wanted to say in a shape that I myself judge is precisely what I mean, right down to the last mark on the paper.

My rambling, discovering, winding way goes something like this. First I get an idea that I say to myself, "Now, that's something to write about." It may be a sound as musical as an orange leaf whisper past my ears, a sight like the brave far blue of my runaway grandson. Something happens that unleashes an emotion in me. Then I think of the words I like and the ways I can say them to make the emotion audible. It takes all of the forms of imagery, simile and metaphor, and all the ways of using language to get closer and closer to the emotion I felt. I have no other language than that which I have and that with which I am comfortable, hence I must use those words, twist them, turn them, beat them, rhyme them, whatever I can to tell my message. Then I need all the forms anyone ever wrote at my mind's tips to choose the one that best fits what I wanted to say, or combinations of, or variations of, or derivations from, in the possibility

184

that I may create something exact and beautiful.

At first I only wanted to do something that only suited myself. I am older now and want to say something to my husband, to my son and daughter and to my grandson (that little blue runaway), something about me and how I saw and felt, things that must make up my immortality, for I have no concern for beyond-life concepts as popularly conceived, no concern for heaven or hell as yet.

Thus I work my way along, word by word, phrase by phrase, idea by idea, image by image until I *feel* finished. Often an idea comes quickly but the development of it is tedium.

Most of my pieces have been slowly grown and changed and changed and cut and cut. But once in a while one springs forth like a flash flood. I have no description for how it came to me. My adoptive Indian father has said that songs are ''given'' to him. The source may vary; it may be a vision, a dream, a voice. But the process is the same. He receives these as gifts from somewhere. Once in a while I have a poem that just comes, just pours out and is finished in no time, and needs little if any alteration and I'm surprised at its being there. I look at it and it has a strangeness, as if the idea, the words, the form are not mine, as if they came to me in a magic way, as if they were ''given'' to me and I am only the instrument of their expression.

Elnora Old Coyote, Crow Agency, 1975

On Form and Diction in Poetry

As with other arts, at least part of the process of composing poems is not entirely under conscious control. There is a considerable element of ''inspiration'' taking the form of a phrase, a line or sometimes a concept. The poem itself, once the writer addresses himself to writing down what inspiration has given him, may ''glow'' out almost automatically. However, the cooler conscious mind has a large part to play in the finishing of the poem. In two areas, seemingly neglected by amateurs, conscious control is highly important — choice of form and choice of words.

When I write of the form of a poem, I mean patterns of rhythm and sound. Both may come partly with the initial gift of the inspiration, that is, the shape of the poem may dictate itself; but often there is necessity for conscious choice. In some areas the problem has been simplified, as in the case of the Elizabethan poets, who found a traditional subject matter, the Petrarchean version of courtly love, with the sonnet form, and consequently lapsed into sonnets whenever the subject of love presented itself. In our day, however, subject matter and form are by no means wedded, except that the more outrageous poems of the unacademic and beat poets seem to call for free verse. Whether this kind of freedom is a curse or a blessing depends, I suppose, upon the poet.

In its sound rhythms English is an iambic language and most of the great poems in the English language as well as some of the great plays have been written in a basically iambic rhythm. Since all stresses are not equal and poets tend to vary a foot here and there the use of the iamb has never been exhausted. There are numerous rhythmic feet, as any manual of poetics will show, but most of them, such as the trochees of ''Hiawatha'' or anapests of ''Annabel Lee,'' strike us as unnatural, although in more than one sense all poetry is unnatural. Rhythms other than iambic tend to dominate the poem and unless one values poetry mostly for its sound the unity of the poem suffers.

The combination of the iamb has sometimes been felt as pure tyranny, however, and one can find examples of many kinds of experiment in English and American poetry. For a contemporary poet, however, the most significant departures from the iamb are accent verse and free verse. Neither is particularly new, but no third way seems to have presented itself. Accent verse contains a set number of stressed syllables per line, but not in regular patterns. Free verse is the absence of pattern.

Accent verse is used by many contemporary poets, free verse by many others. Robert Frost, an iamb man, once remarked that writing free verse is like playing tennis without a net, and free verse is not satisfying to many poets. Traditionally, the artist's choice is on the side of form. The goal is not pure freedom but freedom in chains, a more difficult thing. Once the basic rhythm or lack has been established consistency is highly desirable, not a slavish consistency but one subtly varied.

In the choice of stanza form again problems pop from behind every bush. One's poem may suggest a form like the sonnet, particularly if it has a two-part structure — question and answer, lament and consolation — but more often it will not, and the writer must experiment a bit to see what stanza, if any, seems most consistent with the total poem. Final sound devices define the stanza, of course, although one may divide up a poem without final sound divices into any division of lines he wishes. Besides rime, consonance and assonance considerably extend the range of sound devices in English.

Once a poem has been wrestled into shape it is probably not finished so far as the actual words are concerned. While I would not go so far as some contemporary thinkers who assert that a poem is simply words. I would

186

agree that what distinguishes true poetry from other uses of language, such as hymns to beer, is the attention paid to the words of the poem. Most of the differences of reading we find in the early and later versions of poems by poets like Yeats and Graves are differences of wording — usually toward more specificity, concreteness and precision.

What the poet must do, after the poem has assumed most of its shape, is to subject it to the most careful scrutiny, asking always, is this the best word for the total effect of the poem? Usually the best word is the most specific word. It is virtually meaningless to say that the day is lovely or the woods mysterious. Generality is the death of poetry, because it says nothing clearly, and clarity should be, in my view, the essence of the poem. Instead of "the day was lovely," the poet will tell us about the greenness of the grass, the temperature in the afternoon, and the lovers beneath the trees. The best poetry is full of specific words, concrete words like bread, wine, shovel, table. Even a philosophical or relatively abstract poet like Milton will have areas of painstaking specificity. Poetry is in part the record of things.

When he is writing the poem the loyalty of the poet to his tongue is above his loyalty to God, nation, family or the Communist Party.

The extreme care that a good poet lavishes on his poem tends to militate against long poems, not that one would concur with Poe that there is no such thing. However, it might be said that the reader cannot always sustain the kind of attention that a good long poem requires. Some well-known good poets, like James Dickey, write very long poems, but one is not always impressed by the necessity of the language.

Anyone who is serious about writing poetry should realize that he must have technical knowledge as well as the gift of the Muses. He should be tough-minded about his poems and ask some hard questions: Is the meter or pattern of stresses suitable to the whole poem? If there is no pattern, is the absence a virtue? Does the stanza pattern lead to padding? Does it seem inevitable a week after composition? Is every word "loaded," or is the poem full of blanks? Only a maniac can always answer yes, but a good poet can answer, I think so.

Robert T. Taylor, Butte, 1967

A Word to the Wise Poet

Because I have been fortunate enough to have had a few hundred poems sold I have had my share of the usual questions: How do you do it? How *do* I do it? This is a brief attempt to answer those questions. In the first place, let us recognize that the world isn't exactly crying for this poetry that it needs so desperately. It is up to us to sell the stuff if we think it's worth it. This is not written for those who write poetry spelled ART, too fine for the marketplace. The whole object of any writing is communication. And to communicate a poet must be read. A great deal of the fault of today's lack of interest in poetry lies with the poets themselves, who have written with the idea that "the public" is incapable of understanding us anyhow and that we are writing for some superior minority. I think an honest writer writes to be read and by as large an audience as possible — consistent, of course, with the standards of quality he demands of himself.

So, recognizing that we are writers who want to be published, who think we have something to say worth hearing, let us go straight to the point. WRITE, and when you have written, send it out. It is necessary to write a great deal and rewrite a great deal. Unless you are different from me not everything you write is poetry. I estimate that I have written and thrown away a hundred lines for every one I've kept. Cutting and polishing should be endless, especially if you expect crass payment for your efforts.

The same thing goes for sending out. Don't be afraid to send them and send them and send them. I know a lady who has written poetry all her life and has never sent any out. She speaks of her poems as dream children and can scarcely bear to let even another poet see them. This is not written for her. You and I who want to see our stuff in print will have to send it out. We will have to beat our brains out, and the editor's too, to get a hearing. They are pretty tough customers, though often very nice people who have a pretty good idea as to what will communicate and certainly a hard-headed idea of what they want. It's a matter of not getting discouraged. When you've sent out a hundred poems and got a hundred rejection slips, you haven't even got your feet wet.

Another thing. I've heard surprise and shock expressed that so many excellent poems have been wasted on the so-called small markets, newspapers, little journals and such. But why wasted? They are read. And if they appeal they will prepare the way for a larger hearing. You will become known. If it takes a hundred of them to get one into the so-called

188

bigger markets, what of it? How else would you get a hearing? We can't
guard our precious stuff so carefully that no one gets to see it just because
we think it's too good for a little market. We are writing for people, I hope.
I say start at the top and try them all the way down. But if your poem ends
up in a newspaper or some little struggling poetry journal be grateful and
happy that someone is going to read it. You will be developing an audience.

Finally, don't think that every rejection slip is a slap in the face or is
necessarily final. Remember, you are dealing with people. In the case of
the bigger markets you have to pass a whole battery of editors, each one a
person with changing moods, different tastes and personal ideas. I've sold
poems to the same magazines which had previously refused them a
dozen times — different times — different requirements.

There you have it. Write endlessly. Send out tirelessly. Treasure your
rejection slips. They represent experience. And again, don't despise the
little market. After you've sold to a hundred of them you'll get a lot better
and warmer hearing from the better pay mags. Remember, their editors
are just people, too, but they're in the marketplace. And they are
businessmen. I haven't found any easy way to slip past them. But they're
good guys when you get to know them. Luck —

Don Manker, Broadus, 1967

A Word or Two for Poets

Bold. Be bold. Be alarmingly bold. That's what you are if you are really
living. For many years I have worked with scores of amateur poets in
Montana, in almost every state in our country. Fully half of their writings
have been pallid, timid, soft, evergentle, pussyfooting. Think how bold
you are in feeling, thought and expression in your privacy. Don't write as
though you were sucking existence from routine and monotony. Nobody
need live a life of monotony — "My mind to me a kingdom is . . ." and it is
your kingdom, no one else's, *yours.* Don't trim what you think and feel,
speak and write out of timidity, out of modesty, out of fear of criticism.
Every day think and feel and write something bold. It's good for your
writing. It's good for your thinking. It's good for you.

Fresh. How much verse have we all read that was stale, trite, ordinary,
hackneyed, stereotyped, threadbare. Use your dictionary. Each day think
of a fresh thought — for exercise if for nothing else. Feel strongly about
something each day. Express these fresh feelings and thoughts in words
and phrases and images that may seem to you perhaps even outrageous.

189

Thousands of writers of verse have felt and thought about sunsets, weather, landscapes, lakes, love, friends, death, about what not, and expressed them in such conventional words and images and dull rhythm that one can almost read their verse blindfolded. Don't do that. Seek fresh expressions. Every day write them if only single words of phrases. Don't let your writing smell of the conventional.

Experimental. In your daybook place thoughts and feelings just as you experienced them, with the thought that no one is ever going to see them anyway. (After a while you will dare to show them to a friend and later, perhaps, to a publisher and the public.) Put down your exact feeling — *your* feeling. The English language has a conventional expression for every ordinary thought and feeling, but your thoughts and feelings are not ordinary, they are yours. Insist on freshness. Experiment with fresh thought and fresh feeling every day — at least one fresh item in that book each day. Even smart expressions, clever expressions, extravagant expressions will help you to be alive in your writing. Above all, put down exact expression.

Imaginative. The sky has been called millions of times just sky, the blue heavens, the blue vault, the dome of blue. Omar called it an inverted bowl. How about the fierce eagle's way; the jet's blue channel; the mottled mirror; the angry, depthless blue; the peaceful, depthless sky, and a hundred other imaginative expressions? If your thought, if your expressions aren't imaginative you can't write a poem. If your feelings are flaccid, mild, limp, inactive, negative you can't write a poem anyone will care to read. If your language doesn't explore words and images and symbols you will write ordinary verse. The positive, assertive, searing make your thoughts and feelings and expressions alive for readers, waited for by them, invigorating, pleasure-giving, dawn fresh.

Well now, doesn't all this apply to writers of fiction, too? To any creative writer? To an artist in any medium?

H.G. Merriam, Missoula, 1967

Section IV

POEMS
ARTICLE
SHORT STORIES

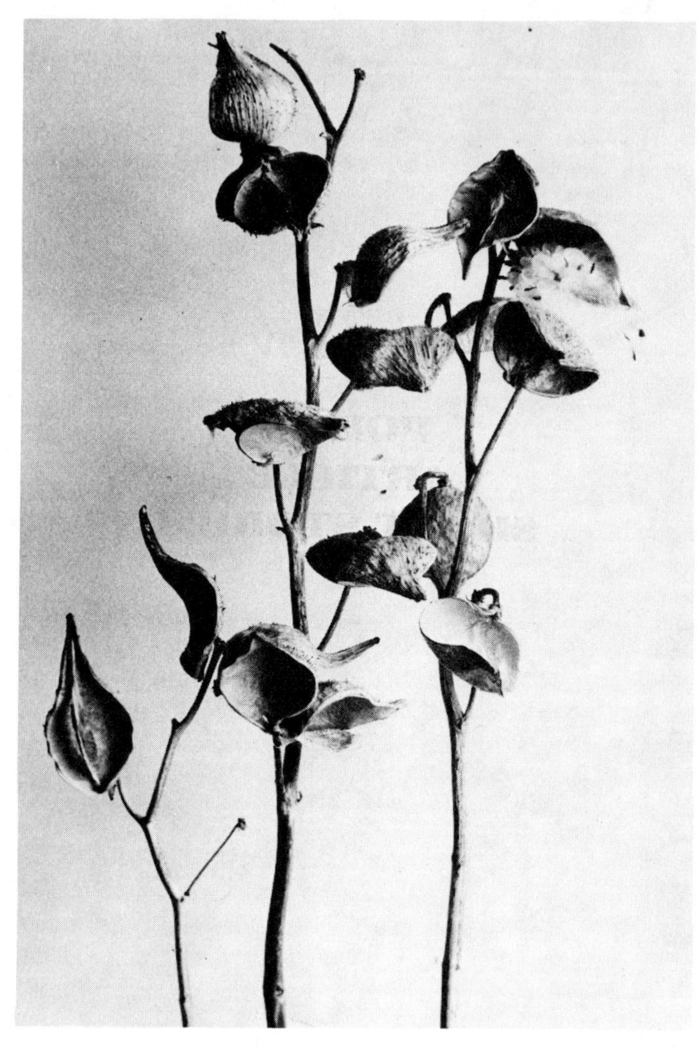

Milkweed Pods, LaDonna Fehlberg

POEMS

SOUNDWAVE

It may be harmony, a technic music, to those mechanics
who outspeed sound and burst the drums of air,
who shatter the waves of space, test the decibels of planets,
there where the awful silence subdues invasion.
They may well have conceived new consonance, cadence,
   measure,
to which one who prefers pianissimo is as yet unaccustomed.

Surely some new god is born from this jettish efflux,
a jinni of gas or golem sprung from a marriage of gears:
this latest intruder motor-gendered, grinding, grating,
sleepless through dark and day, thunderbolting time ...

This evening brings again a curious star, pulsing shimmerly,
which would dance on the bowstring of a sphere once strung in
   melody,
Quickly it pales; it quits horizon, beyond audition.
Perhaps it awaits a melt of tone, a familiar rhythm...

              William W. Chance, Butte

THE SEARCHER

Again he came to explore the darkened home,
far-hilled, withdrawn, like a forted citadel,
the portals closed, barred windows, spectral hall;
no sigh of breath (Or did a bell roll doom?)
he heard, nor warder hail nor welcome "Come"
The gates were gordius-locked. Is it possible —
the mansion mocked him like a leering skull —
that some before had fed but for him no crumb?

But he beat stubbornly till his rapid heart
pumped sound into the hollows — still no sign,
no echoing voice. He had heard of rarest wine
fermented there, past iron that bled and hurt.
What word unbolts? What ghosts must he subvert?
Should crevice crack, he might then sneak within,
break webs, break fast, and assume a sovereign
survey of the burning worlds till all depart ...

* * *

Time aged. Somehow through mercy making rich the poor,
he entered ... and in awe looked out the opening door.

William W. Chance, Butte

ROOM IN ETERNITY

Not like Penelope may I unravel
What through the day I patterned on my loom,
For Time is my Ulysses, not returning,
Part of the used warp in a storied room.

The suitors clamor for their place in the pattern,
Hope, fear, ambition, grief, remembered love.
I weave their symbols in marginal acrostic,
Seeing the web forever from me move.

Mary Brennan Clapp, Missoula

AT BETHANY

Three sat at table, with sparse food: bread, wine,
Olives. Summer sun showed motes in the air. Leaves
Barely stirred. Because they had so much to think of
The three at table were quiet. Mary touched absently
Her long gold hair. Lazarus sipped the wine and gazed
At purpling distance. Martha noticed how little he spoke
Since the day, pale, gaunt, but rising to Christ's eyes,

He shed the shroud. He looked as if he were listening or
    remembering
Something. There was a new grievous beauty in Mary, but she
    was
All kindness. Her heart was an alabaster box.

Martha thought of the years of keeping a house where they
Could come for rest or food or clean, mended clothes.
She hardly knew when they would come and go, but, without
Intention, she had been faithful in this "least." She remembered
Among the hills Christ saying, "Do unto others ..."
And sharper and clearer now, His voice to the multitude,
"When thou doest alms, sound not a trumpet before thee."

Alms had not seemed in any way connected with dusting
And baking and mending. Hostess pride and, no doubt, some
    weariness
Had sounded the trumpet, though. Christ's rebuke — it had
    turned
Her into a beggar. All are beggars sometime, needy
    Some way. and she...
Her face softened. She passed the smooth
Brown olives. Lazarus seemed to shrink from them. She did not
Urge, remembering the Garden of bitter fruit not yet
Ripened. Mary did not even look at them.
Martha put them down gently with a new understanding.

Mary Brennan Clapp, Missoula

RIVER MUSIC

As surely as an orchestra
blends the reeds, the strings
and the percussioned sounds
the river plays its tune.

Upon the sandy bar the wavelets,
from the rock midstream
that split the flood,
lap against my feet.

Theirs is a repetitious theme,
scarcely audible
beneath the crash of cymbals
on the rock.

And while I listen to the water talk
I hear a plaintive note,
almost like a human voice,
that calls beseechingly.

Half-notes and whole, rests and runs
over pebbled bed
the river's music stimulates
and lulls.

Harriette E. Cushman, Bozeman

ABANDONED MAIL BOXES

Where grass-grown wheel ruts meet the range
abandoned mail boxes stand like lopped off crosses
etched against the sky
and brace themselves against the prairie winds
which buffet them and sand the wooden grain
of lidless frames to a painting grown grey and deep.
No postman passes by.
The gophers burrow at their feet
and gnaw the rotting wood.
No rider stops.
These boxes have no tryst to keep.
They are like crossroad crosses set
for those who've hastened their own deaths
and cannot rest in consecrated ground
but for eternity must sleep a troubled sleep.
  And yet last spring
  a bluebird built in one.

Harriette E. Cushman, Bozeman

196

PLEA

You, whom I love, go take another trail.
I want to walk this mountain path alone:
My searching foot will seek the cruel shale,
The damp, caressing moss, the flat hot stone.
Go take another trail where none may see
My nervous face in rapturous repose,
Arms flung in wild abandon. I would be
A wild bird, dressed in a woman's clothes.
Let go your hold and let me fly away
A little while, then hold me tight again,
And walk beside me on another day,
Perceiving this, when I fall wordless then
I'm worshiping in silence as I walk
The curved, the graceful shoulder of a hawk.

Jaculyn Cory, Hamilton

A SINGLE PERFECT THING

Once we were young and in love with each other
(Morning of life when the minutes ran long),
Willingly bound by a silken white tether,
Held by it briefly, this long-ago spring.

Never a trap so enchanting since, truly!
Lovely and light as a snowflake new-formed,
Wild-flower frail, and given as freely,
First love surprised us, and warmed us, and charmed.

Nobody broke it, nor yet was it stolen,
Nobody trampled or turned it to stone.
Of itself somehow it vanished, unfallen,
Poised for an April, by May it was gone.

Love to us then was a gift, not a giver,
How were we patient, while we were young?
And wise, letting go when love freed us, for never
Would it have stayed perfect if it had stayed long.

Ida Isabel Donohue, Great Falls

PORTRAITS

1

Do not wonder at my darting mind!
I am one who walks on crevassed ground
Where unsuspected fissures
Continually alert the contemplated step
Arresting confidence midway in hope.

2

He swam among the cycles of prestige
With just enough of logic to direct
His path where he must ask no favor.
It was a bitter price,
The comfort of the senses
For the comfort of the soul.

Frieda Fligelman, Helena

ON LOVING GRASS

Barefoot
  to the thigh
    in the summer sun ...

Naked of saddle
  and thought
    we race
      through the meadow grass.

Ocean sweet waves
  I dabble my feet in
    the stinging sweet grass
      to his belly and chest ...

We race
  through the fragrance
    the tall stalks around us
      and reap so much more
        by the passing

In the end
    on my back
        I lie between grass and sky
            while he eats
            and I eat
                the sugar-stemmed grass.

                        Irene Gilskey, Bozeman

PARTING

Let there be a song or two, then silence,
        Not a tear
Not a sigh upon the stillness say
        A friend was here;
Let us sing and singing let us part
        And singing know
They who say farewell at noon will meet
        In the after glow.

                    Paul A. Grieder, Bozeman

I DIDN'T WARN THE BOY

I saw him in a five-and-dime store
Buying a book. A cheap western, for God's sake!
I wanted to know if he shouldn't, somehow couldn't,
Do better. But I didn't dare say anything —
His mother was there: a lank-haired woman
Getting stout, a coat originally not hers
Buttoned tight in front, no purse, her money tied
In a handkerchief held wrapped in her fingers
(She'd given him enough for a book, and books
Are never cheap), and she guarded
A small daughter with eyes that saw everything
But the Future.
My duty, had I been the responsible kind,
Would have been to say: "Look here, son,

A few rows over are Tolstoy and Dostoevsky,
And Melville and James, and those other longhairs.
They may not be exciting, but gee, they have flair,
They are *in,* they are *psychological.*
Don't grow a permanent sulk — there are no heroes
Life to imitate: And Grey faked a lot, anyway.
You should read Proust and copy his style,
Then you can hold your head up —
Because, by God, the way you are going now
It's nothing but trouble ahead, I predict!''
I started out to warn him but I lost my courage.
Time's arrow pointed him and me out the door,
And we didn't speak, not for 30 years.
Then, this morning, rummaging around, I found that book,
And meeting the young naive buyer again, I told him
It could have been a lot worse, and we both waited
For a ghost of tomorrow to walk by
And hoped *he* would dare speak.

Philip Gray, Bozeman

COLLAGE

To see my life the way
I see my life
You must cut it up
Into child-pieces
And girl-pieces
And woman-pieces;
There is a lot of sticky laughter
And moist, spongy tears
To paste it all together.
I wish I could decide
How it all fits
Into a pattern.
Is there any design?

Nancy M. Harvey, Kalispell

PASSING

There ought to be some huge, loud movement
      when a man dies
Some trembling of the earth
A splitting of the skies
Some far-flung tolling of thunderous bells.

The gleaming jet that parts the blue
Causes the walls of my house to shake
And all the earth below takes notice
      of its passing.

But my neighbor gathers in her wash
And cooking supper scents the air
Children coming home pass by unaware
A life ended here, today
      and no sign is made.

           Jean Hough, Broadus

APPLE TREES

The boughs bend, the boughs sway,
And turn their tranquil gaze my way.
A blossom drifts to earth below
Resting where gentle grasses grow.

Soft the air, soft the breeze
That walks through all the apple trees.
The blossoms blush beneath the sky
Teased by a passing butterfly.

The boughs bend, the boughs shake
Like ripples on a quiet lake.
The tender lullaby of bees
Is sung up in the apple trees.

The boughs bend, the boughs sigh
And earth has dewdrops in her eye.
Only the blossoms do not cry.
Lightly they fall, lovely they die.

Dorothy Johnson, Butte

APRIL SONG

I dread the softness of another spring.
The misty rains and balmy, scented air —
Mornings when I hear a robin sing
I will feel your presence everywhere.
A ghost will walk each lonely avenue
And phantom footsteps haunt each busy street,
Dreams we dreamed of things we meant to do
Have vanished, leaving bitterness, defeat.

I walk the winter scene, wind in my face,
And feel the sly derision of the storm;
Rejoice to see the gusty snow embrace
The lilac in a bleak, distorted form.
Welcome, every frosty-whiskered imp!
Welcome, too, vicious winter king!
Tempest, beat the weeping willows limp!
Dump a cloud of frozen tears on spring.

Marty Kelly, Great Falls

DEEP FOREST

Beyond the roar of the waterfall,
This cone of living sound,
Wilderness hush is all,
All is the hush of the ground.
    Something is holding its breath,
    Something whose face is a leaf.
Under the cloud and the open sky,

202

Under the breeze's wing,
Shadows are walking, sly,
Shadows of something are forming a ring.
   Somewhere a step without sound,
   Somewhere a print on the loam.
Dare not to venture beyond this sound,
Stay in the water's roar!
Scream and run, you'll be found
Though your feet leave no mark on the forest floor.
   Somehow your watching will fail,
   Something primeval is all.

Margaret Kraenzel, Bozeman

MOUNTAIN JUNE

June is the hot yellow heads of dandelions
And sunlight sliding on brown water,
June is the warm humped boulders
In cold channels where the run-off rivers race.
June blooms around us with a reaching radiance
But we, still bitter here from cold Spring's
Bright delusion,
Fold close our winter-pallid hands.
The high blue sky of June uncovers us to light;
Our stature is revealed
Unaided by the glow of shaded indoor lamps.
Dusted with the pollen of butter yellow flowers
June dares us to remember
By the sliding sunlight's dazzle
That once we stood where trees are standing.
June is a wind-striped lake
Over which we hesitate
And catch our breath
And plunge.

Margaret Kraenzel, Bozeman

A TRIP TO THE STORE

An ounce of justice, please.
          Sorry, we're all out.
Do you have any mercy?
          Nope, haven't had it in stock for a long time.
You wouldn't happen to have a quart of peace, would you?
          Hah!
How about hope?
          Sorry, we've never carried that item here.
Well, okay, then, give me a bag of greed
                    a box of prejudice
                    a head of deceit
                    and a couple pounds of hate.
          Gotcha.

                              William P. Luckenbach

TRANSFORMATION SCENE

The curtain falls. The spells of silence mark
A changing scene. A splendid play is done.
Now come the dimming light, the lowering arc,
A long and dismal play now starts its run:
While shadows move across a barren scene,
The villain, Boreas, with a piercng breath,
Howls, "Massacre!" Yet he, in his routine,
Inspires no panic with his threat of death.
The while he roars and cuts a mortal gash,
Two pantomimists, old and reverent, turn
Toward the warmth of flame and glowing ash,
Upon the grate where seasoned pine logs burn.
One lights his pipe. The other, who is sitting
At ease before the mantel, tends her knitting.

                              Berdina Lane, Great Falls

SUMMER SUNRISE

The sun is slowly climbing
over low, tree-hinged hills.
The fence-scattered fields
of small farms will have
only a few more unbroken
bird songs before tractors
begin bending the morning
toward clock-born purposes.

James Magorian, Helena

THE WIND IS RESTING IN THE BITTERROOT VALLEY

The wind is resting in the valley;
Suspended stillness .... holding
The fragrance of the day,
    Which in this instance
    Is leaf mold, rich and heavy,
    Red apples stored away;
The pungence of a fruitful fall,
The last few purple grapes left
To feed the birds that stay;
    Still harboring some summer sun
    That clings like perfume to
    The stacks of crisp alfalfa hay.
Redolent with heady smells
Of cedar, breathing the pine's
Magnificent bouquet;
    The wind is resting .... Hush!
    For soon its weighted wings will stir
    And waft those aromatic scents away!

Irene McPherson, Billings

TWO GERMANS

1

These towers
are Bach's, I think;
see .... how they sing
with grace?
And this
melodic arch ....
how perfectly
it bridges space —
translating
the German stone
to an exotic
and other place.

2

Beethoven thought
cathedrals,
pyramids of sound,
piled block on block,
square on square,
and out of mind
raised Gothic towns
and cities to astound
the ravished air.

Don Manker, Broadus

LOVE POEM

2 is a poem,
according to Robert Frost a game
delightful from the start,
a 7 come 11 thing, "the same
as the figure for love" —

1 plus 1
(a trick of the heart!)
You see?
Now turn it around; the game is done ...
2 is a poem
according to me.

Don Manker, Broadus

KINETIC PRODUCTS, INC.

"...this is the latest
and, considered
from any standpoint
you please, must be
      the greatest

single line
to come from assembly
It is, we think,
      an original design.

We feel
that Homo Sapiens
may be the toy
to end all toys — the final
      great Mobile

He seems
to have all attributes.
He laughs, cries,
makes love and war
and reproduces
      and dreams...

too much?
We know. That last
thing is a flaw
and dreams can be dangerous —
surely an extra
      and unnecessary touch...

but then
nothing to worry
a responsible company.
Home is, of course,
programmed for self-destruct
      — if and when

          Don Manker, Broadus

YOU POINTING YOUR FINGER

You did not wish for any tears. You said,
"Please do not mourn for me when I am dead."
And I do not. I mourn for apple trees,
And April rain, and roses, and things like these.
I mourn for a special view from our special hill,
Which no one saw quite as you did — nor ever will.

My tears are for unimportant, irrelevant things:
Cloud shapes, and the bright pattern of wings
You traced for me against an autumn sky —
You pointing your finger, I following with my eye.
Oh! I do not mourn for you at all, you see,
But only for the disenchanted earth — and me.

Don Manker, Broadus

MOUNTAIN REQUIEM

When death comes in the hills, quick to still a valiant heart,
And men, awed by the unawares with which death plays its part,
Bend down to strengthen stalwart limbs and fold work-calloused
    hands,
The very hills bow, too, and ask their God for peace,
The peace that He has made and understands.

Not tragedy. Just a woodsman's stop for rest
Along the trail that often knew his stride,
And, facing the east of the old rugged range,
He made camp on the other side.

Bessie K. Monroe, Hamilton

METALLIC WEATHER

Winter wears metal; in its stride
Ice-iron clangs; in leaden skies
A platinum moon and steel stars glide.
A brassy sunrise
Glitters and then plies
Tin and silver to achieve
Needle daggers at each eave.

At day's end long bronze pikes
Lance out in battle line,
All along the harsh incline.
In the cold I grope
And stare, as gilded spikes
Brazenly strike
And burnish all the mountain slope.

Kit Miller, Bozeman

TO A RING-NECKED PHEASANT

Be still and hear the tuning of the vines
Of crisp wild hops that grimly tendril-clutch;
The whining warning as the cold winds touch
At each taut stem along the roughened lines
Of tree trunks. When old autumn has the smell
Of ripe cut melon, Leaves, come, whisper down
And kiss the loam with fading yellow-brown,
And in the message of the rustle tell
That raucous cock who struts his gaudy plume
Against the bareness of a fall gone by
To fly, and mourn him as he curves the sky
Too late, and flutters down into the bloom
    Of cattails, still on dark swamp pool, to where
    The ripples tighten arms and hold him there.

Elnora A. Old Coyote, Crow Agency

THE VILLAGE

August —
>Painters and crafters
>Display their art around the square.

Blond woman,
Unwashed and old,
With earrings to vend,
In a canvas chair
Along the walk at noon,
Sits and smokes her breakfast.
>If she sells the copper
>She will drink her supper.

>>Surrealist,
>>With high-priced canvas
>>Of bloodless hearts on desert sand,
>>Bits of this and that
>>In misplaced places,
>>Knows his stuff good.
>>>He'll sell — for a price;
>>>He shrugs otherwise.

Bald, chubby,
Painter of ballet
>Poises his little coquette
>Before an orange
>Red and yellow glow —
>Of heaven, of earth, or hell?
>>Where is she pirouetting?
>>What is this bright light setting?

Young negro
With burning eyes
Paints his "Green Girl."
Does not want to sell
His love for bread.
With gaunt belly,
>His awed hands touch her.
>A customer asks, "How much sir?"

September —
The artists barter
Their naked hopes
        around the square.

Elnora A. Old Coyote, Crow Agency

PRYORS WEST

In the summer's dry ghost dust,
Brown back against his evening's light,
He descended the foothills to harvest.
His horse was a running dapple
In the gray of the sage and diminishing
        green of the June grass,

Cherries just turning on season,
Half-red cheeked, half green in the shadows
Where auxins drift, orbitting the flesh
On the stony pit,
Always at ripe face with the sun.

His song pushed downwind before him,
A native, high, savage note;
His eyes pleaded loud in their challenge;
One maccasined foot he held down for a stirrup
And with brown hand beckoned up.
Like a lark the homesteader's child
Arose on his bidding,
Arms tightly entwining the deerskin
As wild hops on a willowing stem,
Laughing, rode the swift gradient valley.

Dark brown, the peaks of the Pryors alerted
To swift arrows impaling
The blue and white of the sky.

Black in the west lifted
Thunderheads streaking quick fires;
Hail mounted the high winds
And rattling its absolute bones
Rode, direct, horizontal, at the fields.
The crop turned to summer to autumn,
Leaned with the clear frozen rain
(Bullets abreast and ice sharpened for flight)
And fell in wetted windrows;
Like chaff the grain spilled on the prairie;
  The gold turned to gray to ash,
Lifted and sifted on the end of the season
  Wind weaving the loams on the sage, on the June grass,
Scattering, replanting at random.

On early owl light, the striped shadow
Mounted the crest of the hill;
At the precise place of his passing,
Etched on the full-ripe cherry moon,
A coyote lifted his muzzle.
The cry, like a cord down the hillside,
Curled round the young lark fallen, kneeling
Ground-tethered at the feet of the moonlight,
Straining to run at the hill.

Wild cherry bark bitter,
Lay the image abstract on the tongue.
At dawning, the snows came that season,
Drifting deep in a frozen heart's hollow.

Elnora Old Coyote, Crow Agency

FARM WIFE TRANSPLANTED

I thought it was the town I wanted,
But now I know
That the soft sound of snow
And a wood fire burning
Mean more than a knock, a doorknob turning.

212

Better far,
The deep content of quietness,
And one lonely star.

Lenore Olsen, Bozeman

NEW HOMEPLACE

my new love pours me pools of tumbling water,
sings me songs of whispers,
decorates my rooms with greens and blues
and drops October colors in my hair.
he makes a bed so crisp and white and cool
and lights the way so softly
and takes me up so gently ...

but the morning finds us crying
for i have talked all night
of places i have been.

Julie Reid, Bozeman

MUTED DAYS

I love the softly winded,
Cloudy days that linger
Like a veiled grey mood
Across the waning year,
When the frail, denuded branches
Of winter-waiting trees
Sway and wave and pause
And murmur intermittently
Like muted instruments
That whisper in a minor key.

Jo Stepanoff, Missoula

LET ME SLEEP

Wrap the winter blanket over me,
Let me rest,
Like a tired patient
Whose hovering kin
Have left at last.

Don't stand around my grave,
Pinching off dried buds
That aren't even there,
Pulling at long-forgotten weeds,
Don't send for water at the gate
To nourish me now.

      Let me sleep.

Jo Stepanoff, Missoula

THE BELLS

The bells beat, like muffled drums of bronze
To the trudging feet from the hills that sleep
Like ragged burros, under the night-fading sky.

Clutching her tattered rebozo
Against the cathedral's chill,
A brown girl stops at the grille by the doorway
And gives the drowsing confessor
Her tight-clasped centavo.

Disburdened of sin, she lights a candle
To one dead, kneels to pray
Entranced and exalted,
And joins in the chants
With the rich and the great.

She touches the hem of the Blessed Madonna,
Kisses the smudged picture of her Saint,
Presses her face to the screen
That protects a relic,
Moving aside for the tourists
Without a glance at their elegant burdens,
Unmindful of their curious, pitying stare.

Trudging back to the mud hut in the hills
That shine like domes in the sunlight,
Her heart beats like the bells,
With the pulse-beat of the serene and the eternal.

Jo Stepanoff, Missoula

NOW IN MY THIRTY-EIGHTH YEAR

Now in my thirty-eighth year, here in the winter
garden, watching the wary birds eat bread,
transmuting paper into the gold of flame,
I wonder at mutability and time.
Even knowing as I know, reading the poems I wrote
twenty years ago, that I am different, yet love
rising like incense from those thumbed pages smells
to me familiar, and this latest word I write
as the clock hums on toward its midnight climax,
is informed with an adolescent hope. Ah, yes,
some of us never learn! The master sweats
to pound his lessons home; the heedless scorn
him to their peril; and in this burning man,
ignorant of his doom, there sings a boy.

Robert T. Taylor, Butte

215

WHAT ARE YOU DOING SATURDAY NIGHT?

Not forces
more capricious
stroke their fiddles
bright and night
to jig the sea,
the land
the atmosphere,
than told me:
"She."
But wry in
contradiction,
paralyzed my
will for months
the while I
watched her by.

At last, with effort
pledged to youth,
I —
who knows? —
cajoled too much?
revealed too far?
perhaps the roughly words?

And so we tumble,
Leaves before the wind.

Walter W. Stevens, Bozeman

MEXICAN SUNRISE

The cocks of Hermosillo crow
Across the desert in the slow
Awakening of morning.

Red-rising from the swales of sand
The sun spills heat upon the land
Lizard-like in warming.

216

I sleep, half-sleeping in a dream
Where deserts are not what they seem
At first awakening,

And startle at my heart's quick beat —
Can infinite and finite meet
In a moment's breaking?

Here the sand is full of sound,
Dogs bark and children pound
The air with calls and laughter.

And I, with cockcrows in my ears,
Rejoice above my temporal fears
And run, run laughing after.

Veris Wessel, Bozeman

LEAVES FROM A MONTANA OCTOBER

The antelope
        put outposts on the ridges
    like a Rotcie exercise
    in setting up machine guns.

The Noah's Ark black Anguses
stand in stiff-legged squares
all pointed one way
on their slanted mountain parking lot.

From a fluff of cloud
in the bluebell sky
a snowberry hail
clicks softly down
        an aspen shaking yellow castanets
        on twisted candelabra of sage
        on the hump of a beaver lodge.

The trees heap snowflakes on the ground.

A splash of mustard on the hot-dog hills
with evergreen piccallili.

Milicent Ward Whitt, Bozeman

ARTICLE

What's There to Lose?

"Lost" is one of the saddest words in the English language. It conjures up all sorts of emotional scenes involving keepsake jewelry, whimpering puppies, and wailing little kids. Then there are lost games, lost elections, lost causes, lost control, lost tempers, and lost hair. Bad scenes, all of them!

Conversely "found" is a happy word: found a friend, found a job, found the answer, found a clue, found happiness.

But this can be confusing. One doesn't find an election, or find a temper, and one doesn't lose and answer or lose a clue.

People have been losing things ever since Adam and Eve lost their innocence in the Garden of Eden. People have been finding things ever since the cavemen looked for edible foods and rock missiles.

Probably half of the crises in your home stem from someone having lost something. Dad can't find his car keys. Mother can't find her scissors. Sis can't find her contact lenses, and brother can't find his baseball glove. Our little world is spinning along rather nicely until something gets lost. Then everything seems to fall apart. We spend half our time looking for lost things. Even the best-ordered home does not escape. You are all familiar with the efficient housewife who puts things away so carefully that they are lost forever.

Trying to turn lost things into found ones requires a lot of imagination and ingenuity. Where would I be if I were a ballpoint pen? Where could the mate of one of your favorite gloves manage to hide?

Some sure-fire rules for finding lost articles are:

1. Look again, carefully this time, where you've looked in a panic six times already.

2. Look where you're sure it isn't.

218

3. Look for some other missing article. You won't find it, of course, but something interesting will turn up.

4. Eat some raw cucumbers, hot tamales, and a generous portion of butterscotch pie. Then go to sleep and dream where the missing article is.

5. Forget the whole thing and you'll run across the missing item, in the cuff of your pants, inside a pillow case, in a pocket of the jacket you wore fishing summer before last, in the dog house, in the kids' sandpile, or in the family Bible.

The more imaginative you are, the more fun this impromptu game of hide and seek can become. You'll stumble onto things you haven't seen for years: your high school commencement program, thirty-two pairs of mismatched socks, Grandma's recipe for castor oil bread (that one is for real, and is better off lost), and several pounds of old ticket stubs. Check these latter items. They might be valuable if they're from some event like the 1920 World Series, the Dempsey-Gibbons fight, or an Aimie Semple McPherson rally.

If you want to really boggle your mind, just try to picture the number of lost things that you yourself may have unwittingly banished. What about those depression glass dishes that got mixed up with the junk you sent to the Salvation Army? And do you dare to contemplate what you may have left in the pockets of old clothes on their way to Good Will? Even if you think you have checked these things thoroughly, the awful possibilities will arise to haunt you when something "turns up missing."

There is probably no person alive who hasn't lost something, possibly at least once a week. But unfortunately, not everyone has such a good record at finding things. That talent seems reversed for a special few. Some of these star-favored souls can't go across the street without coming up with a watch, a wallet, or at least a cigarette lighter. We all know kids who can trot down an alley any time of day and fish dollar bills out of garbage cans, or who can always finance a hamburger spree by just picking up coins off the sidewalk. Our envy-ridden admiration may be somewhat disturbed, though, at the thought of the germs they may be collecting or of their imminent chances of getting run over.

Probably there are times when you don't want to find something, like the list of jobs you had to do (for kids, the homework assignment), the address of that acquaintance in Cleveland that you really didn't want to look up anyway, or that insulting gag gift you got at the office party. Even worse, there may be times when you deliberately tried to lose something, such as a cat. Hades couldn't possibly have an apartment warm enough for a person who could thinkingly do that. Because of such people with a big problem and a small conscience, our family last year alone had to find homes for three female puppies, and a full grown crippled St. Bernard.

Losses can become a fatal chain. You are probably familiar with the story of the horse that lost a shoe, and consequently lost its rider, a battle, and eventually the whole war. It is amusing to contemplate how history might have been changed had Ben Franklin lost his key, Caesar his manuscripts, Henry the Eighth his head, or Mr. Goodyear his wife's permission to use the kitchen.

Our eldest daughter says that when she was a little girl she used to think that when you died and went to Heaven, all the things you had lost on earth would be piled up there, waiting for you. Her mound would have towered above the Pearly Gates before she got out of junior high.

How about you? Are you careless, half-conscious, or just a born loser?

Alice Schumacher, Great Falls, 1975

SHORT-SHORT STORY

In Beauty It Is Finished

Hugh Zahonie sat in his hogan contemplating the morrow. In his spirit, he knew that tomorrow he would die. He was ready. He had lived over a hundred years. He had been a child when his people, the Dine, were herded like cattle and driven by White Eyes in Blue Coats to Bosque Redondo in New Mexico. That Trail of Tears was almost a forgotten memory to him now, so long ago it was. The Long Walk was in the year 1864. It was now 1973. One hundred and nine years had passed. he was about five years old on the Long Walk to confinement at Bosque Redondo by Pale Faces. So he was at least one hundred and fourteen years old. So much had he seen come and go.

He had seen the coming of the automobile. Across the pale desert sky, he had watched jet aiplanes stream past. He had seen his children's children go off to many Pale Face wars — to France, to the South Pacific, to Africa, to Korea, to Viet Nam. His children's children had been in intelligence operations, because the Japanese could not decode the difficult Navajo tongue, so strange to the ear. They had been unheralded heroes in espionage. They had fallen on the desert sands of Africa, drowned at sea in the Korean confrontation, been imprisoned in North Viet Nam. They had fought for an ancient enemy, the Pale Faces of George Washington's government. They had never fought at Navajos against the

220

whites of the United States, for the Dine' had promised not to war again against the Blue Coats.

Ah, it was to be over soon. All the contemplations of an old man were coming to an end. He had sent word to his great grandchildren and he had this morning given away the last treasures of an old man's heart — his bows and arrows, his old repeating rifle, his canteen, his squash blossom necklace, his heavy turquoise earrings, his concho belt, his knee-high moccasins, his silver and turquoise rings. There was just one thing left to do, and he postponed it because just thinking of it gave him much pleasure. He had one last debt to settle.

The debt was to the fat owner of the Trading Post — the man with the little, beady eyes of a rat. He had grown to middle age taking over the treasures of the Dine' and reselling them at great personal profit. He had come in his early thirties and now he was in his fifties, and for over twenty years he had bested a people whose understanding of money and what it would buy was very meagre. The Pale Face had been friendly to the Navajo people, but he had never as much bought them a case of pop. Hugh had been told not all operators of trading-posts were so tight-fisted. No generous deed could Hugh ever remember the trader doing for him in over twenty years of acquaintanceship. Ah, what fun to repay such a debt!

Hugh signaled his great grandson it was time to get the Medicine Man. Before the sun went down, the debt would be repaid. The old man put on his heavy felt stetson of six beaver and went out into the sun. It was three o'clock. By five, the sun would be westering and a chill would come over the desert. The Medicine Man's work would be finished, and the old man would go back into the hogan.

In front of his dwelling, Hugh sat on a faded saddle blanket. In a half circle about him sat his relatives and friends. Before them in front of Hugh who faced into the sun, the Medicine Man worked his magic in sand, doing for the old man the last Sand Painting of Hugh's life. These two men, both ancient, had been friends for almost a century. There was nothing about Zahonie's life this man of medicine did not know. Today, he was putting it all in sand, and the painting was so exquisite that it hurt the heart.

As Behai Yazza worked, he hummed. No one spoke. But all watched in reverance and mixed emotion. Never had Hugh seen so many paints in the pot. Never had he seen a Sand Painting with such a display of color and action. There was his mother and father, and he, the child, walking over the sand to Bosque Redondo. There were the Blue Coats on their horses pushing the Navajos like cattle. There was the journey home again after four long years in exile.

There was his first sweetheart and wife-to-be, and his children and Hugh's hogan and crops. There was his favorite horse, whch he had known for 30 years, longer than he had known his first wife, who died with their fifth child. There was his second wife, and their children. And there was the first Pale Face school he had ever entered with two of his sons. There were his sheep, his goats, his mules and his children tending the flocks, and there was the second wife's departure to the Shadow Land.

Then there was his middle age, when he had herded flocks east, north, south and west. As the Medicine Man worked, he put it all in, the beauty before Hugh, the beauty behind him, the beauty all around him. Ah, it was good. It was glorious.

There was the gold of the desert poppy and brittle brush in bloom; the green of the saguaro, cactii and juniper; the fiery red of the octillo blossoms; the yellow of the yucca; the orange of the Easter Bonnet; the blue of the lupin; the pink of Owel's clover; the crimson of the hedgehogs. Never, never had Yazza painted such a thing of beauty, and Hugh knew it was his friend's last present to him. There were gold pieces in Hugh's pocket which were over 60 years old that would be his last payment to his medicine friend. Now, before the painting was finished, it was time to send for the trader.

Hugh had schooled his great grandson well. He was to tell the trader that his great grandfather was dying, and that the old man had a give-away present for him. Within half an hour, the pink Cadillac was making dust as the trader hurried to the hogan, this time granting the great grandson a space on the seat beside him.

The fat, over fifty-year-old man descended and bowed to all present, showing white teeth filled with gold. Oh, the trader knew how to be ingratiating, Hugh conceded. The air seemed electric, as if suddenly in the big half-circle of seated Navajos, they felt something was going to happen that had never happened before. Even the trader seemed keyed up, anticipating his gift.

"You sent for me, Hugh?" he purred. "Your grandson said you had some present you wished to give me."

"Yes," said Hugh. "I have this Sand Painting for you." Sweeping out one arm to the painting, Hugh extended the other to the painter, opening a hand which held six gold pieces. Hugh dropped them into the old Medicine Man's hand. The gold did not escape the eye of the trader, but his attention passed to the beauty of the painting. The greedy Pale Face stared in fascination, the painting was so extraordinary.

"It's the most beautiful Sand Painting I have ever seen," said the trader. "But how do I take it? How do I lift it off the desert floor without destroying it?"

That was when the silent laughter began to rock the Navajos in the semi-circle. Ah, the old man had not lost his wisdom. He was still able, on the eve of his death, to give a fat Pale Face his comeuppance. The vibrations of silent laughter racked the Indians, and the old man shared within himself their inner mirth.

"Sand Paintings not lifted from desert floor," said Hugh. "My gift feeds eye. Perhaps you will not forget. Only eye and memory can hold Sand Paintings. This you not know?"

"But — but — " stammered the white man.

"It yours," said Hugh. "Enjoy before Yazza destroy it — the story of my life."

The forlorn impoverished look which crossed the white man's face was cause for a new vibration of mirth, and the Indians laughed their silent full. At a nod from Hugh, the Medicine Man quickly wiped out the beautiful story of Zahonie's life. It was over. The old man rose to go into the hogan. The white man shook his head in frustration and slowly departed. The Indians stayed to visit one another into the dusk, as did the Medicine Man.

It was over. The old man knew his sunrise would be his last. He pulled the loom-woven blankets about him. He began to sing quietly the Blessing Way Chant: "With beauty all around me, I walk. In beauty I walk. In beauty it is finished."

Helen Clark, Butte, 1973

SHORT STORY

The Weight Lifter

Javad leaned without repose against a wall in the autumn sunshine of Iran.

A year ago he would not have believed that he, a teacher from Karaj, would be leaning beside a country road that passed into the village of Lalezar, warming his back like any villager beside the big jube canal where brown water flowed between the old village walls and the new brick of the American Foundation school. A dull pain near his heart reminded him why he had given up his long teaching hours and taken what seemed a quiet job as interpreter for the new Doctor Professor from America who had come to teach the Iranian farmers about "Co-operatives." But Javad felt now that there could be no quiet when working for such a man, a man like a furnace with banked fires throbbing with energy. A terrible man, in his way, was the Doctor, and one who should never have met up with the young man Askar, the Weight Lifter.

At the thought of Askar, Javad flexed his hands in fists that had not forgotten his youth. But boxing was for young men and Javad had a wife and two small lovely daughters — *mashalla!* Yet he would have liked to take both fists to this weightlifter who had lifted the funds of the new village co-operative, money trusted to his care as manager. It was a matter of 140,000 rials in Bank Melli notes with the Shah's proud face looking up from the red and green papers, but it was even more a matter of betrayal and destruction. Askar the gay, the friendly, the strong, elected by the villagers to be manager of their new venture.

And now the stored wheat sold, without permission!

Javad groaned and pushed his gray fedora back off the thinning curls of his sun-browned head. "I am a fool, a fool! Because I spent a year in America as the guest of the nation at one of its universities, must I forget the ways of Persia?" And then because his mother was of the tribe of the Kurds and honesty was bred into him, Javad faced a further thought. "How did I let this thing happen? And why do I not in reality want to hunt down the weight lifter?"

Three ragged little girls with tangled, shaggy hair stopped by the jube and stared across at him, and he wondered if he had spoken aloud. He looked at them with interest because they did not have the disease scarred skins and shrunken legs of children in the villages farther south. He knew he sought justification for the new program and wondered if he saw it in these children, born after clean water was piped down the village streets where the women could draw it off from faucets instead of dipping water from the ditch. Beyond the children he could see the screen door on the new co-operative store where the villagers bought and sold, and where a she donkey with her toy-like colt grazed at the sparse thorns along the edge of the mud walls. If the animal had been really hungry, he supposed it would wander farther from the village street. But it waited for the grain which could be fed by its owner from the new village silos.

And then he remembered again the wheat. There might be some reason for delay in delivering the other money in the manager's charge, but the wheat should not have been sold. Askar had not the right.

To his own surprise, tears came suddenly into the eyes of Javad as he saw again in his mind the face of the Doctor as they stared together into the empty wheat bins, this morning. It was the face of one whose friend had stabbed him in the back. Did the Doctor suppose that he, Javad the counterpart, might also wield the knife? Javad, who was suppose to be the interpreter not only of the words but of the minds and hearts of these two great nations which wanted to be friendly. It was a task Javad had undertaken, but perhaps his heart was not wholly in it.

Moving swiftly, he straightened up and went over to the ranchwagon standing in the shade of the young chenar trees along the road. It was time for the Doctor to come back from his meeting, and for them to return to Teheran and the offices of the Foundation. He climbed into the car and stared out through the windshield across the fields where the long weeks of cool nights and warm days had made it seem that life was easy. Perhaps an autumn like this, with melons and grapes and pomegranates in abundance, and tomatoes and cucumbers still growing in the gardens begun by the school, was not good for this old nation of sufferers. The soft life could make for temptations, perhaps, and the old trick of dog eat dog rise among them more viciously still. Then he remembered the round limbs of the children.

He saw the Doctor come striding quickly across from the compound gate, and as the Ford moved off with a spurt of gravel, Javad could tell by its motion that the Doctor was deeply troubled and drove well only from long habit. But when they had passed three camel trains and six overloaded trucks without the usual caustic comment from the Doctor, and when the gendarme with the big mustache got no response to his friendly wave, Javad wondered if the blow from the deceiver had been a mortal one to the Doctor's spirit. He knew it would take more than eight months in Persia for an American to learn that here no one trusts another completely. But why then had he, the Mohandes Javadi of Karaj, trusted this weight lifter? Was it because of his boyish smile, his willingness to work when others slept? Or because he felt that here was a young man pliable in either direction to Javad's own secret indecision? Alas, I am neither Persian nor American, I, now that I have the mind of both and the heart of neither. Disturbed too greatly, he spoke.

"Askar was already an employee of the Foundation when you arrived, Doctor," Javad said, "and the village board elected him manager of the Co-operative. To them goes the responsibility, does it not?"

The American guided the car between two buses whose drivers were carrying on a conversation while they drove. "When I would go out to check the work of the tractors," the Doctor said, "he used to take the wrench from me and say, 'Let me do that for you, Doctor'." The American's voice was quiet but baffled, following his own train of thought. And then he turned a brighter face toward Javad. "You know, I still think he may have spent some co-op funds, and now he's gone to try and borrow the money to pay it back."

Javad looked straight ahead. "Why would he take also the wheat money, then?" he asked, almost against his will.

There was another kilometer of silence and dust and the darting of green birds.

"We have his note which he left in the office — that at least is concrete evidence that he had the money," the Doctor said, at last. Javad was silent, reading the note again in his mind. "I will be in the office on Charshambay (Thursday) to deliver the money. Keep the Doctor calm. Signed, Askar, manager." Something was wrong about that, something did not fit, Javad thought — something besides the fact that Thursday had come and gone. Perhaps it was not planned that he would leave any note.

"Well, I've been calm haven't I?" The American turned to stare at Javad.

"It is true," Javad said, cautiously. "You wanted to go after him at once, to check the immigration offices, and I persuaded you that it would make much trouble for Askar and his family — in whom one still believes." Besides, Javad thought to himself, if Askar went to visit his sick father, as his friends claim, he is one to know ways of going without records and permits. All the young men know it, because of the strictness of the military police.

"And when we called on his sister-in-law and asked for the name of the woman Askar wants to marry," the Doctor continued, "I was calm when she assured me that for strange men to call on an unmarried woman would bring her father and brothers down on our necks."

"True," Javad nodded again, and surreptitiously grasped the handle of the door as a woman in a floating robe seemed to disappear under the long engine cowl, only to reappear unscratched and when he looked through the rear window. "And you were very generous in your conversation with the brother of Askar, a teacher of good reputation who no doubt weeps for the absence of the brother whom he raised from a boy." But even to himself his voice lacked conviction. What direction were his inner thoughts taking?

Only the manager could sell the wheat, and with it gone, the villagers had no concrete evidence that their work was good and their debt being repaid to the new co-operative which had loaned the money.

"If we go to the police now," the Doctor was saying, "the Co-op Board will hear about Askar and the money — gone — and it will destroy the whole spirit and purpose of this organization we've created — and in which the poor devils are beginning to believe."

Javad saw a flush of anger rise in the Doctor's face, and he felt a gladness that the banked fires still burned. "There is another week before the matter needs to come to anyone's attention," Javad found himself suggesting. "Much can happen before another Thursday comes around, and perhaps I have a plan."

The Doctor looked closely at him as the car drew up before the iron grill-work gates of the Foundation offices in Teheran. "We must employ the methods of Persia for a little while," Javad said, gently, and smiled with more confidence than he felt.

"All right," the Doctor answered, "I'll wait till Thursday before I go to the police." And he walked into the building, but without his usual energetic stride.

Now I am committed to action, thought Javad, and action is a thing which no Persian likes. I must give it much thought. And as he got into one of the small taxis which buzzed constantly along the crowded street, he forgot to watch the driving although it was something to fear. The traffic lanes were crowded with water carts and hand carts and laden donkeys and women in trailing robes and street boys with daring disregard for anything. And through it all went the shouldering big buses and the slipping and speeding American cars with their powerful engines, and the second-hand cars with no mechanical assurance of lasting out the block.

Javad paid off his taxi on the main street and walked down the short road to where he could inspect the progress of his new house. It was necessary to see how much of the workman's time was spent in laying brick and shaping molding, and how much in drinking tea and washing out their sweaty shirts in the running water of the open gutters that passed down the little street where his house was being built. He told himself he must get his new garden started, too, in the walled enclosure back of the house. It would never do for next summer to come and find his garden less luxuriant than those of the other homes which abutted his and whose garden walls were also the side walls of his own yard. This responsibility was surely a good thing, and he was happy to feel that he must give it his attention now. But as he went to work and sanded vigorously at the cement sides of the small garden pool, he thought about Askar.

One nearest point of contact with him is his brother, the teacher of Teheran, and whose wife's sister this weight lifter was to marry, Javad mused. He sat back on his heels and rested, lighting a narrow Iranian cigarette and smoking it daintily. Moreover, he continued in his thoughts this brother promised the good Doctor that he would send a telegram to their father, inquiring whether Askar was with him. The thing for me to do is to see again this brother and hear what news he has received. Although my American mind regrets to hear it, my Persian mind says, *enshalla, farda, pasfarda* — God willing, tomorrow, or the day after. But my heart which bleeds for the new ways urges my feet upon the road. The evening is still young.

But at the door he met his eldest daughter who brought tea and bread from his wife, and she was full of small chatter about her day at school. And so it was not until the next day that Javad's sense of duty took him to the door of the brother of Askar.

The home of this brother was in a wide street of fairly good brick apartment houses, made not of the sun-dried mud bricks but of the kiln baked product from the smoky yards south of the city. He rang the bell and stood back, watching some boys across the street who were throwing stones at a dog confined to the roof of an adjacent building. The dog was barking excitedly, but Javad was sure he could hear voices inside the house before which he stood. He rang again, and then heard the voice of a servant shouting, "Kee-ay, who is it?" And when he rang a third time, she came to the door which she opened a crack and told him, in answer to his inquiry, that her master was at his teaching at the high school. Something in her manner bothered Javad, but he retreated, nevertheless, and sought another taxi. But at the high school they told him that the Aga was at home. He had sent word that he was ill and could not teach for some days.

Thoughtfully Javad approached again the door to the brother's home. It was a good door, he noticed, panelled and painted, but the paint was peeling around the edges and the door was dirty and scratched. Some poverty here. But then, teachers were never paid according to their worth. He rang the bell.

This time the servant came quickly to the door, as though she might have been watching from a window. There was a child with her, hiding behind the folds of her dress, a little boy of six or seven years.

"I have been told at the Madressee that your Aga is at home. I wish to see him." Javad spoke quietly, at first.

But the servant shook her head. "*Mazel nist* — he is not at home." There was a sullen quality to her voice, and Javad saw the child look up at her in surprise.

"Lies ascend like an evil smell to Allah," Javad said sternly. "Why do you take for yourself the odors of another? My name is Mohandes Javadi, and I intend to see the master. You may tell him so."

He followed the servant into the house.

In the livingroom sat the brother of Askar, a shawl about his knees as he half reclined on a low couch. His face was hidden in shadows, but he waved an arm. "Please come in," he said in a weak voice.

"I inquire for your health," Javad said, bowing from the waist, "which I

228

am told is not good." He seated himself on another couch draped in a worn Kashani rug of faded elegance. He waited, but was not surprised when no explanation was forthcoming on why the man was not "at home," before. "I also wish to inquire," Javad said, "about the answer to the telegram you were to send, concerning the strange disappearance of your brother Askar." The servant had followed him into the room, and the child as well, and a strange silence hung momentarily. He waited, wondering.

"Excuse me," the man on the other side of the room said, gratingly, his voice seeming harsh with a cold. "You and the Doctor have been very kind. But the answer has not yet arrived." He waved his hand vaguely in the direction of the servant. "Bring tea!" he ordered.

"Yes, Aga," she answered, "but — the telegrams are here!" She smiled anxious to show that she had the education to understand an American word.

Again the silence hung momentarily.

"That is so — I had forgotten," the man said, sullenly. Javad could not blame him for fearing that his younger brother might be caught for a criminal, perhaps. But what had the man heard?

The servant was opening the drawer of a low table, the child helping her, and between them they withdrew and dropped on the floor two telegraph forms, marked with the script of the local office. With an exclamation, the man under the shawls threw off his coverings and swooped at the sheets of paper, but he was too late. The child had handed both telegrams to Javad, and although the other man took them immediately from him, it was not before the words of the top form had been seen.

"Askar is in Tabriz — proceed with the plan."

Javad sat still. Like the pictured story on a scroll, the whole thing began to unroll before him. Askar, the younger brother owing everything in life to this man, perhaps looking up to him because he is a school teacher; Askar, the weight lifter, the athlete whose brains are all in his back. Suddenly he is elected to a position of authority, handling large sums of money which may have meant nothing to Askar but everything to someone else. And the poorly paid school teacher will suddenly become a man of wealth if he plays it right, with the funds of a whole village area at his command. And because of Javad's own indecision, his loyalty divided between the old ways and the new, he had blindly allowed this thing to happen.

The brother of Askar was showing him another telegraph form which Javad swept aside as false, since it had not the official stampings and was not the first he had glimpsed. The man was standing there before him with a strange look congealing on his face. Javad noted how the western style suit he wore hung on his lean frame, and pity stirred in Javad, weaving like a faulty thread through the fabric of his consternation, pity for a man of learning who taught of the great days of Darius, yet lived on bread and tea, most likely. Maybe some way could be found —

And then the man was speaking a sly smile flickering about his thin mouth, his eyes not on Javad's face but on his hands.

"We would not have dared, of course, to proceed without planning adequate rewards for all concerned," he said. "Many years ago we Persians learned to turn beneath the heel of our conqueror and steal his shoes, to be sold at a profit. And much money has been made by those who pretend to serve the master while they worked with the slave."

And then shame flooded in hot color to Javad's face. Not only had this theft been accomplished under his wavering nose, but he, Javad, was to be the open sesame to the whole shameful affair. "We Persians," indeed! This was a fool who ran with jackals, not a true Persian.

Javad knew suddenly and completely what he believed in, what he had learned from the sight of village farmers working together in trust, and from his life among those who served the welfare of others. Freedom was an inner light in which man could draw the breath of self-respect. And that was the new Persia of which he dreamed. The indecision that had ridden him for months was gone.

"Let it be as if those words were never spoken, never thought," Javad said distinctly, and at the bright anger in his face the man before him began to wilt like a desert bloom too long without water. "A record of all telegrams is kept at the central office, and may be read by those with the authority to request it," Javad continued, his voice still hard with his anger. "I do not think your brother Askar will live beneath your roof again, or that the roof will long protect you — unless the entire amount of the missing funds is presented in three days' time to the Director of the Foundation."

He stepped closer to the man, who retreated hastily, awkwardly. "I had supposed the matter to be a simple defection on the part of a young man not too smart," Javad said, "yet here I find a conspiracy — and I, the Mohandes Javadi, was to be included. Baksheesh, bribes, for the son of the daughter of a chieftain of the Kurds!"

A cough that was more like a sob broke from the teacher's graying mouth, and Javad remembered his moment of pity and put it behind him. Compassion, yes — but pity, no.

"The full amount by Thursday," Javad repeated, his voice steady. And as

230

he looked into the eyes of the other man, he knew that the matter was settled. The money would be returned. And he swung about on his heel and went out, closing the door carefully behind him lest it swing like a hand that strikes a culprit's cheek.

With increasingly rapid strides, Javad walked out to the main street, to find a taxi. His spirit was light because his mind was clear. Who now, he asked himself, is the lifter of weights from old Iran?

Margaret Kraenzel, Bozeman, 1970

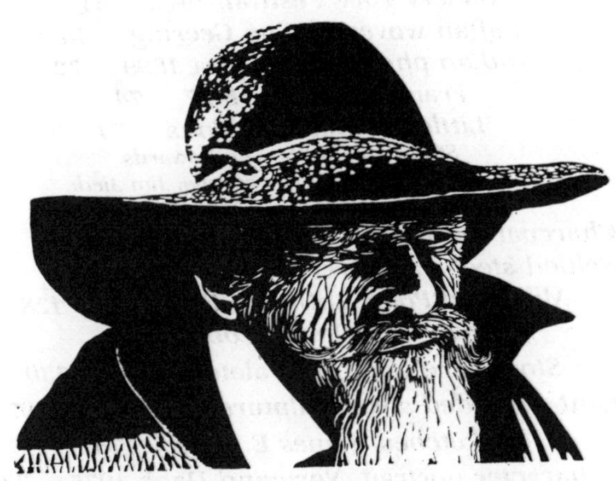

Character portrait, Normand Dahl, 1975

List of Illustrations

Glass, Dave Cornell   Frontispiece
The Market Place, E.H. and Virginia Loeffler, chairmen
Billings Festival, 1975   vi
Sheep, Bill Stockton   xi
Sketch, Bill Stockton   2
Gallery Talk, Festival, 1972   31
Caftan woven by Sue Geering   46
Indian photograph, circa 1899   72
Frances Senska, 1957   74
Little Festival Selections   74
Stoneware bottle, Ken Edwards
Moon Struck, cut paper collage, Jim Jiede
Stoneware berry bowl, Mary Tavener
Charcoal drawing, James M. Haughey, 1958   95
Welded steel sculpture, Lyndon F. Pomeroy   128
Milkweed Pods, LaDonna Fehlberg   128
Painting, Donna Loos   130
Stoneware vase, Peg Valeton, 1971   130
Covenant, a welded steel sculpture, Leo Olson, 1975   148
Sketches, James E. Dew   175
Character portrait, Normand Dahl, 1975   231

Color Insert

Cutting Out the Big One, J.K. Ralston
The Pit, Raymond Campeau
Zebras, Jessie Wilber
August, Lela Autio

APPENDIX

About the Montana Institute of the Arts

President, Mark Browning, Miles City
Secretary-Treasurer, Aurethia Harris, Helena
Editor, *Montana Arts*, LaDonna Fehlberg, Billings

The idea for forming the Montana Institute of the Arts originated with H.G. Merriam. The Institute was founded by 86 people in the Rathskeller of the Placer Hotel in Helena on April 3 and 4, 1948. H.G. Merriam in November of 1947 asked Mary Brennan Clapp, poet, Missoula, Naomi Babson, novelist, and her husband Paul A. Grieder, Professor of English at Montana State College, to join him in circulation of a letter to about 100 persons in Montana known to be interested in the arts which proposed formation of an Institute of Arts, Letters and History. By December more than 80 Montanans had responded favorably sending membership dues and voluntary contributions. The sum of $682 was soon available for effecting the organization.

Mary B. Clapp in the fall of 1947 in a talk on the proposal at a meeting of the instructors in English of the Greater University of Montana, stated that she had found "no set-up of institutes whose proceedings were available, so simple, so sensible and so inclusive as those proposed" in the plans for the Montana Institute." That plan was sent to the founders together with a questionaire about many pre-organizational matters and especially about what groups of activities should be set up. Later a proposed agenda for the founding meeting was sent.

Some weeks before the founding meeting, in behalf of his associates, H.G. Merriam had asked Merrill Burlingame, Bozeman, to prepare a tentative constitution and by-laws. With the help of Robert Dunbar, Bozeman, he did that and their document was presented at the founding meeting. Also, he had asked Branson Stevenson, Great Falls, to prepare a slate of chairmen for the various art groups — painting, weaving, and so on. Norman Winestine, Helena, was asked to come up with proposed names for the Institute, Peter Meloy, Helena, to chairman a committee on arrangements, and Tate Peek, Helena, to set up a banquet for the founders' first evening session. The home work had been done. At the founding meeting H.G. Merriam presided and Mary Peterson was the able recording secretary.

The constitution states the general purpose of the Institute as "the bringing together of persons interested in original and creative work, in teaching and in recreational use in the fields of the arts for mutual cooperation and stimulation.'' The purpose was stated more specifically in the preamble to the constitution: ''To preserve the heritage of the state as found in its history and folklore, to stimulate creative work in the several arts and to make cultural resources available for the benefit and enjoyment of the people of Montana.'' It was thought that though the Institute was primarily a grassroots organization professionals and amateurs would work together to their mutual advantage.

H.G. Merriam at the close of the founding meeting said, with looks in the audience of surprise, doubts, and affirmation, ''This may have been an historical meeting.'' Now, in its twenty-ninth year, MIA flourishes through its state organization and its twenty-three Branches in as many Montana towns. The present membership is 825.

PRESIDENTS OF THE MONTANA INSTITUTE OF THE ARTS
In order of service

Harold G. Merriam, University professor of English and editor, Missoula
Paul A. Grieder, University professor of English, Bozeman
Verne Dusenberry, professor of Anthropology, Bozeman
R.A. Athearn, musician and teacher of Music, Butte
Cyril Conrad, artist and professor of Art, Bozeman
Larry Gill, newsman and editor, Great Falls
Fred Mass, artist and forester, Butte
Robert Fehlberg, architect, Billings
James Logan, artist and mill superintendent, Great Falls
Herbert Jacobson, architect, Helena
Archie Joscelyn, writer, Missoula
Leo Olson, artist and high school teacher of Art, Billings
Ray Campeau, artist and high school teacher of Art, Bozeman
Archie Elliott, artist and school superintendent of Art
Mark Browning, artist

234

SECRETARIES-TREASURERS OF THE
MONTANA INSTITUTE OF THE ARTS

Ruth Robinson, Missoula

Ruby Montgomery, Missoula

Josephine K. Howard, Great Falls

Howard Place and Margaret Kenck, Butte

Harriet Cushman, Bozeman

Edith Maxwell, Great Falls

Peggy Ross, Butte

Anne Pekovich, Billings

LaDonna Fehlberg, Billings

Esther Warford, Missoula

Aurethia Harris, Helena

EDITORS OF THE
MONTANA INSTITUTE OF THE ARTS MAGAZINE

Archie Clark	Great Falls	Quarterly Bulletin of —
Ruby Montgomery	Missoula	Quarterly Bulletin of —
Paul Grieder and Verne Dusenberry	Bozeman	Quarterly Bulletin of —
Verne Dusenberry	Bozeman	Quarterly Bulletin of —
Bo Brown	Havre	Quarterly of —
Bo and Margery Brown	Havre	Quarterly of —
Robert T. Taylor	Butte	Quarterly of —
H.G. Merriam	Missoula	Quarterly of —
Margaret Kraenzel	Bozeman	Quarterly of —
La Donna Fehlberg	Billings	Montana Arts, Fall, 1967

FELLOWS

Harold G. Merriam, Missoula, 1957
Merril G. Berlingame, Bozeman, 1958
Branson G. Stevenson, Great Falls, 1959
Harriette E. Cushman, Bozeman, 1960
Cyril H. Conrad, Bozeman, 1961
Mabel Bjork, Helena, 1962
Lillian Miracle, Helena, 1962
Ruby Montgomery, Missoula, 1963
Frances Senska, Bozeman, 1964
Robert E. Fehlberg, Billings, 1965
James M. Haughey, Billings, 1966
Louis O. Brockmann, Fullerton, California, 1968
Joseph Kinsey Howard, posthumously, Great Falls, 1968
Helen A. Conrad, Bozeman, 1968
LaDonna K. Fehlberg, Billings, 1971
Maxine Blackmer, Missoula, 1972

FOUNDERS

Before the organizational meeting on April 3, 4, 1948, there were 101 founding members in 24 Montana towns who had paid dues. Six weeks after that meeting, May 17, there were 149 founders in 30 towns. The Directors extended the designation of founding member to persons who joined by December 31, 1948, but the editor has not found a printed list of such late founders.

This list is dated May 17, 1948:

Basin

Harriett C. Douglas

Belgrade
Florence M. Gray
Raymond Hulster

Big Timber
Mr. and Mrs. C.T. Irvine

Billings
Vernon Cooper
W.D. Copeland
Mrs. Henry Lohof
Mary J. Meek
Blaine E. Mercer
Myron Tripp
Glengolin Wagner
Ann Whitmack

Bozeman
Mrs. Mitrofan Afanasiev
Mrs. John Blankenhorn
Donald C. Boyd
Merrill G. Burlingame
Mr. and Mrs. Cyril H. Conrad
Harriette Cushman
Jeannie Dixon
Ruth Doering
Robert Dunbar
May G. Flanagan
Robert Galer
Mr. and Mrs. Paul Grieder
Bert Hansen
Martha Hawksworth
Leslie M. Heathcate
Bernice Lamb
Mrs. Hadleigh Marsh
Mrs. R.H. Palmer
Madge Peck
Mrs. Arthur Roberts
Frances Senska
Sarah Vinke
Jessie Wilber
Doris Wilson

Butte
R.H. Fletcher
Stephen P. Hogan
Alexander Leggat
Elizabeth Lochrie
Helen McDonald
Caroline McGill
Dorothy D. McIntosh
Eamon O'Sullivan

Chester
Etta Armstrong

Conner
Mrs. Henry Twogood

Conrad
Mrs. J.C. O'Brien
Mrs. L.C. Marsh

Deer Lodge
Mrs. Frank Shaw

Dillon
Genevieve Albertson
Robert Finch

Dixon
Mr. and Mrs. C.C. Wright

Ennis
Fay B. Jeffers

Fromberg
Jessie L. Duboc

Glasgow
Grace Van Duser

Great Falls
Charles Bovey
Patricia Brennan
Mrs. E.L. Dana
Norman Fox
Margaret Fulmer
J.K. Howard
Mr. and Mrs. James Logan
Mildred Schemm
Branson Stevenson
Sister Mary Trinitas
Mrs. R.K. West

Hamilton
Mark J. Boesch
G.M. Brandborg
Mrs. G.G. Jellison
Mrs. W. McCracken
Bessie Monroe
Mrs. M.J. Watt

Havre
Margaret Skinner

Helena
Harold Barnes
Mrs. Ray Bjork
Archie Bray
Frank J. Casey
Ernest T. Eaton
Susan Eaker
Mrs. Grace Erickson
Frieda Fligelman
Hugh D. Galusha
Bishop J.M. Gilmore
Ethel Goodale
Ralph C. Henry
Fay Kirkpatrick
Leonard Larsen
Mr. and Mrs. H.E. Longmaid
Mrs. W.B. McClatchey
Mrs. Arn McDonell
Clyde McLemore
Peter Meloy
Mrs. Ralph Miracle
Tate W. Peek
Mrs. William Pippy
Mrs. Frank Porter
Kathleen Ramey
Dr. and Mrs. T.P. Regan
Rt. Rev. Msgr. Emmet J. Riley
Lucinda Scott
George Selke
Victory Sullivan
Mrs. E.G. Toomey
Mr. and Mrs. Norman Winestine
Doris H. Young

Kalispell
Grace Baldwin

Lewistown
Mr. and Mrs. Al Attwell
Elizabeth R. Turner

Martinsdale
Grace Coates

Miles City
J.W. Masterson

Missoula
Aden Arnold
Rev. Guy Barnes
C.B. Bartholomew
Mary B. Clapp
Ken Cooper
Rufus A. Coleman
James E. Dew
John Crowder
Mrs. Douglas Fessenden
Edmund L. Freeman
Archie Joscelyn
Mrs. R.C. Line
Edna Mann
Mrs. Luce F. Martin
Mr. and Mrs. H.G. Merriam
Lyle W. Noble
Paul C. Phillips
Dr. and Mrs. J.P. Ritchey
Ruth Robinson
Mrs. A.N. Stepanzoff
R.P. Struckman
Ellen Torgrimson
Dorothy Tupper

Outlook
Mrs. C. Mills

Ramsey
Mrs. Howard Place

Sidney
Geneva Combes

Springdale
Helen McAuslin

West Yellowstone
Mike Kennedy

Whitefish
Agnes Sloan

PUBLICATIONS OF THE MONTANA INSTITUTE OF THE ARTS

Pamphlets of Poems

For Me, For You, 1956
When Comes Tomorrow, 1961
The Death of John Bozeman, and Other Poems, 1964
Sang It All His Life, 1965
Winning Poems from the Mary Brennan Clapp Memorial Contest, 1968

Paper Cover — Poems
Seedlings, Poems by Poets of the Montana Institute of the Arts,
Edited by Lillian Dove, H.G. Merriam, Jo Stepanzoff, 1973
MIA Poets Gallery, Edited by Lillian Dove, 1973

Cloth Bound — Poems
Seed in the Soil, Poems by Poets of the Montana Institute of the Arts,
Edited by Ida Isabel Donohue, H.G. Merriam, Elnora Wright, Mountain
Press, Missoula, Montana, 1967

The MIA Magazine, 1948 —